CAMBRIDGE LIBRARY COLLECTION

Books of enduring scholarly value

British and Irish History, Seventeenth and Eighteenth Centuries

The books in this series focus on the British Isles in the early modern period, as interpreted by eighteenth- and nineteenth-century historians, and show the shift to 'scientific' historiography. Several of them are devoted exclusively to the history of Ireland, while others cover topics including economic history, foreign and colonial policy, agriculture and the industrial revolution. There are also works in political thought and social theory, which address subjects such as human rights, the role of women, and criminal justice.

Archbishop Herring's Visitation Returns, 1743

In 1743, the appointment of a new archbishop of York, Thomas Herring (1693–1757), led to the creation of one of the most useful historical records of parish life in eighteenth-century England. This five-volume edition of visitation returns was first published between 1928 and 1931. It contains the responses made by hundreds of clergymen to the archbishop's enquiries as to the social and religious character of their parishes. Incorporating records detailing clerical matters and covering subjects ranging from the number of families in residence to the popularity of Methodism and the provision of schools, these volumes comprise, in the words of the editors, 'a collection of facts which are valuable for the economic and social, as well as the ecclesiastical history of England'. Volume 5 contains biographical notes, an index of place names and an index of persons.

Cambridge University Press has long been a pioneer in the reissuing of out-of-print titles from its own backlist, producing digital reprints of books that are still sought after by scholars and students but could not be reprinted economically using traditional technology. The Cambridge Library Collection extends this activity to a wider range of books which are still of importance to researchers and professionals, either for the source material they contain, or as landmarks in the history of their academic discipline.

Drawing from the world-renowned collections in the Cambridge University Library and other partner libraries, and guided by the advice of experts in each subject area, Cambridge University Press is using state-of-the-art scanning machines in its own Printing House to capture the content of each book selected for inclusion. The files are processed to give a consistently clear, crisp image, and the books finished to the high quality standard for which the Press is recognised around the world. The latest print-on-demand technology ensures that the books will remain available indefinitely, and that orders for single or multiple copies can quickly be supplied.

The Cambridge Library Collection brings back to life books of enduring scholarly value (including out-of-copyright works originally issued by other publishers) across a wide range of disciplines in the humanities and social sciences and in science and technology.

Archbishop Herring's Visitation Returns, 1743

Volume 5

Edited by Sidney Leslie Ollard
and Philip Charles Walker

CAMBRIDGE UNIVERSITY PRESS

Cambridge, New York, Melbourne, Madrid, Cape Town,
Singapore, São Paolo, Delhi, Mexico City

Published in the United States of America by Cambridge University Press, New York

www.cambridge.org
Information on this title: www.cambridge.org/9781108058773

This edition first published 1931
This digitally printed version 2013

ISBN 978-1-108-05877-3 Paperback

ARCHBISHOP HERRING'S VISITATION RETURNS.

Vol. V.

THE YORKSHIRE

ARCHÆOLOGICAL SOCIETY.

FOUNDED 1863. INCORPORATED 1893.

RECORD SERIES.

VOL. LXXIX.

FOR THE YEAR 1931.

ARCHBISHOP HERRING'S VISITATION RETURNS, 1743.

VOL. V.

(CONCLUDING VOLUME WITH INDICES).

EDITED BY

S. L. OLLARD, M.A.,

Rector of Bainton, East Yorkshire,
Member of the Council of the Yorkshire Archaeological Society,

AND

P. C. WALKER, M.A.,

Rector of Lockington, East Yorkshire,
Member of the Council of the Yorkshire Archaeological Society.

PRINTED FOR THE SOCIETY,

1931.

Printed by
THE WEST YORKSHIRE PRINTING CO. LTD.,
WAKEFIELD.

CONTENTS.

	PAGE.
Appendix D.	1
Appendix E.	31
*Index of Places	39
*Index of Persons	65
*Miscellanea Index	104
*Addenda and Corrigenda	106

* Compiled by the Rev. P. C. Walker.

APPENDIX D.

ARCHBISHOP HERRING.

By S. L. Ollard.

The principal authorities for the career of Archbishop Herring are :—

A. Mss.

1. The letters of the Archbishop to his friend and patron, Philip Yorke, first Earl of Hardwicke (1690-1764) preserved among the Hardwicke papers in the British Museum (Add. Mss. 35598).
2. A Ms. endorsed "Extracts from the Returns of the Incumbents at The Abp.'s Visitation 1743," with "Observations," apparently in the Archbishop's hand (G.2.13), a few miscellaneous papers, and very exact accounts of part of the Regiment of Foot, raised largely by the Archbishop's exertions in September, 1745 (Bundle 27), among the Mss. of the Archbishop of York at Bishopthorpe.
3. A collection of letters from Archbishop Herring to Matthew Kenrick, Esq. in the possession of his lineal descendant, Miss Kenrick of Reigate.

B. Printed.

1. The Preface (xli pages) to *Seven Sermons on Public Occasions by the Most Reverend Dr. Thomas Herring,* London, 1763. The author was the Archbishop's intimate friend, William Duncombe, Esq. (1690-1769).
2. *Letters from Dr. Thomas Herring to William Duncombe, Esq., deceased,* London, 1777. The editor was the Rev. John Duncombe (1729-1786), son of the writer mentioned above.
3. *A History of the Antiquities of the Town and Church of Southwell, etc.,* by W. Dickinson Rastall, A.M., London, 1787. The account of Archbishop Herring in ch. iv is so particularly full and careful that it is clear the writer had access to some first-hand authority.
4. *Memoirs of a Royal Chaplain,* 1729-1763, *etc.*, ed. Albert Hartshorne, London, 1905. This contains many references to Archbishop Herring. Both Dr. Pyle (1702-1776) and Dr. Kerrich (1696-1768), whose correspondence the volume contains were at Corpus Christi College, Cambridge when Archbishop Herring was Fellow and Tutor there.

5. *The Life and Correspondence of Philip Yorke, Earl of Hardwicke, etc.*, by Philip C. Yorke, 3 vols., Cambridge, 1913. This prints the more important letters from the Hardwicke papers referred to above.

6. *Correspondence of Archbishop Herring and Lord Hardwicke during the Rebellion of* 1745, edited by Dr. Richard Garnett, in the *English Historical Review, vol. xix,* pp. 532, *seq.*, 719, *seq.* (1904). These articles contain letters from the Hardwicke correspondence already referred to, by no means all of which are printed in the *Life and Correspondence of the Earl of Hardwicke.*

7. *Hist. Mss. Commission Report on Mss. in Various Collections, Vol. I,* p. 226, *seq.*, London, 1901. Two letters from Archbishop Herring in 1752.

8. *Dict. of National Biography,* ed., 1908, vol. ix, pp. 710, 711. Article by the Rev. Richard Hooper.

9. *The Primates of the Four Georges,* by A. W. Rowden, K.C., London, 1916. This contains a careful study of the Archbishop and is based on nearly all the foregoing authorities.

These Visitation Returns seem to require for their completeness some account of the Archbishop at whose request they were made. Further, having been born at Wisbech and being connected, on my father's side, with a former Rector of Walsoken, I confess that a certain local patriotism has urged me to try to sketch the story of the man amongst whose printed and Mss. remains I have spent a great part of the last six years.

Archbishop Herring has not been well treated by the historians of Wisbech. Colonel Watson in his *History of Wisbech* (Wisbech, 1827) does indeed commemorate the Archbishop, but three of the four pages allotted to him are occupied by a reproduction of his anti-Jacobite speech at York in September, 1745.[1] Walker and Craddock in their *History of Wisbech and the Fens* (Wisbech, 1849) dismiss the Archbishop in two sentences and allow themselves to write, with equal disregard of grammar and good taste : "He does not seem to have been celebrated for anything except being an archbishop, which in itself is a very questionable title to remembrance, much more posthumous celebrity."[2] The most recent historian of Wisbech, though his book deals, nominally, only with the period 1848-1898, at least mentions the Archbishop among the famous men connected with the town.[3] Yet Archbishop Herring's name is one of the two most eminent names on the roll

[1] Watson, *op. cit.* pp. 431-435.

[2] Walker & Craddock, *op. cit.* pp. 470, 471.

[3] F. J. Gardiner, *History of Wisbech, etc.*, 1848-1898 (Wisbech, 1898), p. 398.

of Wisbech School; it is equalled only by that of Thomas Clarkson (1760-1846) who shares with William Wilberforce the honour of liberating the slaves. Clarkson has, deservedly, his fine public monument in Wisbech; Archbishop Herring has no public memorial there or elsewhere, save his attractive portraits at Bishopthorpe, at Lambeth and in the Hall of Corpus Christi College, Cambridge.[1] Yet of the 76 Archbishops and Bishops of York before him only three had been translated to Canterbury: Herring made the fourth. Since then there have been only three such translations, including that of the present Primate of All England, to whose kindness this book owes very much. That Wisbech can claim to be represented in that rare company should not have escaped the attention of those who have tried to tell the glories of that ancient and delightful town.

Thomas Herring was born at Walsoken in Norfolk, a mile and a half from Wisbech, across the Norfolk county boundary. The house in which he was born still stands among the fruit orchards which now cover much of that country-side, but the house is no longer the rectory. John Herring, his father, had been Rector of Walsoken since 1681. He had been a Scholar of Trinity College, Cambridge whence he took his B.A. degree in 1664; he was ordained Deacon and Priest on the same day in 1667 by the Bishop of Peterborough and had become M.A. in 1688. How he obtained the rich rectory of Walsoken does not appear; he held it 36 years, being buried on 2nd June, 1717 before his son had become famous. His wife, Martha, daughter of Thomas Potts of S. Gregory's, London, was some 18 years younger than her husband; she had died nineteen years before him having been buried on 1st January, 1704, aged 44, when her son was a schoolboy of 11. The home was evidently a good one, if the Archbishop's integrity of character be an index to it; rather strangely he delayed until 1750, when he was a man well over 50, to erect a monument "in grateful memory of his excellent parents" on the south wall of the sanctuary in Walsoken church. On that monument he describes himself as "their only son, Thomas, Lord Archbishop of Canterbury."

The family of Herring came, apparently, originally from Montgomeryshire, which may partly explain the devotion to the Archbishop displayed "by a Welch curate from the bottom of Merionethshire, 6 foot and ½ high," who wrote during the anxious days of October, 1745, when Prince Charles Edward and his army were marching south, to offer to attend his Grace "at an hour's warning," if his own Bishop (of Bangor) "did not call upon him for ye same service." There was evidently a Puritan strain in the family, Julines Herring (1582-1644) achieved some fame as a divine of that school; and Archbishop Laud is alleged, on Puritan

[1] There is also an engraving of the Archbishop in the Combination Room of Jesus College, Cambridge. There is, I understand, a fourth portrait, besides the three mentioned in the text. I have not traced it.

authority, to have said that he "would pickle that Herring of Shrewsbury." Julines Herring left England for the more congenial atmosphere of Holland in 1637 and became co-Pastor of the English congregation at Amsterdam where he died in 1644. Probably the Puritan tradition of this ancestor tinged Thomas Herring's upbringing. He went in due course to the Grammar School at Wisbech, then held in the mediaeval Town Hall, where his headmaster from 1708, was a young man only ten years his senior, John Carter, an Etonian who had taken his B.A. degree from King's College, Cambridge in 1704 and been licensed to teach at Wisbech by the Bishop of Ely in 1708. After Herring had left the school for Cambridge Mr. Carter was ordained, became Rector of Newton-in-the-Isle and a Fellow of Eton College. Doubtless from this young headmaster, Herring acquired his classical scholarship, and, perhaps, the very agreeable manners which impressed so pleasantly all who came to know him.

On 21st June, 1710, Thomas Herring was admitted a pensioner at Jesus College, Cambridge. The choice of that college, unless it was dictated by necessity, was strange if John Herring desired his son to carry on the Puritan tradition and become a Whig, for Jesus College was a Tory stronghold. His tutors at Jesus were one of the younger Fellows, Mr., later Dr., Richard Warren, afterwards Rector of Cavendish and Archdeacon of Suffolk, and Mr. Townsend. Herring was elected a Scholar of the college, 13th June, 1712. But he found the Tory atmosphere of Jesus College uncongenial though another member of his family, Julines Herring, of Wisbech, apparently a cousin, was sent there as an undergraduate in 1713; and he had another reason for disliking the college, he attributed his delicate health to his having been put into damp sheets as an undergraduate.[1] Herring took his degree in 1713 and "seeing no Prospect of obtaining a Fellowship" at Jesus[2] he migrated a few months later on 13th July, 1714, to Corpus Christi or, as it was more usually called, Bene't College.

Besides asthma and a horror of Toryism the future Archbishop carried with him from Jesus a friendship for an undergraduate contemporary which was not without result. Matthew Hutton, of the family of Hutton of Marske, Yorkshire, a lineal descendant of Archbishop Matthew Hutton of York (1529-1606) was admitted pensioner at Jesus College a day after Thomas Herring. Like Herring he disliked the Tory atmosphere of the college and, like Herring, left it after taking his B.A. degree. He became a member of Christ's College and was Fellow there from 1717 to 1729. He held three preferments in the diocese of York

[1] *Letters to Duncombe*, p. 44.

[2] The Master of Jesus College, to whose kindness I owe some of the facts above writes, "Probably there was a genuine block in Fellowships in 1714 and statutable restrictions to county may have prevented Herring's election at that time."

when Herring came there as Archbishop, but he was not destined to be one of his clergy for he succeeded him as Bishop of Bangor; and when Archbishop Herring was translated, most unwillingly, to Canterbury, it was decided that his friend Matthew Hutton should succeed him at York. When Archbishop Herring died, the habit of appointing Matthew Hutton his successor seems to have become too strong to be resisted, for Matthew Hutton followed him at Canterbury. Whether all these promotions were due to Herring's loyalty to his friend from undergraduate days is not clear; certainly Matthew Hutton had few distinctions save his gentle birth and the loyal friendship of Archbishop Herring. That he had been private chaplain to the great Whig noble, Charles, 6th Duke of Somerset, "the proud duke" (1662-1748), and had married a chamber-maid from the ducal household at Petworth, possibly helped his fortunes, but it was Herring, his friend from undergraduate days, who urged in 1747 that Matthew Hutton should be made Archbishop of Canterbury. Herring's later connexions with Jesus College were slight.

Dr. John Jortin (1698-1770), was admitted pensioner of that College a year after Herring had left it for Corpus, and, unlike Herring, was elected a Fellow. As archbishop, Herring patronized generously Jortin's now almost forgotten literary work, and Jortin has left on record a not unjust panegyric on his patron's charm of manner. It is possible that Archbishop Herring helped Jortin from affection for his old college, it is more likely that he was attracted by Jortin's real ability and by the fact that Jortin was of the popular Latitudinarian school.

Yet another Jesus man, though of a much later date, Francis Fawkes (1720-1777) was patronized by Herring in his last years. But Fawkes owed this patronage, it would seem, to the Odes he addressed to the Archbishop, of which hereafter.

Thomas Herring's migration from Jesus to Corpus was the decisive event in his career, for at his new college he was elected a Fellow in 1716 and apparently made a Tutor at the same time. Corpus, or Bene't College, to give it its then usual name, was the centre of the Whig interest in Cambridge; to Corpus Whig ministers looked for men who could be trusted to hold high office in the Church with a proper regard for Whig principles. Of the five successive Masters of Corpus between 1698 and 1764 all but one were made bishops, and when Herring became a member of the college in 1714, the Archbishopric of Canterbury was held by one of its former Fellows. "The Old House," so its senior members called the college, was indeed a very snug society of able men, united in devotion to the Revolution of 1688 and to the Hanoverian succession. The standard of work and of discipline was moreover, high; and the sunshine of the favour of the men who had come into power with the accession of George I. shone brightly on the college.

A vivid picture of the circle in which Thomas Herring moved at Corpus is presented in the letters of Dr. Kerrich and Dr. Pyle published under the title of *Memoirs of a Royal Chaplain*, 1729-1763.[1] Herring flits in and out of that correspondence, for Kerrich was his brother-Fellow and Pyle had been an undergraduate when Herring was a Tutor. And both Kerrich and Pyle were, like Herring, Norfolk born. But the letters throw no intimate light on Herring as a Corpus don. Duncombe records that Herring and "the learned Dr. Denne, now Archdeacon of Rochester, were joint Tutors (at Corpus) for upwards of seven years. Mr. Herring read the Classical, and Dr. Denne the Philosophical lectures." Rastall states more fully that Mr. Herring "read the classical lectures, with much approbation to himself and advantage to his pupils." Evidently he was a capable and conscientious tutor. He was ordained Deacon by the Bishop of Ely, Fleetwood, on 23rd September, 1716 and Priest in 1719, possibly by the then Master of Corpus, Samuel Bradford, Bishop of Carlisle.[2] Herring added to his income by accepting the charge of various small parishes, Great Shelford, Stow-cum-Quy and Holy Trinity, Cambridge. Apparently he held these charges successively. Meanwhile he had caught the notice of the most astute Whig bishop then on the bench, Dr. Fleetwood, Bishop of Ely who had ordained him Deacon. A political party in power, to retain its hold, needs constant reinforcement by able men. Bishop Fleetwood, as a devoted Whig, would keep his eyes open for promising young men at Cambridge, and he marked Thomas Herring. In 1722 he made him his chaplain, and presented him to the rectory of Rettingdon, Essex on 1st October, and to that of Barley, Herts. on 7th December. More than that, the Bishop was accustomed in winter to reside at Ely House in London and to preach on Sundays in the beautiful chapel there. But in 1722 his health was failing (he died in August, 1723) and he appointed Mr. Herring to preach in his stead. The bishop was delighted by his chaplain's discourses and declared to his friends "that he never heard a Sermon from Mr. Herring but what he should have been proud to have been the Author of himself."

Bishop Fleetwood was one of the two strong characters which most influenced Herring, the other was an equally strong man and an equally devoted Whig, Philip Yorke, 1st Earl of Hardwicke (1690-1764) who was only three years Herring's senior. Herring possessed a portrait of Bishop Fleetwood which he evidently valued much for, by his will, he left it, most suitably, to the other who had most influenced his life, Lord Hardwicke.

[1] Edited by Albert Hartshorne, London, 1905.

[2] See Vol. 1 of these *Returns*, p. v. The present Master of Corpus, who kindly examined the records of the College in 1929 in order to clear up this point, tells me that there is no record of Dr. Bradford ordaining in the College Chapel.

Both Masters, in his *History* of Corpus Christi College (1753) and Duncombe in his Preface to the *Seven Sermons, &c.* (1763) give 1719 as the year of Herring's priesthood.

Herring's acceptance of the two rectories, and his connexion with Bishop Fleetwood, determined the end of his career at Cambridge; he ceased to be Fellow of Corpus in 1723. The foundation of his fortunes was too well and truly laid to be affected by Bishop Fleetwood's death in 1723, for the clever young barrister, Philip Yorke, who was already making his name both in the House of Commons and in the Courts, had discovered Herring's talents. And as Yorke rose from one post of importance to another, on his way to the Woolsack, he was careful to see that Herring rose with him. How the two men became acquainted is not known, Philip Yorke was never at the University so that Cambridge was not the link between them. Very likely Yorke attended Ely House Chapel and was attracted by Herring's sermons. Certainly in 1726, when Herring was appointed Preacher of Lincoln's Inn, Yorke, then Attorney-General, was a Bencher of the Inn. From 1723 Herring was a country parson, residing at Barley. Though he was a country parson's son he confesses, in 1728, that he found life in the country lacking "a certain cheerfulness and vivacity."[1] These agreeable things were no doubt amply supplied by his friends at Lincoln's Inn when he preached there. Herring still kept up his connexion with Cambridge, he took his B.D. degree in 1724 and his D.D. in 1728, by which time he had become a Royal Chaplain. One of his Lincoln's Inn sermons brought him prominently before the public for the first time. Gay's famous *Beggar's Opera* was first produced at the Lincoln's Inn Theatre on Monday, 29th January, 1728 and won immediate success; incidentally it satirized the Prime Minister, Sir Robert Walpole. Dr. Herring in a sermon condemned the play as injurious to public morality, since it invested thieves and highwaymen with a halo of romance. Dean Swift took up the cudgels for the play, praised it for having done eminent service both to religion and morality, and added that it would probably do more good "than a thousand sermons by so stupid, so injudicious, and so prostitute a divine as Dr. Herring." The controversy was sharp, and not all good men agreed with Herring. Thus Dr. Johnson wrote "it is not possible for anyone to imagine he may rob with safety because he sees Mackeath reprieved upon the stage."[2] But the result was to win for Herring a devoted friend in the writer, John Duncombe, and to make his name known.

Preferments were coming swiftly to him. In 1724 Dr. Edward Waddington vacated the City church of All Hallows the Great on his consecration to the see of Chichester, and the Crown offered the benefice to Herring who accepted it, but withdrew his acceptance before he was instituted. On 31st August, 1731 he was

[1] *Letters to Duncombe*, p. 5.

[2] See the Muses' Library edition of Gay's *Poems*, edited by John Underhill. Introd. pp. lvi., lvii., and Johnson's *Lives of the Poets* (edited by Cunningham) ii., 292.

instituted on the presentation of William Clayton, Esq. (who was created a Baronet in the next year), to the agreeable Rectory of Blechingley in Surrey.[1] He valued it particularly because it was not far from Sir Philip Yorke's house at Carshalton. Some months later he was preferred by the Crown to the Deanery of Rochester where he was installed on 5th February, 1731. He seems to have divided his time between Blechingley and Rochester until on 18th June, 1737 he was nominated to the see of Bangor, vacant by the death of Bishop Charles Cecil. Herring owed this elevation to his friend and patron Sir Philip Yorke who had been created Baron Hardwicke in 1733 and became Lord Chancellor in 1737, and he acknowledged the debt in a letter which has been described as "cringing." "I shall remember to my latest breath, with a quick sensibility that the happiness and honour of my life, whatever it is or may be, has been owing to the distinction with which you have been pleased to treat me and to the assistance by which you have raised me" the bishop-elect wrote, and he declared that he wished "to act in such a manner as may become the station I am going to be placed in, and to do as little discredit as may be to your Lordship's recommendation of me."[2]

The letter certainly displays the inferiority complex in a marked form, but it may be pleaded in its extenuation that Herring who was a gentle, affectionate and sensitive man, was apt to be overwhelmed at all times by the strength of Lord Hardwicke and was writing under the stress of strong emotion, dazzled by the glittering prospect of the pomp and circumstance which belonged to a Bishop in the reign of George II. Certainly Dr. Herring wrote far more coolly, a few weeks later, in reply to the congratulations of his friend Duncombe.

"It is generally looked upon as a point of happiness, and is, to be sure, an honour; yet to say the plain truth, I am in no sort of raptures about it, nay, indeed, not without my apprehensions, that I am making work for repentance, and that my friends may hear me repeating, ere long, *Vitae me redde priori*."[3] There was no hurry in giving Dr. Herring his see. Nominated on 18th June, as has been said, and elected by the Chapter in the following August, the royal assent to the election was not given till the 29th December. The election was confirmed at Bow Church on the following 14th January and on the next day Thomas Herring was consecrated in the Chapel of Lambeth Palace by Archbishop Potter of Canterbury, Bishops Claggett of S. David's, Butts of

[1] Herring's connexion with Blechingley is admirably told by Mr. Uvedale Lambert in his sumptuous history of that parish; it contains an illustration of the Rectory as it was in Herring's time. Herring owed this preferment to his friendship with Matthew Kenrick, Esq., whose sister Mr. Clayton had married. See *Blechingley* (London, 1921), ii, 453 *seq*.

[2] Rowden, *The Primates of the Four Georges*, pp. 178, 179, quoting Hardwicke's *Life and Correspondence*, i., p. 405.

[3] *Letters to Duncombe*, pp. 36, 37.

Norwich and Secker of Oxford. The temporalities of the see were restored to him on the following 25th January, and he was allowed to retain the Deanery of Rochester *in commendam* with his bishopric.

Bishop Herring was a conscientious man and he took his Welsh diocese seriously, more seriously than one of his predecessors, Benjamin Hoadly, who during the five and a half years that he was Bishop of Bangor never once entered the diocese. At the same time the new bishop was leisurely. It was not until the autumn of the year that he travelled "slowly and commodiously" to see his diocese, and found Wales "as interesting as it was new." He had something of the artist's eye for natural beauty, and he described to his friend Duncombe some of the scenery which had delighted him.

Next year, 1739, the Bishop held his primary visitation and he wrote "I determined to see every part of my diocese, to which purpose I mounted my horse, and rode intrepidly, but slowly, through North Wales to Shrewsbury......I set out upon this adventurous journey on a Monday morning, accompanied (as bishops usually are) by my chancellor, my chaplain, secretary, two or three friends and our servants." Again he displayed his artistic temperament in his delicate accounts of scenes through which he passed; and, at the same time, he was evidently anxious to do his duty by his charge.

In 1741 he appears to have made another tour through the diocese and in 1742, keeping the rule of the Canon which orders bishops to "visit" their diocese every three years, Bishop Herring was preparing in 1742 for a formal visitation, which doubtless took place. Some few scraps of evidence that remain show too his real care for his clergy and his desire to help them.[1] But the powerful Lord Chancellor had no intention of allowing Bishop Herring to remain in a poor Welsh see and when, in 1742, the Archbishopric of Dublin became vacant, it was offered to the Bishop of Bangor. He declined it. Next year the Archbishop of York, Lancelot Blackburn died, and if Horace Walpole is right, the vacant Primary was offered to and declined by the Bishops of Salisbury (Sherlock) and Rochester (Wilcox). The powerful Lord Chancellor then secured that it should be offered to the youngest bishop on the bench, the Bishop of Bangor, who was only 49. This time he accepted the offer. He was nominated on April 6th (Archbishop Blackburn had been buried only five days before) and elected between that date and April 13th on which day the royal assent was given to the election. It was confirmed in S. George's, Hanover Square on 21st April, and the temporalities were restored to him two days later. The procedure was as swift as that of his appointment to Bangor had been slow; this was complete within seventeen days, the other had been spread over seven months.

It is unnecessary to repeat what has been said in the Intro-

[1] See Rowden *op. cit.* p. 180.

duction to these Returns about the scandalously slothful rule of Archbishop Blackburn. It was recognised, by all who knew, that the new archbishop was going to a diocese which had suffered from long years of neglect, after being shepherded carefully and conscientiously by two devout and able archbishops, John Sharp, 1691 to 1714, and Sir William Dawes, 1714 to 1724. Of the four archdeacons, to whom naturally an archbishop would turn, two had been chaplains to Archbishop Sharp and belonged to his time, and consequently, in 1743 were old men. The other two had been appointed by Archbishop Blackburn; one was reputed to be that prelate's natural son, the other was a man of immoral life. The new archbishop had, however, a clear outline of what a bishop should do and be, and he set to work at once to arrange for a thorough formal Visitation. Of it these volumes of Returns are the result. He left Kensington, where he had lived when in London, in the middle of May and began his Visitation at Nottingham on Friday, May 27th. He was at Newark on May 30th, Worksop on June 1st, Sheffield on June 3rd and Doncaster on June 6th, whence he proceeded to Bishopthorpe, having been, as he wrote "above a fortnight on the road." An old friend, Dr. Matthias Mawson, who had been Master of Corpus since 1724 and from 1740 also Bishop of Chichester came to help the Archbishop with the confirmations and Dr. Pyle tells how much they had laughed at Corpus over various incidents of the Master's northern expedition. "As he went the Archbishop and his company were magnificently entertained at the Duke of Kingston's[1] seat" [Thoresby, in Sherwood Forest, lying on the Archbishop's way from Newark to Worksop] "though his Grace the Duke was not there, being obliged to be from home himself, and ordering his French mistress to abscond for that day. After their repast, as the Archbishop was admiring the place and expressing his sense of the honours done him there, my Lord of Chichester said, 'Yes, indeed, very fine, Herring, but—I wish we had seen Madame.' "

Equally unedifying was Bishop Mawson's reply to Dr. Pyle who had "feared that the pleasure of his Lordship's tour was much abated by the fatigue that must arise from the share he had had in the work of Confirmation." To which the Bishop of Chichester answered "Why, truly, Mr. Pyle, the places were very large and the people very numerous, but yet I saw nothing in the business of Confirmation but what one pair of hands might very well have performed."[2]

No such anecdotes are related of the Archbishop, whose mind,

[1] Evelyn Pierrepont (1711-1773), who succeeded his grandfather as 2nd Duke of Kingston-upon-Hull in 1726. Horace Walpole described him as "a very weak man, of the greatest beauty and finest person in England." He married the notorious Elizabeth Chudleigh, *vere* Countess of Bristol, in 1769. On his death, without issue, in 1773, the dukedom became extinct.

[2] *Memoirs of a Royal Chaplain*, pp. 88, 89. Letter from Pyle to Dr. Kerrick, 17 July, 1743.

save where Roman Catholics were concerned, was of a finer and more reverent temper. The story of this Visitation clearly illustrates Archbishop Herring's conscientious devotion to his work. Having completed his inspection of Nottinghamshire and the South Yorkshire Deaneries, and arrived at Bishopthorpe, he, in his own phrase "entered upon a new round of compliments and entertainment"[1] for ten days and then entered upon his "second plan of Visitation." He began at Wakefield on 21st June, was at Leeds on 23rd, and at Skipton on the 27th. After a short recess he began again, and visited at York on 25th July, Hull on 28th and Beverley on the 30th. He paused for a fortnight and then went on. He was at Bridlington on 16th August, Malton on 18th, Thirsk on the 20th, and Stokesley on 23rd. Writing on 15th September, he tells Duncombe that his visitation had ended a fortnight before, but in fact he visited at Ripon on 13th October and (by a Commissary) at Hexham on 5th. The Archbishop was greatly pleased with his work. "I bless God for it," he wrote. "I have finished the work, not only without hurt, but with great pleasure to myself, and I returned home with great satisfaction of heart for having done my duty, and acquired a sort of knowledge of the diocese, which can be had by nothing but by personal inspection. I have traversed, by this means, a prodigious tract of ground, seen all possible variety of country, many rich and populous towns, and some of the finest seats of the kingdom, and what may give you, by the rules of proportion, a great idea of the importance of this district of England, I am confident I have confirmed above thirty thousand people." His Grace proceeds to describe the pleasure he took in his "last expedition" (he means, very likely, his return from Stokesley to Bishopthorpe) "which was a visit to Castle Howard[2] (where I spent two days) where there is every provision for elegant life, which pleasure and magnificence, conducted with the best economy, can afford."

Archbishop Herring held the see of York only four and a half years, from April, 1743 to October, 1747, but in that short time he left more material than he left elsewhere, for judging what manner of man he was. The evidence shows his conception of his work as a diocesan bishop, his courage and resolution in the face of danger, and the fascination which his home at Bishopthorpe exercised over him. Taking these three points in order, Archbishop Herring's conception of his work as a diocesan bishop is revealed, fairly completely by these Returns. It is true that the Questions

[1] *Letters to Duncombe*, p. 63.

[2] A seat of the Earls of Carlisle. The owner in 1743 was Henry Howard, K.G., the 4th Earl, who, born in 1684, died in 1758. Two months before the Archbishop's visit, 8 June, 1743, the Earl had married a second wife who bore him six children. The youngest of these, Lady Juliana Howard, died in her 100th year in 1849, and thus linked the reign of Charles II. to that of Queen Victoria. The Earl, her father, was, apart from his territorial possessions, a quite undistinguished Whig nobleman.

which the Archbishop sent out to his clergy were not original, there were in all but a few details, the questions issued by Bishop Edmund Gibson to the diocese of Lincoln in 1718,[1] but the fact that Archbishop Herring was willing to follow the lead of Bishop Gibson in such a matter shews his practical sagacity. The Archbishop's comments on the Returns, many of which have been printed in these volumes, show the care with which he noted the digest of the Returns, which he had prepared for him.[2] He was specially careful to note the answers about catechising, which shows that he was a parish priest of experience. Apart from these Returns there is among the Bishopthorpe Mss. a letter to the Archbishop from the Vicar of Scarborough, endorsed with the notes of the Archbishop's reply, which shews to some extent, his method of handling minor diocesan problems. The letter is dated from Scarborough, 15th February, 1746 (1747 in the modern reckoning),[3] and is as follows :—

May it please Yr. Grace

Coming to York Unfortunately the Monday Evening before You set out for London, as it was my chief Business to have paid my Duty and most humble Respects to yr. Grace; And then by the Suddainness of yr. leaving us being disappointed of an Opportunity in Person to consult You as to some Particulars, may it please You to excuse the Trouble of This, which comes in the most submissive Manner, to desire ye Favour of yr. Answer by any Hand to what follows, viz,

Whether (as This is a very large Parish, and there are frequently a great number of Communicants, Especially at ye Four solemn Times of ye Year; and it has lain & may lye upon One Person to go through with the Communion Service, which makes it very tedious and fatiguing) yr. Grace approve of the officiating Minister's giving Two Cups with the Blessing in the plural Number, which would much shorten ye service.

Whether you approve of a Deacon's using any Form of Absolution in reading Morning or Evening Prayer i.e. Either that in our Morñ: & Evening Service, Or that in the Commination?

Whether as this Living is but £34 a Year *Certain* you wou'd please to accept of a Title for Holy Orders of £16 a Year out of it as the Curate's Salary, He being willing?

Whether a Licence to a Curacy (the Living being worth £80 a year) of £24 a Year Salary (the Duties expected and set forth in ye Nomination not being almost half so Great as they were when such Licence was granted) may not be set aside; Especially the Curate having Since taken on him another Curacy, the supplying of which

[1] See above, Vol. I., p. viii.

[2] It is preserved among the Mss. at Bishopthorpe. G. 2, 13.

[3] Bishopthorpe Mss., Bundle 28, No. 130. For the writer and the allusions to his other charges see Scarborough, Stainton (Cleveland), and Thornaby Chapel. Vol. III., pp. 133, 56, and 169 above.

often deprives the first Curacy of Part of their Service, as Prayers on Sundays in the Afternoon.

And whether yr. Grace have a power to Dispence with my keeping Residence at *Stainton,* which I hold by a Royal Dispensation, as I am nigh 65 years of Age and infirm? And now (having ask'd yr. Pardon for this Trouble) with my Prayers for the long Life and Health of so great and worthy a Patriot both of our Church and Nation I am

My Lord
Yr. Grace's
Most Obedient humble Servant
Theoph. Garencieres.

The Archbishop, on 22nd April, 1747 endorsed this letter with the following notes :—

1st. Request not granted.
2ly. Deacon forbid reading the Absolution.
3d. Left to his Discretion.
4. Consult Mr. Abraham Clarke, Curate of Stainton.
5. Mr. Garencieres indulged to go reside at Stainton (wch. was his meaning) putting in a competent Curate on a sufficient Salary at Scarborough.

These short notes show not merely the clear-headedness which made Archbishop Herring a most competent administrator, but also the stiffness of his Churchmanship, at least in his adherence to the rubrics of the Prayer Book. It was, perhaps, the horse-sense of the Archbishop which made him realize the value of knowing not only his clergy and the condition of the parishes they served, but the important laity as well. And he set out seriously to do this. His visits on his Visitation tour to such great territorial magnates as the Duke of Kingston-upon-Hull and the Earl of Carlisle, have been already noticed, the seats of those Whig noblemen lay upon his road; but when the Archbishop was on holiday, in the summer of 1745 and had hoped to be "snug and private" on a visit to a kinsman in Nottinghamshire, he found it "quite otherwise." For he "paid some compliments to great folks, who love to be complimented, and got into the acquaintance and characters of some of the principal gentry in that part of my diocese."[1] And writing on 16th April, 1746 to Lord Hardwicke the Archbishop described his keeping of the Duke of Cumberland's birthday the day before "Many of the gentlemen took it into their heads to dine with me [at Bishopthorpe], the Lord Mayor and the Church and many of the soldiery and some young rakes, who made a shift to be demure for an hour or two. I sent for the city cook and did the best I could for them."[2]

[1] *Letters to Duncombe*, p. 79.

[2] *Life and Correspondence of Lord Hardwicke*, i. 521.

The most spectacular event in Archbishop Herring's career was his action when Prince Charles Edward sought to regain the throne for his father in 1745. The Prince unfurled his standard at Glenfinnan on 19th August, 1745, and on 21st September, by his victory over King George's troops at Prestonpaus, he became master of Scotland. The news of the progress of the Rising had stirred the Archbishop greatly. On Sunday, 22nd September he preached at York Minster a sermon such as a convinced Whig would have preached at such a crisis. Two days later, at a meeting of the leading gentlemen of the county in York Castle, the Archbishop addressed them in a rousing speech and led them, then and there, to form an association for the defence of the realm and to promise subscriptions to the large sum of £40,000, to equip troops. So eager was he in the cause that he told the clergy that "he should think it no derogation from the dignity of his character, or the sanctity of his function, in times when the religion and liberties of his country were at stake, to change his pastoral staff for a musquet, and his cassock for a regimental coat,"[1] a declaration which led the Welsh curate to offer to attend the Archbishop at an hour's notice[2] and makes it evident that the Archbishop must have possessed a pastoral staff. The Archbishop's military zeal led others than his Welsh friend to believe that he had "put on scarlet," and this myth, for myth it was, earned for him the nickname of "the Red Herring." The Archbishop became the principal representative of King George's government in the North of England as the danger from Scotland increased, he concerned himself greatly with the Yorkshire regiment that was being trained, thanks chiefly to his efforts. At Bishopthorpe are preserved the very exact accounts for five months of the seven companies raised from the East Riding; the accounts begin on 25th September, 1745.[3] The Archbishop in a letter of this time tells how successful General Oglethorpe had been in winning the admiration of the citizens of York, and how, at a military parade, he himself, at the General's desire, had ridden "upon the ground with him for what he called Countenance."[4]

As the news of Prince Charles's march south became known, the Archbishop shewed his courage by remaining at Bishopthorpe. He wrote on 22nd November "As to my own safety for the present, I will stay till the last moment, and if any scheme of defence of any likelihood can be formed, I will share in the common danger. If not, I know of no duty that obliges me to run the hazard of being knocked on the head or taken prisoner. I stand ready to escape at half an hour's [warning] and shall

[1] Rastell, *History of Southwell, etc.*, p. 317.

[2] See above, p. 3.

[3] Bundle 27.

[4] The letter is endorsed "Recd. Octr. 4th." *English Historical Review*, xix, 548.

endeavour to do so. This is upon supposition that these ruffians take the York road. If they take the other I am determined to fix my abode and wait the fate of, and, as I may, serve my country here. I have taken the best methods I could think of to persuade the Lord Mayor, if he can't stand it out, to fly rather than submit to proclaim the Pretender."

The moral effect of the stand taken by the Archbishop was probably of untold value to the Government and must have steadied many waverers. He shared, indeed, the fears around him and he was specially credulous of any reports which reflected on the loyalty of the Roman Catholics. Possibly a modern psychologist might be able to discover the cause of this obsession for, in the phrase of to-day, Roman Catholics were the Archbishop's "blind spot." As early as 7th September he is writing to Lord Hardwicke about the Roman Catholics in York, "a place where the number & spirit & boldness of the Papists is such that their public Mass House joins in a manner, to the Cathedral, their service is performed daily there, & their congregation formed by the same public notice, & their congregation as large or larger than that of the Protestant Church."[1] On 27th September, three days after the meeting in York Castle and the opening of the defence fund, the Archbishop writes "Some of the Papists here I am told have subscribed—*Timeo Danaos et dona ferentes*," and he proceeds to suggest that the excellent Mr. Tempest of Broughton "who is said to be very artful and zealous" and Mr. Constable of Holderness, who, as he has heard "has a troop of three hundred at his command" should be secured.[2] Happily for these two perfectly peaceable gentlemen Lord Hardwicke was able, after making inquiries in London to reply on 3rd October "I know nothing, nor can I find that anything is known by others here, relating to the two considerable Gentlemen you mention."[3] On 1st October the Archbishop writes "We were thoroughly alarmed on Tuesday with danger from the Papists and particularly that Lord Fairfax of Gilling was on the point of rising. Search warrants went out instantly, & returned with the fullest justification of that noble Lord; who, I believe, is the King's friend. The alarm struck us the more, as we had more certain intelligence at the same time that the Papists at Egton, a little town on the Moors full of them, had made public rejoicings on Cope's defeat, & had all like to have been cut to pieces by the protestant ship-carpenters of Whitby."[4] How vain these fears were the event proved, when the Roman Catholics of Egton refused, a month or two later, to give shelter to their two priests when they were flying to avoid arrest; conduct which caused one of those priests, Monox Hervey to write

[1] *English Historical Review*, xix, 533.

[2] *Ibid.*, p. 544.

[3] *Ibid.*, p. 547.

[4] *Ibid.*, p. 548.

in his Register "From the Moors in Yorkshire, Good Lord deliver us—Amen."[1]

Archbishop Herring seems in all other respects to have been a just, humane, and gentle man, but where Roman Catholics or Jacobites were concerned those virtues disappeared and an ignoble and ungenerous temper replaced them. Thus he wrote on 6th October about Lord Fairfax and Mr. Tempest of Broughton, "Fairfax and Tempest's houses have been searched, but no appearance of mischief,"[2] and there is no spark of humanity or generosity in his reference to the Jacobite prisoners, taken as the Prince's army retired to Scotland. "Our castle is being full of prisoners, & of so low and dirty a sort, that when the wind sets fair, I can almost fancy that I can smell them, as they do the hogs (i.e., hogsheads) at a distillery."[3] The conditions in York Castle became so vile, however, that the Archbishop was moved, on 14th February to approach the Lord Chancellor on the condition of the jail. "The prisoners die and the Recorder told me yesterday when the turnkey opens the cells in the morning the steam and stench is intolerable and scarcely credible. The very walls are covered with lice in the room over which the Grand Jury sit."[4] When the last hopes of the House of Stuart had been scattered at Culloden and the process of exterminating its adherents was well on its way, Archbishop Herring received the Duke of Cumberland at York, ceremonially, at the head of the Dean and Chapter and Clergy and presented an address on 23rd July, 1746. The language of that address can only be excused on the supposition that the Archbishop was ignorant of the atrocious cruelties[5] sanctioned by the brutal and licentious young man he was addressing. "Your conduct, Royal Sir, has been glorious," he said, and he proceeded to applaud "the greatness of your understanding and the goodness of your heart, which make every subject of Great Britain not only to admire and love and serve you...... but trust and depend upon you, as the happy instrument of Heaven."[6] Such words used to a young man who had caused wounded men to be dragged out and shot, and a building in which twenty disabled Highlanders had sought shelter to be burnt with the fugitives inside it, cause the most recent biographer of Archbishop Herring to write "We may think that the Archbishop's language was too strong."[7]

[1] See above Vol. IV, pp. 196, 203.

[2] *English Historical Review*, xix, 719.

[3] *Ibid.*, p. 738. A letter of 6th January, 1745-6.

[4] Lord Hardwicke's *Life*, ii, 501.

[5] For the atrocities committed upon the defeated Jacobites after Culloden see *The Lyon in Mourning*, 3 vols. Scottish Hist. Soc., 1896.

[6] The address is printed in full in Herring's *Sermons*, pp. xxvi-xxix.

[7] Rowden, *The Primates of the Four Georges*, 1916, p. 191.

This performance shews a side of Archbishop Herring which is weak and unpleasant. He had had a tremendous fright but he had risen to the occasion and met the danger with unusual ability and courage. His friend and patron Lord Hardwicke had helped him by his letters but his principles needed no stiffening. Unconsciously, in rallying the forces of Yorkshire to meet a Scotch attack, Archbishop Herring was following the example of his predecessor, Archbishop Thurstan, six centuries before. For Thurstan, in the case of a disputed successor to the English crown in 1138, had organised a force to beat back the Scotch army supporting the Empress Matilda at the Battle of the Standard. Archbishop Herring would not have relished the comparison, for, as he was to show later at Canterbury, he had an almost vulgar and ignorant contempt for a mediaeval predecessor.[1] But, in fact, when the throne of King George II was in danger, he, by his energy and courage, protected it very much as Archbishop Thurstan his predecessor had protected the throne of King Stephen. Whether such activities are admirable in a Christian bishop is another question. Undeniably Archbishop Herring acted from the highest motives that he knew, and his action was to have a result most undesired by him, for it forced him, most unwillingly, to leave the diocese of York and his house at Bishopthorpe.

Bishopthorpe Herring loved. As Bishop of Bangor he had resided either at his deanery at Rochester, or, when Parliament was sitting, at a house in the village of Kensington; when he was translated to York he succeeded to an historical see-house, the sole survivor of the manor houses once belonging to the Archbishops. Cawood had been dismantled after the Restoration, Southwell was dilapidated, Laneham, Scrooby, Bishop Burton, Otley, like the old palace in York, were in ruins. Bishopthorpe Archbishop Herring cared for in every sense. He spent much money on its buildings and its gardens, a fact that he urged in vain on Lord Hardwicke as a reason for refusing the See of Canterbury. In the anxious days of October, 1745 when he was hourly expecting news of Prince Charles Edward's approach, the Archbishop found solace in the grounds of Bishopthorpe, he "could not help putting up an ejaculation at the Pond's side to-night. God grant I may feed my swans in peace !"[2] And among the few remains of Archbishop Herring in the miscellaneous MSS. at Bishopthorpe is a receipted bill for a new copper for the brewhouse, put in in October, 1744.[3] It was more than twice the size of its predecessor, weighing 5¾ cwt. as against the 2 cwt. of the copper it replaced, and it cost, deducting £9. 6s. 8d. allowed for the old one, £39. 8s. 4d. To-day the clock over the gateway alone remains to witness to Archbishop Herring's care for the place of which he was so fond.

[1] S. Anselm, see below, p. 20.

[2] *English Historical Review*, xix, 719.

[3] Bishopthorpe MSS, Bundle 20, No. 31A.

On 10th October, 1747 Archbishop Potter died suddenly in an apoplectic fit at Lambeth. The vacant see is said to have been offered to and refused by Gibson, Bishop of London and Sherlock, Bishop of Salisbury, in turn, and on 13th October Lord Hardwicke wrote to Archbishop Herring to tell him that the King intended to move him to Lambeth. In vain the Archbishop struggled to avoid the translation. "I am come to a very firm and most resolved determination not to quit the See of York on any account or on any consideration," he wrote on 17th October, before the formal offer had been made. When the offer came he was resolved to refuse, but the domination of Lord Hardwicke was too strong and the Archbishop, having burnt three letters of refusal, accepted. Even in his acceptance he begged that the authorities might promote his friend Matthew Hutton, Bishop of Bangor to Canterbury and leave him at York. But the Lord Chancellor was inexorable and to Lambeth Herring went. His just over 9 years as Archbishop of Canterbury add no lustre to his fame. With the rest of the Bishops he opposed the clause in the penal Act against the Scots clergy which made Letters of Orders from the Scots Bishops illegal, and the clause was struck out by 32 votes to 28. But Lord Hardwicke was determined to have the clause, and on the Report stage a motion to re-insert the clause was carried, Archbishop Herring, and other Bishops, absenting themselves. Lord Hardwicke had convinced him that the State was not attempting to decide questions of validity of ordination. A mild storm arose in 1753 over the renewal of a temporary Act permitting Jews to become naturalised. The Archbishop, who had been at first indifferent, with the other Bishops voted for the Act, which passed, only to be repealed in the next session. At Lewes, in that summer he had been received with shouts of "No Jews" and he was greatly shocked "to see how easy it is to raise this foolish people to an inhuman and savage spirit, in spite of all the light and moderation which has of late years prevailed."[1] Had the mob been shouting "No Popery," as in 1746 instead of "No Jews," the Archbishop would certainly have written differently of them. Strangely these demonstrations served only to confirm his prejudices against what he called "High Church"; "Faction, working upon the good old spirit of High Church, has made wild work with the nation," he wrote.[2]

For the rest the Archbishop gave polite and friendly interviews to leading divines of the "Dissenting Interest," Presbyterians and Independents, encouraged scholars like Birch and Jortin (who were wholly free from High Church and Tory principles) and was much concerned in the various political crises as they arose. Herring's Whig politics were a part of his being. Thus in December, 1735 the question of appointing a new Master for Sir J. Williamson's

[1] *Life of Lord Hardwicke*, ii, 56.

[2] Quoted by Rowden, *op. cit.*, p. 205.

school at Rochester arose. Herring, as Dean, was a Governor of the school and his friends, Matthew Kenrick and others, were interested in a candidate who was a good mathematician, but a Tory. The Dean wrote frankly that he could not vote for "a Man of that Denomination, if I did so I should make a scurvy Figure" as seeking to defeat his old friends: "I can neither from Reasons of Integrity nor Policy engage my word to serve any man in that application, who goes under ye denomination of a Tory."[1] It was fortunate for so pure a Whig as Herring that the Whigs were in office for the whole of his public life, for he was no opportunist, and unquestionably he was prepared to suffer for his principles. He held them with an enthusiasm which he disliked and deplored when it was manifested in the strictly religious sphere. Hence, partly, his profound dislike for Roman Catholics, High Churchmen and the Methodists.

The Archbishop's theological opinions are not of importance for he was not a theologian; he displays no trace of being well-read either in the Fathers or in the Anglican divines. His intellectual interests lay in the Classics and in *belles lettres*, in which last, to judge from his printed letters, his taste was poor. Yet he was a constant reader, indeed as a bishop he would read a French novel in his coach, "a book of gallantry, but very modest,"[2] he says of one such work which he recommends to his friend Duncombe. Herring's theological standpoint he described himself to his friend Lord Hardwicke: "Men of science must have their systems, but yet for all the good that their disputes and subtleties have done in the world, I believe we may venture to say that the gospel is infinitely better for common instruction and practice that it has neither enthusiasm, nor metaphysics, nor school divinity in it."[3] The Archbishop has been accused of Arianism, apparently because in 1733 he thought Hoadly's *Plain Account of the Lord's Supper* "a good book" (chiefly because of the temper of its prayers), and because he approved "the temper and wisdom" of Dr. Samuel Clarke's suggested "Book of Common Prayer." But in fact he was not sufficiently a theologian to be attracted by Arianism, such speculations were alien from his very practical mind.

Of one charge brought against his theology he is certainly guiltless, viz., that he suggested that "it would be necessary to order that the Lord's Supper should be administered after the Evening as well as after the Morning Service" to discourage the "superstitious reason" of fasting before communion. The passage is from "A new form of Common Prayer" published in London in 1753, and the learned Dr. Wickham Legg, whose name I mention with grateful veneration, supposing Archbishop Herring to have

[1] MS. Letter of 10th Dec., 1735 to Matthew Kenrick, Esq. in the possession of Miss Kenrick.

[2] *Le paysan parvenue* to Marivaux. *Letters to Duncombe*, p. 42.

[3] *Life, etc. of Lord Hardwicke*, i, 422, a letter, apparently, of 22nd Dec., 1737.

been the author of the book, fastens this charge upon him.[1] But Dr. Wickham Legg was misled by a note in the British Museum Library Catalogue.[2] The crusader against fasting communion was merely an anonymous "Clergyman of the Church of England" who addressed his work to the Archbishop.

Dr. Wickham Legg had, indeed, a horror of Archbishop Herring, writing of him as "The Leist Herring" and as "the Archbishop of Canterbury of ill fame, Dr. Herring."[3] This horror was based, presumably, not only on the mistaken ascription of the "new form of Common Prayer" of 1753 but on an episode which shows the Archbishop at his worst and which cannot be defended. It was first brought to light by Dr. R. L. Poole when examining the muniments of the Dean and Chapter of Canterbury for the Historical MSS. Commission and was printed by him in his Report published in 1901.[4] Briefly, on 23rd December, 1752 Archbishop Herring was approached by Count Perron, the Sardinian Ambassador in London, to know whether his master, Charles Emanuel I, might be granted the relics of S. Anselm from Canterbury Cathedral. Archbishop Herring, astonished and amused by the suggestion, wrote at once to sound the Dean, Dr. John Lynch, as follows :

"Dear Mr. Dean.

I had a Request communicated to me to Day of a very singular Nature; and it comes from the Ambassador of a great Catholic Prince. Arch Bishop Anselm, it seems, lies buried in our Cathedral and the King of Sardinia has a great desire to be possess'd of his Bones, or Dust and Coffin. It seems he was of the Country of Oost, the Bishop of which has put this Desire into the King's Head, who, by the by, is a most prodigious Bigot, and in a late dispute with Geneva gave up Territory to redeem an old Church. You will please to consider this Request with your Friends but not yet capitularly. You will believe I have no great Scruples on this Head, but if I had I would get rid of them all if the parting with the rotten Remains of a Rebel to his King, a Slave to the Popedom & an Enemy to the married Clergy (all this Anselm was) would purchase Ease and Indulgence to one living Protestant. It is believed, that a Condescension in this Business may facilitate the way of doing it to thousands. I think it is worth the Experiment, & really for this End, I should make no Conscience of palming on the Simpletons any other old Bishop with the Name of Anselm. I pray God send you and yours many happy new Years......

Your affectionate Friend"

Lambeth House, Decr. 23, 1752. [T. Cant.]

[1] *English Church Life*, 1660-1833 by J. Wickham Legg, M.D., D.Litt. (London, 1914), p. 55. The mistake is copied from Dr. Wickham Legg's book by Mr. U. Lambert in his fine *History of Blechingley* quoted above, p. 8.

[2] B. Mus. Libr. Catalogue (Lond. 1899) vol. *Liturgies*, p. 506.

[3] *Op. cit.*, p. 26 and p. 55.

[4] Hist. MSS. Comm. *Report on MSS. in Various Collections*, i, pp. 226, 227.

This letter was followed by a formal request by the Archbishop:
"Dear Mr. Dean

Count Perron has been with me just now, and signified his Master the K of Sardinia's request as to the Coffin and Bones of Arch Bp Anselm. The Count is desirous to apply to the Dean and Chapter of Canterbury in the most respectful Manner, and most agreeable to them. Upon which Subject I told him I would consult you. The Count intimated, that if any Thing is found and a removal made, it will be necessary for him to be upon the Spot an ocular Witness in order to testify in the most authentical Manner the reality of this pretious Deposit.
I suppose the old Tomb has ponderous and marble Jaws so that it will make some noise to effect this important Work, but sure you have no Protestant Virgers that can look upon this as Diana of the Ephesians. This you will consider. I have said no thing to the Count, but declared your and my Readiness

Yr affect Friend

Lambeth House,
Jan. 6, 1753.

This outrage was prevented by some unwillingness, it would seem, on the part of the Prebendaries. A letter to the Archbishop, signed S.S., (the initials may represent either Samuel Stedman or Samuel Shuckford, both were Prebendaries at the time, but Dr. Shuckford is slightly more probable as he was something of a scholar and an historian) gives some facts about S. Anselm's tomb in the cathedral and considers the matter "impracticable." The writer urges also the neglected state of the undercroft, which would give offence to the Ambassador if he came, and makes it clear that he was opposed to the design. Meanwhile the Ambassador submitted to the Archbishop a report on the probable site of S. Anselm's tomb, drawn up by "P. Bradley," evidently an antiquary, and the Archbishop on 14th April, 1753 sent it on to the Dean for his "reverend consideration." But there the matter seems to have ended, thanks to the obstruction of the Prebendaries.[1]

The callousness and coarseness displayed by the Archbishop in the affair were due partly to his ignorance of history, partly to his unbounded contempt for Roman Catholics. In his printed sermons he appears most stirred when he is urging "the iniquity of the Roman Church."

Thus preaching the Annual Sermon for the S.P.G. on 17th February, 1737 from the text "And the Poor have the Gospel preached unto them" (S. Matthew xi, 5) Bishop Herring (as he then was) is concerned with the simple nature of the Christian message, its suitability for rich and poor alike. Explaining exactly what the content of this message is, the preacher defines it as "the knowledge and worship of the true God, the divine Mission of our

[1] *Op. cit.*, pp. 227-230.

Saviour", "a plain and clear rule of duty", "the addition of two most wise and significant Institutions" (apparently Baptism and Holy Communion are meant), and the assurance of the Forgiveness of sins.[1] The reasonableness of this revelation is then considered at length, which leads to the consideration of the iniquity of the Roman Church "in shutting up the Holy Scriptures, where they can do it, in an unknown Tongue" and to "the very monstrous Absurdities practised in their public Service."[2] Roman Catholics omit, the Bishop sneers, to claim that through their communion "the Poor have the Gospel preached to them." There lies the excellence of the work of the S.P.G. Further, the Bishop urges "Every Convert to Christianity, or Member secured to our Establishment upon Gospel and Protestant principles is a Friend to our Country & Government, as well as to our Religion; an Argument that ought exceedingly to weigh with us, when we consider the indefatigable Zeal of Popery, both at home and abroad, in propagating the shameful Cause of Tyranny and Superstition." Another sermon, preached at the Anniversary of a Society for Promoting English Protestant Working Schools in Ireland, on 18th March, 1740, from the text of the story of the Good Samaritan, is concerned with "the Practice of universal Love and Charity......to do Good to all......whether they be of the Eastern or the Western Church; whether they dwell in the North or in the South."[3] Consequently it is well to "enlighten the Minds, & sweeten and civilize the Natures of thousands of poor ignorant Children, brought up in a sort of Profession of Christianity, but in reality in Heathen Ignorance and Savageness of Temper."[4] And the sermon ends with an exhortation to Roman Catholics "*Go then,* all ye of that peevish and narrow-spirited Religion, *Go and do likewise*" and the preacher enforces his remarks with a quotation, on the need of extending religion by the practice of virtue, from "a great Ecclesiastic of your own Persuasion," the Abbé Fleury.[5] Had any Irish or British Roman Catholics been among Dr. Herring's congregation they must have reflected on the singular contrast between his exhortations and the bitter severity of the penal code which cut them off from almost every privilege of citizenship. In a sermon of 1748, at Kensington, the Archbishop was greatly shocked by the evils of the times: "our Nation is most apparently in a declining State," he declared. "Religion has lost its Power on the Heart, and by the most natural Consequence, things every Day proceed from bad to worse"[6] and he proceeds to illustrate this in detail. And this in spite of our being

[1] *Seven Sermons, etc.,* London, 1763, pp. 16, 17.

[2] *Ibid.,* pp. 31-32.

[3] *Ibid.,* pp. 143-145.

[4] *Ibid.,* p. 147.

[5] *Ibid.,* pp. 156, 157.

[6] *Ibid.,* p. 213.

"reformed from the Errors of a corrupted Church." Yet "a sober and regular, though weak and deluded *Romanist* is a Character preferable to a loose & immoral *Protestant*."[1] But this admission is succeeded by an attack of unusual ferocity. "The strange & alarming spreading of" Popery "continues, & is our greatest and most immediate danger." The words are strange in 1748, when all danger of a Roman Catholic rising had been crushed, savagely, in 1746. His Grace went on "No Nation (speaking in the gross), can possibly be happy & flourishing under *Popery*, because the Influence of it is of so baneful a Nature, that it does not only sink the Spirits of Men, damp the Vigour and Life of Industry, stop every Avenue to religious Knowledge from the Scriptures, make Princes Tyrants, and their People Slaves, but it in a manner countermines the Wisdom and Goodness of Providence, and converts (as it has done in fact) the most beautiful and fertile County into a desolate Wilderness ......For *Popery*, as a fine Writer expresses it, is really an usurpation upon Christianity, and, like Usurpers, lives within its Guards, Inquisitions and Dragoons, it settles and supports itself by Gibbets, Axes, Halters, Fire & Sword, and all the Instruments of Death & cruel Execution."[2]

The language of the preacher applied very exactly to the doings of the Duke of Cumberland in Scotland two years before, and to the actions of past English commanders in Ireland, but it is not easy to find contemporary justification for these violent charges against Roman Catholicism "in the gross." Louis XIV had indeed used dragoons in the Cevennes, but the Duke of Cumberland had done so far more recently against Scotch Episcopalians and Roman Catholics. Archbishop Herring had never crossed the Straits of Dover, and his highly-coloured language about Popery seems due partly to that fact. He had lived in a very secluded *enclave* and was not only personally unacquainted with any Roman Catholic country, but, apparently, even with any living Roman Catholic.

There is another explanation of this outburst. On 9th March, 1746/7 Dr. Pyle wrote to his friend Dr. Kerrich, "Pray have you seen his Grace of York's fast-sermon? It is a fine one, and has recovered him the credit he lost by his sermon at York last year. N.B. To page 15 it is the very sermon he preached against the 'Beggar's Opera'."[3] Evidently the reference is to the sermon quoted above; and the abuse of Roman Catholics was possibly put in to order, for the Archbishop's sermon at York in September, 1745 had been strangely free from that particular seasoning which the Whig taste of the day liked strong and plentiful.

The Archbishop had made his reputation by his preaching. Philip, 2nd Earl Hardwicke (1720-1790), son of Herring's patron

[1] *Ibid.*, p. 215.

[2] Ibid., pp. 222-3.

[3] *Memoirs of a Royal Chaplain*, p. 120.

declared that the Archbishop "was a popular preacher, and though his delivery or elocution had something particular, it was captivating and agreeable. He was not fond of printing his sermons, perhaps they were better to *hear* than to *read*. I believe he ordered them all by his will to be burnt." He witnesses also that "of all the clergymen I ever knew he was most acceptable to the laity in general."[1] One further point in Archbishop Herring's position deserves notice: he was sternly opposed to the Methodist Revival and one of his printed letters, written in the year before his death, expresses his attitude clearly.[2] "Whitefield is Daniel Burgess *redivivus*," he wrote (Daniel Burgess, 1645-1713, was a Presbyterian minister, noted for his vivacious preaching). And John Wesley he considered an "author, with good parts and learning" but "a most dark and saturnine creature. His pictures may frighten weak people, that, at the same time, are wicked, but, I fear, he will make few converts, except for a day......For myself, I own I have no constitution for these frights and fervors; and if I can but keep up to the regular practice of a Christian life, upon Christian reasons, I shall be in no pain for futurity."

As might be expected, Herring declared to the Prime Minister, the Duke of Newcastle his resolution "never" to "teaze the Administration on the Foot of Episcopacy in America....I have hitherto endeavoured and shall continue so to do to keep clear of the rancour of High Church."[3] Four years earlier he had written that when the King commanded him "to consider that affair" he would do so, "but not before." Yet notwithstanding this, and the expression of his opinions quoted previously, Rastall in his very careful account of the Archbishop, having stated that "Herring was certainly a very sincere Protestant; and, as such, a steady friend to the house of Hanover" has "no hesitation in asserting, upon good authority, that his politics were monarchical, and his religion high church."[4] Rastall (1756-1822) had considerable opportunities for learning about Archbishop Herring, for his father was Vicar General of the Church of Southwell and he himself was a Fellow of Jesus College, Cambridge, and had married Harriet Kenrick of Bletchingley, a family with which the Archbishop was on terms of close friendship.

The term "high church" as used by Rastall may connote no more than a strong belief in the privileges of a State Church and a keen sense of its "established" position; and whenever Archbishop Herring uses the term, he uses it in an opprobrious sense. But Rastall wrote with considerable knowledge and care, and possibly Herring was akin ecclesiastically to Bishop Gibson and Archbishops Potter and Secker, who were, to some extent,

[1] Hardwicke, *Life*, i, 422.

[2] Letter XLVIII in the *Letters to Duncombe*, p. 171 seq.

[3] Letter of 24th July, 1754 quoted by Rowden, *op. cit.*, p. 206.

[4] W. D. Rastall, *History, etc. of Southwell*, London, 1787, p. 234.

High Churchmen in the theological sense. Such printed and MS. remains of Archbishop Herring as survive hardly suggest that he held such opinions.

One strange link connected him with his martyred predecessor, William Laud. Archbishop Laud had kept a tortoise in the gardens at Lambeth, and it survived the storms both of the Commonwealth and of the Revolution. Early in Archbishop Herring's reign at Lambeth this historical tortoise was killed by the spade of a gardener who was digging the border in which it was hibernating. The Archbishop, with a light allusion to Archbishop Laud, wrote to Lord Hardwicke that he had replaced it.[1]

The place of Bishopthorpe in Archbishop Herring's affections was taken not by Lambeth House, as he always calls it, but by his other palace at Croydon. He spent much money on both houses and on their gardens. Of Croydon he wrote on 24th April, 1754, "I love this old House, and was very desirous of amusing myself, if I could finds means to do it, with the history of its buildings."[2] But his care for Croydon palace was wasted, so far as the See of Canterbury was concerned, for neither of his two immediate successors occupied it, and in 1780, under Archbishop Cornwallis, it was sold. The buildings which remain still bear witness to Herring's generous care for this ancient house of the See.

In the summer of 1753, the Archbishop's health, always delicate, began to fail and he was seized with serious illness. Removal to Croydon, riding on Banstead Downs and daily draughts of asses milk, restored him for a time. Dr. Pyle, Bishop Hoadly's chaplain, recorded from time to time how ill the Archbishop looked; thus on 20th February, 1755 "I was with the Archbishop t'other day. No man alive was ever so thin and looked so like a ghost. But he says he is well."[3] In March, 1756, on one of his brief visits to Lambeth, the Archbishop went to see his old Corpus colleague, Dr. Mawson, now Bishop of Ely, at Ely House in Holborn. There he caught cold which brought on further attacks of illness,[4] and in June, 1756 Dr. Pyle reported "the poor Archbishop cannot live long," and thought it a matter of a few months.[5] The ebb and flow of the Archbishop's health was marked in a fashion unusual if not unique in such a case, being recorded in English verse by a young divine, Francis Fawkes, son of the Rector of Warmsworth, Jeremiah Fawkes, who appears in these Visitation Returns.[6] Francis Fawkes (1720-1777) had been like the Archbishop, a scholar of Jesus College, Cambridge and had served as chaplain to

[1] Rowden, *op. cit.*, p. 203 quoting Hardwicke, *Life*, ii, 401.

[2] Ibid., p. 212.

[3] *Memoirs of a Royal Chaplain*, p. 232.

[4] Ibid., p. 255.

[5] Ibid., p. 260.

[6] Above, Vol. 3, p. 189.

Mr. Lane at Bramham. He followed the Archbishop to the South, becoming curate of Croydon about 1752. On 25th June, 1753 he inscribed an 'Ode to the Archbishop' "on his Sickness and Recovery." It begins

"Why droops Aurelius by sharp pains opprest,"
"Whose danger saddens every virtuous breast?"

and it laments the recent death of Frederick, Prince of Wales with a warmth of feeling which history does not justify.

"Frederick, alas, the Kingdom's greatest pride"
"Fair in the bloom of all his virtues died."

The poet then turns to the Archbishop:

"Ah! generous Master of the candid mind,"
"Light of the world and friend of human kind,"
"Leave us not cause our sorrows to renew,"
"Nor fear the falling of the state in you."

He alludes to his conduct in the Rising of 1745.

"Your righteous zeal the brave Brigantes warm'd,"
"Silent they heard, approv'd, united, arm'd,"

and concludes, fulsomely:

"Oh, by kind Providence to Britain given,"
"Long may you live and late revisit Heaven;"
"Continue still to bless us with your stay,"
"Nor wish for Heav'n till we have learnt the way."[1]

A little later Fawkes composed an ode "to Mrs. Herring," presumably the wife of a cousin of the Archbishop, and on 12th March, 1754, composed a Vernal Ode to his Grace himself. In this composition the poet urges Health to "descend and scatter pleasures, as she flies,"

"Where Surrey's downs extend:"
"There Herring wooes her friendly power;"
"There may she all her roses shower;"
"To heal the shepherd all her balms employ,"
"So will she soothe our fears and give a nation joy."[2]

In 1755 the Archbishop presented the poet to the vicarage of Orpington with the chapelry of S. Mary Cray and in 1756 Mr. Fawkes wrote another Ode to his Grace, praising "the generous hand" that had placed the writer "Fast by the fountains of the silver Cray."[3]

But the hopes of Mr. Fawkes for the Archbishop's health were not realised. His last letter to his friend Duncombe was written from "Croydon house" on 3rd January, 1757 thanking him for his "noble present," a Yorkshire pie.[4] Six months before, on 22nd June, 1756, he had written to the same friend "life is over with me," and in the reserved and sincere manner of his piety he declared

[1] *Johnson's English Poets* (ed. 1810), Vol. XVI, p. 242.

[2] Ibid., p. 243.

[3] Ibid., p. 244.

[4] *Letters to Duncombe*, p. 177.

"I know who sent me hither, and how much it is my duty to attend his summons for a removal."[1] On Friday, 11th March, 1757 Dr. Pyle tells that the Archbishop "desired to be by himself—and spent some hours in burning papers; the family were not pleased at his being so long alone; but nobody cared to disobey his order, about not going in to his room. At last he rang the bell, and was found unable to speak intelligibly. So he continued till Sunday morning, March 13th, when he died." Dr. Pyle adds "this good prelate lived till he was reduced to the resemblance of a skeleton covered with bladder, or parchment: And was, really, a sad sight."[2]

By his own directions the Archbishop was buried privately in a vault in Croydon parish church. He had forbidden the erection of any monument, but a plain black stone over the vault was inscribed, "Here lieth the body of the Most Revd. Dr. Thomas Herring, Archbishop of Canterbury, who died March xiii, A.D., MDCCLVII, aged LXIV." Croydon church was burnt down in 1867 but a tablet on the wall of the Southern Chapel records that Archbishop Herring lies buried near.

In his will made on 6th July, 1756 with three codicils added, one on 13th October and the others on 14th December[3] the Archbishop shewed his care and affection for his servants, his relations and for "the Old House," Corpus Christi College, Cambridge, to which last he left £1000 in South Sea annuities. He left a like sum to the Corporation of the Sons of the Clergy.

The list of beneficiaries shews the staff employed by the Archbishop as well as his generous remembrance of it. First on the list is the Receiver, Mr. Thomas Parry, who is left £200, next come the butler and the coachman who receive a like sum, then two women housekeepers and nine men servants who are left each £100, and then three men servants who are left £50 apiece. A further £100 is to be divided among the servants not mentioned, and to "my faithful servant William Burnett" is left £500 and the Archbishop's body-linen. In the first codicil the Archbishop leaves bequests to his postillion, under-gardener and under-cook, and in the second codicil a bequest to yet another servant. In all twenty men servants and two women, the housekeepers, are named. In his last codicil the Archbishop bequeathed his "options"; the Precentorship of Chichester to Thomas Herring, Rector of Chevening, the Archdeaconry of Gloucester to Henry Herring, Rector of Topsfield, and the Rectory of Rothbury to "Mr. Berdmore, Residentiary of York." He directed that all his written papers and sermons were to be burnt. Dr. Pyle reckoned that the Archbishop died "worth only 18 thousand pounds," and that when the legacies were paid "there will be somewhat better than £1000 apiece for his relations i.e., Dr. Will Herring of York, Herring the

[1] Ibid., p. 176.

[2] *Memoirs of a Royal Chaplain*, p. 296.

[3] The will is in the P.C.C., 1757, fo. 77.

draper, and their children"[1] "Herring the draper" had his business (in 1728, at least) "at the golden artichoke, in Lombard-street."[2] The Archbishop's fortune was, apparently, even less than Dr. Pyle estimated, the *Gentleman's Magazine* gave it as £10,000. It was in striking contrast to the sum left by his predecessor, Archbishop Potter, which was variously reckoned at £90,000 or £70,000, and to the £50,000 left next year by his successor, Archbishop Hutton "saved out of the Church in 12 years" Dr. Pyle writes "and not one penny to any good use or public charity."[3]

One bequest in Archbishop Herring's will is interesting because it links together the two men who probably influenced him most; it was the gift, along with his topaz seal, of the "head of Bishop Fleetwood of Ely painted by Richardson" to the Earl of Hardwicke.

The executors evidently carried out most thoroughly the Archbishop's direction to burn his papers, for very few survive; chiefly the letters in the Hardwicke MSS. and those in the possession of Miss Kenrick. In the Library of Corpus Christi College, Cambridge are preserved two fragments which are believed to be in the Archbishop's hand: one consists of the rough notes for a sermon on the text "An Evil and Adulterous generation seeketh after a sign, etc.," S. Matthew, xii, 39 and 40, and is almost entirely a collection of parallelisms from the Synoptists on the Entombment and the Resurrection on the third day, with a reference to S. Jerome; the other is a sheet of note paper of the modern shape covered on both sides with rather illegible and incoherent sentences. Among them it is possible to decipher "I don't think yt I shall live—but I have nothing on my conscience to give me any bitterness." "I am now dying" and "I am going to great happiness." The fragment, if it is the Archbishop's, was evidently written in his last conscious hours.

Portraits of the Archbishop were painted by Hogarth twice, by S. Webster, and by Thomas Hudson; they can be seen at Lambeth, at Bishopthorpe and in the Hall of Corpus Christi College, Cambridge. The portrait at Bishopthorpe is particularly pleasing; the face, almost feminine in its delicacy, suggests a rather fastidious man, at once gracious and graceful. There it is certainly true to life, for those who knew the Archbishop best unite in praising his kindness and charm. A few details of his manner of life are preserved; he was an early riser "the sooner my friends call upon me in the morning, so much the better. I am at leisure constantly by nine" the Archbishop wrote from Lambeth to Dr. Doddridge in July, 1749, and in another letter to the same

[1] *Memoirs of a Royal Chaplain*, p. 296.

[2] *Letters to Duncombe*, p. 7.

[3] Rowden, *Primates of the Four Georges*, pp. 158, 225. *Memoirs of a Royal Chaplain*, p. 305.

divine two years later, he wrote "remember, I am an early man."[1] There is a certain fastidious simplicity, in his invitation to the Duke of Newcastle to dine at Croydon in July, 1753 "Your Grace shall find *concha salis puri*, a clean table-cloth, good mutton, and the best claret I can procure."[2] Among the Bishopthorpe MSS. is a letter to Archbishop Drummond from Bishop Terrick then of Peterborough recommending to his Grace as his wine merchant at York a relation of Mrs. Terrick, whose Port wine, supplied to Archbishops Herring and Gilbert had always won, the Bishop said, their Graces' approval.

Archbishop Herring passes almost unnoticed now in the long list of the Archbishops of Canterbury and of York. He is dismissed, perhaps, as 'a typically Georgian prelate.' That he was a Whig, and a wholehearted one is certain, but his strict partisanship was part of his quality of loyalty; he was devotedly loyal to his friends. That he was a really conscientious bishop these Returns prove, he had a clear head which shewed itself both in the very direct English of his sermons and in his dealings with his dioceses. He was simple, unostentatious, and extremely generous in a luxurious, lavish, and selfish age. He was not a scholar nor a man of great learning, but he had been an efficient Tutor at Cambridge and, throughout his life, he liked to keep in touch with his college. He patronized men of learning who were Whigs. But the Archbishop's interests were less intellectual than practical: he was greatly concerned with politics, and it was political pressure and loyalty to his party and to one of its great supporters, Lord Hardwicke, which forced the Archbishop, much against his will, to leave Bishopthorpe for Lambeth.

The key-note of Archbishop Herring's character seems to have been a teachableness which made him absorb readily and thoroughly the lessons impressed upon him by the authorities he recognised. He had been brought up a Whig; Bishop Fleetwood's influence reinforced the Whig tradition; and then the powerful intellect of the Whig lawyer Lord Hardwicke kept Herring firm in the Whig faith. He was intensely loyal and very affectionate, but he gives the impression of a man who was possibly unable, and certainly unwilling, to look over the wall built for him by his stronger friends. Consequently he took for granted the Whig views and practices of the day, without questioning their truth or rightness. His contempt for his mediaeval predecessors is an example of this, yet, greatly as he would have disliked the comparison, Thomas Herring bears a stronger likeness to the Archbishops of the Middle Ages than most of those who came before him or who came after him. He stood directly in succession to Archbishop Thurstan when he raised the men of Yorkshire to withstand a Scots army in 1745, he showed his kinship with not a few of the mediaeval archbishops

[1] Rowden, *Primates of the Four Georges*, pp. 202, 203.

[2] Ibid., p. 225.

when he spent money lavishly on the houses of his sees, he carried on their tradition by the generous charities of his last will, and he was the last English archbishop until the 20th century, who lived and died unmarried. He cannot be reckoned among the great Archbishops of Canterbury or of York, and his outlook was too limited and his achievements too few to entitle him to be called a great man. Even as a Christian bishop of the period he does not attain the spiritual stature of his predecessor, Archbishop Sharp of York nor of his aged contemporary, Bishop Wilson of Sodor and Man; but he was without question a good man, and according to his lights, a good bishop, conscientious, businesslike, accessible, and free from pomposity, self-seeking and self indulgence.

He was a generous and kind master, a most true and affectionate friend, and, very evidently, he had the elusive and indefinable gift of charm. He did not lack courage, he was a persuasive preacher, after the manner of that day, though his sermons read dully now, and his personal religion, though it lacked the glow and fire of the religion of William Law or the Wesleys, was sincere and deep. It enabled him to face with courage years of steadily failing health and to meet death, when it came, with untroubled calm. Francis Fawkes wrote a poem on the Archbishop's death, entitled *Aurelius, an Elegy*.[1] It is of twenty-two stanzas and is marked by the unctuous flattery and exaggeration which appear in the same writer's works noticed above, though to a less degree. Three of its stanzas bear quotation here:

"Mild was his Aspect, full of Truth and Grace,"
"Temper'd with Dignity and lively Sense;"
"Sweetness and Candour beam'd upon his Face,"
"Emblems of Love and large Benevolence."

. . . .

"How will the Poor, alas! now truly poor,"
"Bewail their generous Benefactor dead?"
"Who daily, from his hospitable Door,"
"The Naked cloth'd, and gave the Hungry Bread."

. . . .

"Thus mild, thus humble, in the highest State,"
"The 'one Thing needful' was his sole Regard;"
"Belov'd, and blameless, he prolong'd his Date"
"By Acts of Goodness, which themselves reward."

[1] It is printed in the edition of Abp. Herring's *Sermons*, 1763, p. xlii seq., and elsewhere.

APPENDIX E.

By S. L. Ollard.

A list of the clergy of the Minsters of York, Southwell, and Ripon, and of the Proctors in Convocation, in 1743, shewing their other preferments within, and as far as possible outside, the diocese.

YORK MINSTER.

Dean. Richard Osbaldeston, D.D. 19th September, 1728. Res. on election to the See of Carlisle, to which he was consecrated 4th October, 1747.

R. of Hinderwell, 15th January, 1714. C. of Muston Chapel, 22nd March, 1714. V. of Hunmanby, 1st July, 1715. R. of Folkton, 5th March, 1727.

Sub-Dean. Thomas Hayter, M.A. 26th November, 1730. Res. on consecration as Bishop of Norwich, 3rd December, 1749.

Archdeacon of York, 26th November, 1730. Preb. of Strensall, 20th January, 1735. R. of Kirkby Overblows, 23rd April, 1729. R. of Kirkby [Cleveland], 24th February, 1737. Preb. of North Muskham at Southwell, 21st September, 1728. Preb. of Westminster, 12th February, 1738. Formerly Domestic Chaplain to Archbishop Blackburn.

Archdeacon of York. Thomas Hayter, M.A. 26th November, 1730. See above.

Archdeacon of the East Riding. Heneage Dering, LL.D. 7th March, 1701. Died 8th April, 1750.

Preb. of Fridaythorpe, 1st May, 1708. R. of Scrayingham, 24th March, 1711. Dean of Ripon, 3rd March, 1710. Master of Hospital of S. Mary Magdalen at Ripon, June, 1711. Master of Hospital of S. John Baptist at Ripon, June, 1711. Formerly Domestic Chaplain to Archbishop Sharp.

Archdeacon of Cleveland. Jaques Sterne, LL.D. 17th November, 1735.

Precentor and Preb. of Driffield, 17th November, 1735. R. of Rise, 5th Feb., 1722. V. of Hornsea, 3rd May, 1729. R. of Hornsey-cum-Riston, 3rd May, 1729. Preb. of South Muskham at Southwell, 11th April, 1734.

Archdeacon of Nottingham. Robert Marsden, B.D. 18th February, 1715.

R. of Rempston, 28th August, 1702. Preb. of Norwell Palishall at Southwell, 2nd June, 1720. Formerly Domestic Chaplain to Archbishop Sharp.

Precentor and Prebendary of Driffield, and Canon Residentiary. Jaques Sterne, LL.D. 17th November, 1735. See *Archdeacon of Cleveland* above.

Chancellor and Prebendary of Laughton-en-le-Morthen. SAMUEL BAKER, D.D. 12th January, 1740.

Canon Residentiary. Proctor in Convocation for the Archdeaconry of Cleveland. R. of Settrington, 7th March, 1721. R. of Dunnington, 18th May, 1722.

Succentor Canonicorum. MATTHEW HUTTON, D.D. 21st January, 1735.

Preb. of Langtoft, 18th May, 1734. R. of Spofforth, 1st April, 1730. R. of Tunstall (Holderness), 21st January, 1735. Preb. of Westminster, 18th May, 1739. Chaplain to King George II. Elected Bishop of Bangor, 23rd April, 1743, consecrated 13th November, 1743.

PREBENDARIES.

1. **Apesthorpe.** ROBERT REYNOLDS. 17th September, 1736.

R. of S. Cuthbert's, York, 4th June, 1740. V. of Holy Trinity in King's Court, York, 5th June, 1740.

2. **Ampleforth.** HENRY COOKE, M.A. 10th April, 1722.

Preb. of Rampton at Southwell, 14th October, 1721. R. of Stokesley, 26th December, 1723. Preb. of 2nd Stall at Ripon, 19th October, 1743. Formerly Domestic Chaplain to Archbishop Sir William Dawes.

3. **Barnby-on-the-Moor.** LEWIS STEPHENS, M.A. 9th February, 1726.

Archdeacon of Chester, 21st September, 1727. Preb. of Dunham at Southwell, 18th July, 1729. Preb. of Exeter, 2nd October, 1731. Formerly Archdeacon of Barnstaple at Exeter, 1724 to 1731. A benefactor to Exeter Grammar School.

4. **Bilton.** ROBERT WHATLEY. 24th June, 1729.

5. **Bole.** RICHARD GOODWIN, D.D. 23rd March, 1719.

R. of Tankersley, 20th September, 1715. V. of Prestwich, Lancs. Proctor in Convocation for the Archdeaconry of York.

6. **Botevant.** GEORGE LEGH, LL.D. 16th June, 1732.

V. of Halifax, 25th August, 1731.

7. **Bugthorpe.** WILLIAM BERDMORE, M.A. 14th April, 1743.

V. of Bishopthorpe, 22nd March, 1736. C. of Acaster Malbis, 22nd March, 1736.

8. **Dunnington.** NICHOLAS GOUGE, D.D. 18th May, 1722.

R. of Gilling, 29th June, 1715.

9. **Fenton.** THOMAS MEASE, M.A. 2nd March, 1718.

R. of Scorborough, 16th November, 1698. C. of Beverley Minster, 3rd March, 1702. Lecturer there, 14th July, 1727. C. of Beswick.

10. **Fridaythorpe.** HENEAGE DERING, LL.D. 1st May, 1708. See *Archdeacon of the East Riding* above.

11. **Givendale.** William Dodsworth, M.A. 5th January, 1741.

C. of S. Olave, York, 6th August, 1733. R. of All Saints, Pavement, York, 24th June, 1735.

12. **Grindall.** Richard Robinson, M.A. 4th May, 1738.

R. of Etton, 20th April, 1739. V. of Hutton Buscel, 3rd May, 1742. Afterwards Bishop of Killala, 1752, Ferns, 1759, Kildare, 1761 and Archbishop of Armagh, 1765. Created Baron Rokeby of Armagh, 1777. Formerly Domestic Chaplain to Archbishop Blackburn.

13. **Holme Archiepiscopi.** Thomas Clark, M.A. 9th December, 1742.

R. of Kirkheaton, 9th July, 1728.

14. **Husthwaite.** John Clarkson, M.A. 22nd February, 1708.

V. of Silkstone, 6th October, 1708.

15. **Knaresborough cum Bickhill.** Thomas Lamplugh, M.A. 15th February, 1711.

Canon Residentiary. R. of Bolton Percy, 9th February, 1715. Proctor in Convocation for the Chapter of York, 1741. Formerly Domestic Chaplain to Archbishop Sharp.

16. **Langtoft.** Matthew Hutton, D.D. 18th May, 1734. See *Succentor Canonicorum* above.

17. **North Newbald.** Laurence Sterne, M.A. 5th January, 1741.

V. of Sutton-in-the-Forest, 24th August, 1738.

18. **South Newbald.** Hollis Pigot, M.A. 11th January, 1741.

V. of Doncaster and C. of Loversall Chapel annexed, 10th February, 1738.

19. **Osbaldwick.** Benjamin Wilson, M.A. 13th September, 1736.

Headmaster of Wakefield Grammar School, 14th May, 1720. Vicar of Normanton, 10th July, 1727.

20. **Riccall.** Charles Cowper, M.A. 28th January, 1735.

Canon Residentiary. C. of Thorne, 10th August, 1728. R. of Oswaldkirk, 19th January, 1731. R. of Foston (Bulmer), 21st June, 1732.

21. **Stillington.** Richard Levett, M.A. 3rd December, 1730.

Preb. of Oxton and Cropwell, Prima Pars, at Southwell, 2nd March, 1732. Preb. of Tachbrook at Lichfield, 10th July, 1740.

22. **Strensall.** Thomas Hayter, M.A. 20th January, 1735. See *Sub-dean* and *Archdeacon of York* above.

23. **Tockerington.** John Witton, M.A. 30th August, 1743.

V. of Thockrington, Northumberland, 1740.

24. **Ulleskelf.** George Talbot, M.A. 20th December, 1739.

V. of Guiting, Gloucestershire. Clerk of the Custodies of Idiots and Lunatics in Chancery.

25. Warthill. WILLIAM STEER, M.A. 10th July, 1713.

Vicar of Ecclesfield, 2nd August, 1708.

26. Wetwang. JOSEPH ATWELL, D.D. 23rd February, 1737.

Preb. of Oxton and Cropwell, Secunda Pars, at Southwell, 23rd March, 1742. Preb. of Gloucester, 2nd February, 1736. Previously Rector of Exeter College, Oxford, 1732-1737, and subsequently Preb. of Westminster, 9th October, 1759.

27. Weighton. NICHOLAS WOOLFE, LL.B. 10th June, 1732.

C. of Boynton, 22nd August, 1728. V. of Carnaby, 22nd August, 1728. C. of Bessingby, 2nd December, 1730. C. of Awburn Chapel, 13th March, 1739. C. of Fraisthorpe, 13th March, 1739. Proctor in Convocation for the Archdeaconry of the East Riding.

28. Wistow. THOMAS SHARP, D.D. 29th April, 1719.

Preb. of Norwell Overhall at Southwell, 6th March, 1717. Archdeacon of Northumberland, 27th February, 1722. Rector of Rothbury, Northumberland, 12th July, 1720. Preb. of 10th Stall at Durham, 18th October, 1732. Formerly Domestic Chaplain to Archbishop Sir William Dawes.

VICARS CHORAL.

1. JOHN FULLER, M.A.

V. of S. Mary, Bishophill, Junior, York, and C. of Copmanthorpe Chapel, 25th June, 1709. C. of Upper and Nether Poppleton, 30th February, 1739.

2. RICHARD WARNEFORD, M.A.

V. of Kilnwick Percy, 25th May, 1728. V. of S. Martin, Coney Street, York, 14th June, 1729.

3. BRYAN ALLET, B.A. Admitted (as a Deacon) 21st July, 1729.

V. of Sturton-in-the-Clay, Notts., 9th January, 1734. R. of Londesborough, 22nd December, 1736. C. of S. John, York, 2nd April, 1742.

4. WILLIAM FOSTER, M.A. Adm. 19th November, 1731.

R. of Holy Trinity, Goodramgate, York, 23rd November, 1739. R. of S. John del Pike, York, 23rd November, 1739. V. of S. Maurice, York, 23rd November, 1739.

SOUTHWELL MINSTER.

PREBENDARIES.

1. Beckingham. EDWARD WILSON, M.A. 28th September, 1727.

R. of Teversall, Notts., 19th June, 1716. R. of Crofton, Yorkshire, 6th March, 1718.

2. Dunham. LEWIS STEPHENS, M.A. 18th July, 1729.

Preb. of Barnby-on-the-Moor at York, 9th February, 1726. Archdeacon of Chester, 12th September, 1727. Preb. of Exeter, 2nd October, 1731.

3. Eton. JOHN ABSON, M.A., 2nd June, 1720.

R. of S. Nicholas, Nottingham, 22nd July, 1714. V. of Rolleston, Notts., 7th December, 1727. Proctor in Convocation for the Chapter of Southwell.

4. Halloughton. EDWARD PARKER, M.A. 24th September, 1724.

R. of Wadingham, Lincolnshire, 1714.

5. North Leverton. BENEDICT SHERARD, M.A. 7th November, 1734.

R. of Langar with Barnston Chapel, 9th November, 1714.

6. North Muskham. THOMAS HAYTER, M.A. 21st September, 1728.

Sub-dean of York, 26th November, 1730. Archdeacon of York, 26th November, 1730. Preb. of Strensall at York, 20th January, 1735. Preb. of Westminster, 12th February, 1738. R. of Kirkby Overblows, 23rd April, 1729. R. of Kirkby (Cleveland), 24th February, 1737.

7. South Muskham. JAQUES STERNE, LL.D. 11th April, 1734.

Archdeacon of Cleveland, 17th November, 1735. Precentor of York, 17th November, 1735. R. of Rise, 5th February, 1722. V. of Hornsea, 3rd May, 1729. R. of Hornsey cum Riston, 3rd May, 1729.

8. Normanton. MATTHEW BRADFORD, LL.B. 28th April, 1743.

R. of Elton-on-the-Hill, 6th March, 1720. R. of South Collingham, 20th February, 1722.

9. Norwell Overhall. THOMAS SHARP, D.D. 6th March, 1717.

Preb. of Wistow at York, 29th April, 1719. R. of Rothbury, Northumberland, 12th July, 1720. Archdeacon of Northumberland, 27th February, 1722. Preb. of 10th Stall at Durham, 18th October, 1732.

10. Norwell Palishall. Robert Marsden, B.D. 2nd June, 1720.

R. of Rempston, 28th August, 1702. Archdeacon of Nottingham, 18th February, 1715.

11. Norwell Tertia Pars. EDWARD GREGORY, M.A. 6th December, 1733.

R. of Widmerpool, 28th April, 1731. R. of Carlton-in-Lindrick, 15th March, 1731. Minor Canon of Durham. C. of S. Margaret Crosgate, Durham, 1732-1753.

12. Oxton and Cropwell, Prima Pars. RICHARD LEVETT, M.A. 2nd March, 1732.

Preb. of Stillington at York, 3rd December, 1730. Preb. of Tachbrook at Lichfield, 10th July, 1740.

13. Oxton and Cropwell, Secunda Pars. JOSEPH ATWELL, D.D. 23rd March, 1742.

Preb. of Gloucester, 2nd February, 1736. Preb. of Wetwang at York, 23rd February, 1737.

14. Rampton. HENRY COOKE, M.A. 14th October, 1721.

Preb. of Ampleforth at York, 10th April, 1722. R. of Stokesley, 26th December, 1723. Preb. of 2nd Stall at Ripon, 19th October, 1743.

15. Sacrista or Segeston. ANDREW MATTHEWS, M.A. 28th February, 1733.

R. of Lindby, 4th October, 1723. C. of Annesley, 11th August, 1726. R. of Nuthall, 20th September, 1729.

16. Woodburgh. ROBERT AYDE, M.A. 28th May, 1719.

R. of East Mediety of Treswell, 5th July, 1710. C. of West Burton, 21st September, 1726. R. of Barnburgh, 3rd August, 1733.

VICARS CHORAL.

1. SAMUEL BIRD, M.A.

V. of Farnsfield, 20th May, 1725. C. of Halloughton, 7th September, 1726.

2. CHAPPELL FOWLER, B.D.

V. of Upton, 25th June, 1730.

3. THOMAS FELLOWS, M.A.

Lecturer of Southwell Minster. C. of Morton, 20th January, 1742.

4. JOHN LAVERACK, M.A.

V. of Southwell with West Halam, 18th March, 1741.

5. HENRY BUGG. Master of the Grammar School, 23rd July, 1730.

V. of Bleasby, 10th December, 1730. C. of Kneeton, 20th September, 1743.

RIPON MINSTER.

Dean. HENEAGE DERING, LL.D. 3rd March, 1710.

Archdeacon of the East Riding, 7th March, 1701. Preb. of Fridaythorpe at York, 1st May, 1708. R. of Scrayingham, East Yorkshire, 24th March, 1704. Master of the Hospitals of S. Mary Magdalen and of S. John Baptist at Ripon. In 1739 Dr. Dering recorded that he was the eldest member of the Church of York and the eldest Dean and Archdeacon in the Northern Province.

Sub-Dean. WILLIAM ELMSLEY, M.A. December, 1723.

Preb. of Tockerington at York, 31st July, 1721. R. of Ryther, 16th March, 1703. Proctor in Convocation for the Chapter of Ripon. He died as this Visitation was beginning and was buried at Feliskirk, 17th May, 1743. He was succeeded by—

JOSEPH COOKSON, M.A.

Vicar of Leeds, 6th March, 1715. Preb. of 1st Stall at Ripon, 25th September, 1722 till he resigned it for the Sub-deanery in 1743.

PREBENDARIES.

1st Stall. JOSEPH COOKSON, M.A. above. 25th September, 1722. JOHN DERING, M.A. 1743.

R. of Hilgay, Norfolk, 1740. He was the eldest son of the Dean above.

2nd Stall. RICHARD KAY, M.A. 26th December, 1728.

R. of Moor Monkton, 19th January, 1702. He died September, 1743 and was succeeded by Henry Cooke, M.A. for whom see the Chapters of York and Southwell above.

3rd Stall. WILLIAM THOMPSON, M.A. 4th December, 1729.

R. of Escrick, 26th July, 1728.

4th Stall. JOHN WAKEFIELD, M.A. 7th May, 1723.

R. of Sessay, 7th November, 1697.

5th Stall. THOMAS WARWICK, M.A. 17th June, 1742.

R. of Copgrove, 3rd November, 1730. R. of Great Smeaton, 13th December, 1732. C. of Appleton-on-Wiske Chapel, 14th January, 1736.

6th Stall. MARMADUKE BUCK, M.A. 1718.

R. of Long Marston (*al.* Hutton Wanesley), 12th June, 1705.

VICARS CHORAL.

1. JOHN WILSON, B.A. Precentor, 1735.

C. of Winksley with Grantley Chapel, 2nd April, 1741.

2. JOHN WATSON, B.A.

V. of Burton Leonard, 29th November, 1727. C. of Bishop Thornton, 13th April, 1716. C. of Bishop Monckton and Bondgate Chapels.

PROCTORS IN CONVOCATION, ELECTED IN 1741.

Chapter of York. THOMAS LAMPLUGH, M.A. Canon Residentiary, Preb. of Knaresborough and Rector of Bolton Percy.

Chapter of Southwell. JOHN ABSON, M.A. Preb. of Eton, Rector of S. Nicholas, Nottingham and Vicar of Rolleston.

Chapter of Ripon. WILLIAM ELSLEY, M.A. Sub-dean. Preb of Tockerington at York and Rector of Ryther.

Archdeaconry of York. 1. SAMUEL DRAKE, D.D. Rector of Treeton and Vicar of Holme-on-Spalding-Moor. 2. RICHARD GOODWIN, D.D. Preb. of Bole at York, Rector of Tankersley and Vicar of Prestwich, Lancs.

Archdeaconry of the East Riding. 1. THOMAS WAKEFIELD, M.A. Rector of Rowley. 2. NICHOLAS WOOLFE, LL.B. Preb. of Weighton at York, Vicar of Carnaby and Curate of Boynton, Bessingby, Awburn and Fraisthorpe.

Archdeaconry of Cleveland. 1. SAMUEL BAKER, D.D. Chancellor and Canon Residentiary of York, Rector of Settrington and Rector of Dunnington. 2. ROBERT HITCH, M.A. C. of Bramhope Chapel.

Archdeaconry of Nottingham. 1. WILLIAM BRIDGES, M.A. Rector of Gotham. 2. JOHN WARDE, B.D., Rector of Hickling.

Although at this time the Convocations only sat formally it is interesting to see the type of Proctor chosen by the clergy. Of the 8 elected by the parochial clergy, 6 had been Fellows of their colleges at Cambridge, viz., Drs. Goodwin and Drake at S. John's, Mr. Wakefield and Dr. Baker at Peterhouse, Mr. Bridges at Emmanuel and Mr. Warde at Queens'. Of the other two Proctors for the clergy, Mr. Hitch had been Scholar of Trinity and Mr. Woolfe a Fellow Commoner of S. John's. All these 8 Proctors were from Cambridge. None of the Proctors from the Chapters had been on the foundation of their respective colleges; two of them, Mr. Lamplugh and Mr. Abson were from Oxford, the third, Mr. Elmsley was from S. John's, Cambridge.

INDEX OF PLACES.

The spelling of the names alphabetically follows Crockford's Clerical Directory. Where this is not possible, a modern atlas has been used. Figures in black type indicate the main entry. The county is inserted only where the name occurs in other counties. Figures refer to the *pages*.

Aberford, Abberford, i, **9**, 10; iv, 189, 191, 194, 197, 213, 240.
Acaster Malbis, Acaster, i, **6**, 7, 46.
Acaster Selby, iii, 91.
Acklam, East; Acklam, i, **40**, 41; iii, 217, 224.
Acklam, West; Acklam, Intr. xv; i, **30**; ii, 192.
Ackworth, i, **13**; iii, 190.
Acomb, i, **25**.
Adbolton (*see also* Holme Pierrepont) iv, 67, 68, 184.
Addingham (Yorks.), i, **11**, 53, 58.
Addle, *see* Adel.
Adel, Addle, i, **5**.
Adlingfleet, i, **14**; ii, 2.
Adwalton, Intr., xi; i, 61; iv, 240.
Adwick-le-Street, i, **23**.
Adwick-upon-Dearne (Dern), i, **24**; iii, 193.
Agnes Burton, *see* Burton Agnes.
Ainsty, Ainstie, Deanery, New, Intr. ix; i, 6, 7, 8, 9, 25, 42, 43, 44, 45, 46, 47, 77, 78, 79, 80, 123, 124, 138, 139, 164, 203; ii, 2, 20, 23, 103, 104, 105, 118, 144, 173, 174, 183, 196; iii, 2, 14, 41, 42, 43, 44, 64, 65, 142, 143, 144, 178, 180, 181, 197, 250, 252.
Ainsty, Ainstie, Deanery, Old, Intr. ix, 5, 10, 48, 49, 125, 196, 197, 221, 222, 223, 224; ii, 2, 21, 24, 25, 26, 140, 142, 145, 208, 222; iii, 16, 179, 250, 251.
Aire, Eire, River, iii, 81.
Airmyn, Armin, Armine, i, **26**; ii, 54; iii, 67.
Airedale, iv, 241.
Aldborough (Holderness), i, 192, **221**; ii, 13, 88; iv, 236.
Aldborough-juxta-Boroughbridge, i, **221**, 223; iv, 197.
Aldfield-with-Studley, iii, 230, **231**; iv, 197.
Aldwark, Aldwarke, Hall, iv, 9.
Allendale, iii, **244**, 246; iv, 191, 198, 234, 236.
Allerston, i, **34**, 157, 188, 189, 211; iii, 177.
Allerthorpe, i, **39**, 116, 220; iii, 175.
Allerton (Yorks.), *see* Northallerton.
Allerton-Bywater, ii, 106.
Allostock (? Lostock), iv, 230.
Almondbury, Intr., x; i, **15**, 16, 19, 205, 207; ii, 31, 42, 44.
Alne (Yorks.), i, **32**.
Alne and Tollington preb., *see* York.
Alverton, iv, 136.
America, iv, 237.
Amotherby, i, 28, 29.
Ampleforth, Ampleford, i, **33**; ii, 58, 200, 214; iv, 186, 205.
Ampleforth preb., *see* York.
Angram Grange, iv, 196, 202.
Anlaby, ii, 75.
Annesley, iv, **4**, 91, 110.
Anston, i, **27**; ii, 49, 151; iii, 159.
Apesthorpe, iv, **6**, 94, 95.
Apesthorpe preb., *see* York.
Appleton, *see* Nun Appleton.
Appleton-Roebuck, i, 42.
Appleton-le-Street, i, **28**.
Appleton Wiske, upon Wysk, i, **31**, 186; iii, 30.
Ardsley, East, i, **14**; iii, 148, 188.
Arksey, Intr., xv; i, **22**, 23, 180.
Armagh, Abp. of, Intr., xix; i, 190.
Armin, Armine, *see* Airmyn.
Armley, i, **10**, 11; ii, 25; iv, 240.
Armthorpe, Armthorp, i, **20**, 21, 71; ii, 182.
Arncliffe, i, **12**, 13; ii, 29; iv, 236, 237.
Arnold, Intr., xviii; iv, **3**, 4, 224.
Arnoldsbiggin, iv, 227.
Arram, ii, 161.
Arthington, i, 6.
Arundel, iv, 198.
Asenby, iii, 162.
Askham (Notts.), iv, **6**, 42, 149.
Askham Bryan, i, **8**, 9.
Askham Richard, Askham, i, **7**, 8, 47, 148, 149.
Aslabie, *see* Asselby.
Aspley Hall, iv, 211.
Asselby, Aslabie, ii, 93.
Aston (Yorks.), i, **21**, 22.
Attenborough, Attenborrow, Attenborow, iv, **2**, 3, 19.
Attercliffe, i, **25**; iv, 224.
Atwick, i, **36**.

Aughton (Yorks.), i, **35**, 36, 157, 190, 191.
Austerfield, iv, **5**, 22, 147, 148.
Averham, iv, **2**, 69.
Awburn, Awburne, i, **39**, 111, 112, 159, 217.
Ayton, East, i, **39**, 160; iii, 132.
Ayton, West, Great Ayton, Ayton-in-Cleveland, i, **29**, 30; ii, 128, 129; iv, 224, 225.

Babworth, iv, **22**, 23, 113, 114.
Bacup, iv, 241.
Badsworth, i, **65**.
Bagby, i, **88**, 89; ii, 119, 120.
Baildon, Bayldon, i, **49**; iii, 179, 180; iv, 240.
Bainton (Yorks.), Intr., xviii, xxiv; i, **97**, 98.
Bainton, East, Manor, i, 97.
Bainton, West, Manor, i, 97.
Baldersby, iii, 162.
Balderton, iv, **12**, 13, 55, 56.
Balkholme, ii, 93.
Balmes (Hackney), i, 97.
Balne, Baln, iii, 67, 83, 85, 86.
Balne Hall, iii, 68, 73.
Bangor, Diocese, Intr., v, vi, xix; ii, 19.
Bangor, Bp. of, iii, 41, 42.
Bangorian Controversy, i, 35.
Bank Newton, iii, 147.
Banks, iii, 239.
Barbles Moor (Lancs.), iv, 215.
Barden, iii, 45.
Bardsey, i, **46**; ii, 146.
Barkisland, iii, 20.
Barlby, i, **93**.
Barlow House (Lancs.), iv, 201.
Barmby-in-the-Willows, *see* Barnby-in-the-Willows.
Barmby-Marsh, i, **115**.
Barmby, Barnby, -Moor (Yorks.), i, 40, **116**, 220; iii, 175.
Barmston, i, 38, **109**, 110, 193.
Barnbow, Barnborough, Hall, iv, 195, 198, 214, 221.
Barnborough, i, **68**; iv, 158, 182.
Barnby, Barmby-in-the-Willows, iv, **12**, 46, 107, 154.
Barnby Dun, i, **69**.
Barnes Hall, Barnshall, Hospital, i, 179.
Barnoldswick, Intr., xx; i, 54, **76**; iv, 241.
Barnshall, *see* Barnes Hall.
Barnsley (Yorks.), i, **222**; iii, 62, 189.
Barnston (Notts.), *see* Langar-with-Barnston.
Barrow-on-Soar, iv, 132.
Barton-in-Fabis, in-the-Beans (Notts.), iv, **7**, 8.
Barton-le-Street, i, **89**.
Barwick-in-Elmet, i, **44**, 45; iv, 195, 198.
Basford (Notts.), Intr., xii; iv, 15, **17**, 18, 87.
Batcombe (Somerset), iv, 69.
Bath, Intr., xii; iv, 3, 4, 28, 169.
Batley, i, **62**, 63; iv, 225, 232.
Battle Hill, iv, 206.
Bawtry, iv, 5, 22, 102, 147, **182**, 183.
Bayldon, *see* Baildon.
Beamsley, Beamsly, iii, 45.
Beaufront, iii, 248; iv, 207, 209.
Beckingham (Notts.), iv, **25**, 102, 103, 173.
Beckingham preb., *see* Southwell.
Bedale, iv, 222.
Beeford, Beford, Intr., xviii; i, **108**; ii, 164.
Beeston (Yorks.), i, **221**.
Beeston (Notts.), iv, **16**.
Beilby, *see* Hayton-with-Beilby.
Belby, ii, 93.
Belgium, iv, 193.
Bempton, Intr., xii, xvii; i, **114**, 218; ii, 18.
Benningbrough, ii, 199.
Bentley (Yorks.), iii, 30.
Berkshire, iii, 191.
Berkshire, Archdeaconry of, ii, 116.
Berkswich preb., *see* Lichfield.
Berwick-on-Tweed, ii, 123.
Berwickshire, iv, 227.
Bessenby, *see* Bessingby.
Bessingby, Bessenby, Intr., xv; i, 39, **111**, 159, 217.
Beswick, i, 104, **105**; iii, 113.
Bevercotes, Bevercoates, iv, 53.
Beverley, Intr., xv, xix; i, 42, 102, 103, 104, 152, 155, 190; ii, 60, 88; iii, 74, 80, 83.
Beverley, Manor of, i, 103; Grammar School, Intr., xi; i, 103; iii, 21; Presby. Ch., iv, 225; Visitation, ii, 132, 161; iii, 113, 116.
Beverley Minster, St. John's, Intr., xi; i, 101, **103**, 104, 105, 106; iii, 112, 113; St. Martin's, i, 105.
Beverley, St. Mary's, Intr., xvii, xviii; i, **101**, 103.
Beverley, St. Nicholas, Holme Church, i, **102**.
Bewerley, iii, 239.
Biddlestone Hall, Northumberland, iv, 221.
Bielby, *see* Hayton-with-Beilby.
Bilborough, Bilborrow, Bilborow (Notts.), iv, **13**, 14, 143.
Bilbrough (Yorks.), i, 8, **47**, 149.

Bilsdale, Billsdale (the place), i, **91**, 92; iv, 211, 237; (the valley), ii, 59.
Bilsthorpe, Bilsthorp, iv, **19**, 20.
Bilton-in-Ainsty, i, **77**.
Bilton-in-Holderness, ii, 204; iii, 124, 127, **128**, 131; iv, 218.
Bingfield, St. Mary's, iii, **246**, 247, 248.
Bingfield, St. Oswald's, iii, **247**, 248.
Bingham, Intr., xii; iv, **9**, 10.
Bingham, Deanery of, iv, 7, 8, 9, 10, 11, 27, 28, 30, 33, 44, 45, 58, 60, 66, 67, 68, 75, 76, 77, 78, 85, 86, 87, 112, 116, 118, 119, 120, 121, 131, 132, 133, 134, 135, 137, 151, 152, 153, 160, 161, 162, 163, 179, 182, 183, 185.
Bingley, i, **49**, 50; ii, 3, 110, 111; iv, 225, 226, 231, 240.
Birckshaw, iii, 73.
Birdforth, i, **87**; iii, 164.
Birdsall, i, 208, **222**; iv, 211.
Birkby, i, **94**; ii, 70.
Birkin, Intr., xiii; i, **43**.
Birmingham, Intr., xii; i, 144; iv, 232.
Birstall (Yorks.), Intr., x, xi, xviii; i, **60**, 61, 130; iv, 225, 227, 240.
Bishop Burton, i, **98**, 99, 153, 156; iv, 225, 241, 242.
Bishop Monkton, Monckton, iii, **231**, 232, 233, 234.
Bishop Norton, ii, 198.
Bishop Thornton, iii, 232, **233**, 234; iv, 195, 198, 210, 212, 213.
Bishopthorpe, Bishopthorp, i, 7, **45**; iv, 119, 182, 187, 193; Palace, Intr., xxii; ii, 96.
Bishopthorpe Muniments, Intr., v, viii, ix, xvi; i, 221.
Bishopthorpe MSS., iv, 187, 189, 190, 195, 198, 209, 213, 214, 234.
Bishopton Chapel (Ripon), iii, 230.
Bishop Wilton, i, **119**, 120; ii, 122; iii, 119.
Blackmanstone, Intr., xiv; iv, 64.
Blacktoft, i, 118, 119, 193.
Bleasby, iv, **24**, 25, 78, 79, 185.
Blidworth, iv, **25**, 117, 182, 225.
Blyth, Blythe (Notts.), iv, 5, **21**, 22, 74, 147, 199, 236, 241.
Bodleian Library, ii, 116.
Bointon, *see* Boynton.
Bole, Intr., xiii; iv, **23**, 24, 134, 169.
Bole preb., *see* York.
Bolsterstone, Bolster Stone, Boulsterstone, i, 73, **75**, 76, 179; ii, 223; iv, 199.
Boltby, i, **88**, 209.
Bolthorpe, *see* Bowthorpe.
Bolton (Lancs.), iv, 226.
Bolton-by-Bolland, i, 12, **52**, 58.
Bolton-in-Craven, i, 12, 53, **58**.
Bolton (par. Skipton), iii, 45.
Bolton-juxta-Pocklington, i, 119, 120.
Bolton Percy, i, **42**.
Bolton-upon-Dearne, Dearn, i, **72**, 73; ii, 46; iii, 87.
Bondgate, iii, **232**, 233, 234.
Boothby Graffoe, iv, 2.
Bornhem, iv, 191, 193, 207, 208.
Boroughbridge (Yorks.), i, 221, **222**, 223; ii, 185.
Boroughbridge, Deanery of, i, 221, 222; ii, 222, 223; iii, 242.
Borrowby, iii, 99, 111.
Bossall, i, **85**; ii, 208.
Bothamsall, Bothomsall, Botthomsal, iv, **20**, 53, 84, 85.
Boughton (Notts.), iv, 81.
Boulsterstone, *see* Bolsterstone.
Bournsall, *see* Burnsall.
Bowthorpe, Bolthorpe, ii, 67.
Boynton, Bointon, i, 39, **110**, 111, 112, 158, 159, 217.
Bracewell, Bracwell, Bracewel, Intr., xvii, xx; i, **53**, 54, 76, 77.
Bradfield (Yorks.), i, **73**, 74, 75, 76, 179; iii, 156, 251; iv, 199, 225.
Bradford (Yorks.), Intr., x; i, **58**, 60; ii, 39; iii, 149, 188, 189; iv, 226, 229, 232, 234, 236, 237, 241, 242.
Bradford, Grammar Sch., i, 59; Presby Ch., iv, 225, 227; dungeon, iv, 240.
Bradmore, iv, 27.
Brafferton, i, **86**, 87.
Braithwell, Intr., xvii; i, **71**, 72.
Bramcoat, *see* Bramcote.
Bramcote, Bramcoat, Bramcoate, iv, 3, **18**, 19.
Bramham, i, **79**; Park, i, 79; ii, 144.
Bramhope, i, **222**.
Bramley-juxta-Leeds, i, **48**; iv, 242.
Bramley-juxta-Rotherham, i, 72.
Brandesburton, Bransburton, i, **107**.
Brandsby, Bransby, Intr., x, xiv; i, **82**, 83; ii, 60; iii, 161; iv, 191, 199.
Bransburton, *see* Brandesburton.
Bransby, *see* Brandsby.
Brantingham, i, **118**, 119, 193.
Brawby, iii, 108.
Brayton, i, **80**; iii, 66.
Breers, Briers, Chapel, i, **63**, 64; ii, 33.
Bridgford, Bridgeford, East, iv, **182**.
Bridgford, West, iv, **8**, 9.
Bridlington, i, **112**, 113, 218; Visitation, i, 38; iii, 133; Quay, Key, i, 113, 114; Zion Ch., iv, 225, 226; Bapt. Ch., iv, 241.

Briers, *see* Breers.
Brighouse, iv, 236, 238.
Broad Bush, iv, 62.
Broad Marsh (Nottingham), iv, 211.
Brodsworth, i, 20, 21, **70**, 71; ii, 181, 182.
Brompton, Bromton (Cleveland), i, 35, **95**, 174.
Brompton-with-Snainton, i, **90**; iii, 98, 99, 204.
Bromsgrove, iv, 241.
Brotherton, i, **78**, 79, 198, 199.
Brotton-in-Cleveland, i, **92**, 93; iii, 103, 104, 110; iv, 216, 236, 239; *see* Skelton-in-Cleveland.
Broughton-in-Airedale (Craven), Intr., x; i, **54**, 55, 56; iv, 190, 191, 194, 200, 219.
Broughton, Great (Cumberland), iv, 242.
Broughton Sulney, iv, **10**, 11.
Broughton (Lancs.), ii, 99, 100.
Brussels, iv, 188.
Bubwith, i, **100**; iv, 200.
Buckrose, Deanery of, Intr., ix; i, 40, 106, 117, 157, 222; ii, 19, 81, 133, 134, 162, 203; iii, 31, 32, 118, 119, 120, 121, 122, 171, 214, 216, 228, 251, 252.
Buckton, i, 114.
Budby, Budbye, iv, 52.
Bugthorpe, Bugthorp, i, **117**; ii, 134; iii, 13, 14.
Bulcote, Bulcoat, iv, **15**, 226.
Bulmer (Yorks.), i, **81**.
Bulmer, Deanery of, Intr., ix; i, 32, 81, 82, 85, 86, 87, 88, 93, 94, 140, 142, 147, 171, 172, 181, 182, 183, 207, 208, 209, 222; ii, 55, 56, 65, 67, 68, 69, 70, 119, 120, 121, 184, 185, 193, 199, 212, 213, 217; iii, 25, 28, 90, 91, 92, 93, 99, 104, 105, 106, 107, 109, 160-167, 170, 202, 203, 209, 210, 250.
Bulwell, Intr., xii; iv, **14**, 15, 18, 87.
Bunney, Bunny, iv, **11**, 27, 120.
Burghwallis, Burgwallis, i, **64**, 223; iii, 64; iv, 200, 202, 205, 221.
Burlees, ii, 37.
Burley-in-Wharfedale, i, **221**; ii, 95.
Burnby, i, **95**; ii, 12.
Burnsall, Burnsal, Bournsall, Intr., xxi; i, **50**, 51; ii, 26, 27, 146, 147.
Burntacres, *see* Erringden.
Burscough, iv, 194.
Burstwick, Bustwick, i, 138; iii, 10, **126**, 127, 172, 173; iv, 216.
Burton Agnes, Agnes Burton, Burton, i, **37**, 38, 109, 110, 193; ii, 91, 92.
Burton Constable, iv, 203, 206, 216, 217, 218.
Burton Fleming, i, **111**, 121; ii, 19; iii, 36, 37.
Burton Joyce, Burton, iv, **15**, 16, 226.
Burton Leonard, iii, **232**, 233, 234.
Burton Pidsea, Pidsey Burton, Pydsey-Burton, i, **117**, 118; ii, 137.
Burton-on-Trent, iv, 10, 11.
Burton, West (Notts.), i, 69; iv, 158, **182**, 185.
Burythorpe, i, **106**; ii, 203.
Buttercrambe, Buttercoombe, i, 85, 86.
Butterwick (Yorks.), i, **114**, 215.
Byland, Old, i, **93**, 148.

Calderdale, iv, 241.
Calton (Yorks.), iv, 227.
Calverley, Calverly, Intr., xi; i, **128**, 129; ii, 26, 95; iii, 5; iv, 226, 228, 229, 238.
Calverley Hall, iii, 16.
Calverton (Notts.), iv, 175, **176**, 177, 226.
Cambrai, iv, 197, 205, 216.
Cambridge, iv, 227.
Cambridge, University of, Intr., xix, xx, xxiv; i, 22, 64, 87, 101; ii, 173; iii, 110; Librarian, iii, 251.
Cambridge Colleges (text), Trinity Hall, ii, 16; Trinity, iv, 137; St. Cath., iv, 240.
Cambridge. For *Alumni Cantabrigienses, see* Venn.
Cambridgeshire, iv, 229.
Cammerton, iii, 172.
Campsall, Campsal, Intr., xvii, xxiii; i, **133**, 134, 135.
Camston (?), *see* Ganton.
Canterbury, Abp. of, Intr., v, xix; i, 1, 14, 38, 69, 71, 126, 128, 190, 215, 223; iii, 42; iv, 22, 64, 80, 108, 114, 124.
Canterbury, Dean of, Intr., xxiv; diocese, iv, 64; six preacher, Intr., xiv; iv, 64; 2nd preb., iii, 192; Prerog. Court, ii, 37.
Cantley (Yorks.), i, **135**, 136, 179; iv, 184.
Carburton, iv, **39**, 40, 53, 115, 116, 118.
Car-Colston, Carcolston, iv, **30**, 31, 68, 69, 135.
Carleton-in-Craven, i, **125**; iv, 236.
Carlisle, Bp. of, Intr., v, xiii; diocese, Intr., xxii; registry, Intr., v, xxiv; i, 33, 87, 94, 114; ii, 65, 67, 127; iii, 102, 104, 107, 222, 248; iv, 97.
Carlton (Bulmer), Intr., xix; i, 143, **147**; ii, 69.
Carlton-in-Cleveland, i, **146**, 211;

ii, 219.
Carlton-in-Lindrick, iv, **38**, 163.
Carlton Miniott, Minniott, i, **222**.
Carlton-juxta-Snaith, i, **139**, 140; iii, 67; iv, 196, 197, 201, 215.
Carlton-on-Trent, *see* Norwell.
Carnaby, i, 39, 111, 112, **158**, 159, 217.
Cartagena, i, 221; iv, 228.
Castleford, i, **126**, 127; ii, 177; iv, 52, 101.
Castle Howard, ii, 219, 220.
Castor, preb. of, *see* Lincoln.
Catcliffe, Catcliff, iii, 21.
Catterick, Deanery of, iii, 234, 235, 236.
Catton with Stamford Bridge, i, 8, 47, **148**, 149.
Catton (par. Topcliffe), iii, 162.
Catwick, Intr., xviii; i, **157**, 158, 224; ii, 85, 86.
Caunton, iv, **183**, 184.
Cave, North, i, **149**, 150; ii, 206; iii, 114; iv, 237.
Cave, South, Intr., ix; i, **161**, 194, 195; iv, 226, 229.
Cave, South, History of, iii, 30; iv, 227.
Cawood, i, **138**; iii, 197, 198.
Cawthorne, i, **137**, 138; iii, 6; iv, 114.
Cayton, i, 39, **159**; iii, 132.
Chaddesley Corbett, Intr., xvii.
Chapel-Allerton (Yorks.), i, **125**.
Chapelthorpe, Chappelthorpe, Chapell Thorp, Thorpe, i, **132**, 133; iii, 47, 48.
Chelsea Hospital, iv, 181, 242.
Cherry Burton, North Burton, i, **96**; ii, 163.
Cheshire, iv, 230.
Cheshire, East, History of, ii, 50.
Chester, Bp. of, i, 31, 153; diocese, Intr., xxii; i, 31, 32, 123, 153, 221, 222; ii, 6, 222, 223; iii, 30, 164, 232; iv, 240; R.C. diocese, iv, 196; minor Canon, Intr., xiii; iv, 23, 133, 134; ordinations, Intr., xx; registry, xxiv.
Chesterfield, iv, 201.
Chichester, Bp. of, Intr., xiv; Ipthorne preb., iii, 144; Wittering preb., iii, 144.
Chilwell, iv, 2, 3.
Church Fenton, Kirk Fenton, Fenton, i, **203**; iii, 64, 65.
Clapham (Yorks.), iv, 237.
Clareborough, Clarbrough, iv, **39**, 73, 236.
Claxby, iv, 129.
Clayfield, iv, 238.
Clayton, *see* Frickley-with-Clayton.
Clayworth, Claworth, iv, **37**, 38.
Cleckheaton, Intr., xi; i, **129**, 130; ii, 31; iv, 225, 227, 229, 240; Red Chapel, iv, 226.
Cleveland, Archdeaconry of, Intr., ix; i, 172, 222; iii, 36; iv, 209, 220.
Cleveland, Deanery of, Intr., ix; i, 29, 30, 31, 34, 92, 95, 144, 145, 146, 173, 174, 184, 186, 210, 211; ii, 8, 9, 62, 63, 65, 71, 97, 126, 128, 129, 130, 155, 157, 190, 191, 192, 202, 215, 218, 223; iii, 27, 29, 56, 100, 101, 102, 103, 110, 111, 169, 176, 177, 204, 205, 207, 227, 252.
Cleveland, East (R.C. Mission), iv, 203, 209, 212, 219.
Cleveland, Histories of, iv, 202.
Cliff (par. Hemingborough), ii, 66, 67.
Cliff, North, iv, 213, 214, 219.
Cliffe, South, iv, 237.
Cliffe-on-Tees, iv, 195, 198.
Clifford (Yorks.), iv, 232.
Clifton (York), ii, 208.
Clifton (Notts.), Intr., xii; iv, **27**, 28, 169, 201.
Clifton, North (Notts.), iv, **34**.
Clipstone, Clypston, iv, 52.
Cloughton, i, **160**; iii, 133, 169, 228.
Clypston, *see* Clipstone.
Cockan, Intr., xvi; i, **143**; ii, 8, 125.
Cockermouth, iv, 232.
Cockshaw, iv, 206.
Coddington, Codington (Notts.), iv, **35**, 36, 48, 140, 142.
Colchester, iv, 242.
Cold Kirkby, Kirby, i, 94, **147**.
Coley, Intr., xix; i, **130**; ii, 33; iv, 226.
Collingham, Colingham (Yorks.), i, **124**; ii, 144; iii, 143.
Collingham, North (Notts.), iv, **33**, 34, 79, 141, 185, 241.
Collingham, South (Notts.), iv, **32**, 34, 45.
Colne (Lancs.), ii, 43.
Colston-Bassett, Basset, iv, **28**, 30, 37, 194, 201, 210.
Colthorpe, *see* Cowthorpe.
Colton (par. Bolton Percy), i, 42.
Colwick, iv, 30, **36**, 37, 108, 161.
Coneysthorpe, Conisthorpe, i, 90.
Congleton, ii, 49, 50.
Conisborough, Conningsburgh, i, **136**, 137; iii, 24, 157.
Conisthorpe, *see* Coneysthorpe.
Coniston (par. Gargrave), ii, 4.
Conistone, Coniston (par. Burnsall), i, 50, 51.
Conningsburgh, *see* Conisborough.
Copgrove, Copgrave, i, 31.
Copmanthorpe, Copmanthorp, i, **139**; ii, 171; iii, 2, 3.

Coringham, preb. of, *see* Lincoln.
Cortlingstock, *see* Costock.
Cossall, Cossal, *see* Wollaton-with-Cossall.
Costock, Cortlingstock, iv, **26**, 27, 164.
Cotes, iv, 95.
Cotgrave, iv, 8, 9, **183**.
Cotness, ii, 93.
Cottam (Yorks.), i, **161**, 162; ii, 165, 166.
Cottam Hall (Lancs.), iv, 219.
Cottam, West (Notts.), iv, 94.
Cottingham (Yorks.), Intr., xviii; i, 99, **150**, 151, 152, 153, 156; iii, 116; iv, 226.
Cottingwith, Cottinwith, East, i, 36, **156**, 191.
Courteenhall, Courtenhall, iv, 62.
Coventry, *see* Lichfield and Coventry.
Cowesby, Cowsby, Intr., xii; i, **144**.
Cowick, iii, 67, 68, 69, 72, 73, 74, 80, 81, 82, 83, 84, 86.
Cowlam, Intr., xvii; i, 34, **157**, 189, 211; iii, 177.
Cowsby, *see* Cowesby.
Cowthorpe, Cowthorp, Colthorpe, i, **123**.
Coxwold, Coxwould, Intr., xix; i, **142**, 147; ii, 67, 68, 69; iv, 196, 202.
Craikhall, *see* Crakehill.
Crake, *see* Crayke.
Crakehill, Craikhall, iii, 162.
Crambe, i, **140**, 141; ii, 56, 57.
Crathorne, Craythorne, Cratharn, i, **145**; ii, 193; iv, 194, 202, 207, 208.
Craven, Deanery of, Intr., ix; i, 11, 12, 49, 50, 52, 53, 54, 58, 76, 125; ii, 3, 4, 5, 27, 28, 29, 94, 106, 108, 111, 112, 146, 147, 175; iii, 45, 89, 145, 146, 182, 250; iv, 237, 239, 241, 242.
Craven, History of, iv, 236.
Crayke, Crake, i, **222**.
Craythorne, Cratharn, *see* Crathorne.
Crofton (Yorks.), i, **127**, 128; iv, 156, 195, 212.
Cromwell, Intr., xiv; iv, **31**, 32, 64, 141.
Cropton, i, **143**, 144; ii, 153, 155, 189, 190.
Cropwell Bishop, iv, **40**, 41, 68, 182, 184.
Cropwell [Butler], *see* Tithby-with-Cropwell.
Crosland, South, ii, 43, 44.
Crossgate, Durham, iv, 163.
Cross Stone, Crostone, i, **131**, 132; ii, 33, 35, 37; iv, 226, 228, 229, 232, 236, 241.
Crostone, *see* Cross Stone.
Croydon, Intr., vi.
Cuckney, iv, 8.
Cuckney, *see* Norton Cuckney.
Cudworth, iii, 196.
Cumberland, iii, 46; iv, 238, 242.
Cumberworth, i, **222**; iii, 62.
Curborough, preb. of, *see* Lichfield.
Cusworth Park, ii, 45.

Dacre, iv, 238.
Dalby (Yorks.), i, **172**, 173; ii, 20; iii, 171, 172.
Dale Head, iii, 251.
Dalton (par. Topcliffe), iii, 162.
Dalton, North, i, **176**; ii, 73; iii, 212, 213.
Dalton, South; Dalton Holme, i, **175**; ii, 79, 80.
Danby-in-Cleveland, i, **173**; iii, 27.
Danthorpe Hall, iv, 213, 214.
Darfield, i, **167**, 168; iv, 226.
Darlton, iv, **43**, 44, 131.
Darnall, iii, 58.
Darrington, i, **165**, 166.
Darton, i, **168**, 169.
Dawscout Farm, ii, 38.
Deanhead, *see* Scammonden.
Dedham, ii, 144.
Deighton-in-Cleveland, Intr., xvi; i, 35, 95, **174**.
Deighton (par. Escrick), i, 182.
Deighton, North, i, 123.
Denby (Yorks.), i, **170**, 171; iii, 5, 6; iv, 236, 237.
Dent, iv, 240.
Denton (Yorks.), i, **223**; ii, 209.
Derby, iv, 98, 230.
Derby Hundred, iv, 194.
Derbyshire; Co. of Darby, ii, 47; iii, 192; iv, 8, 98, 144, 145, 146, 193, 194, 199, 201, 214.
Dewsbury, i, 221, **223**; ii, 210; iii, 180; iv, 231, 240.
Dickering, Deanery of, Intr., ix; i, 37, 39, 110, 111, 112, 114, 158, 159, 160, 161, 193, 213, 214, 215, 216, 217, 218, 219; ii, 15, 16, 17, 83, 90, 91, 138, 164, 165, 196, 204, 221, 222; iii, 36, 37, 38, 132, 133, 135, 173, 220, 221, 223.
Dieulouard, iv, 191, 193, 207.
Dinnington, Dinington (Yorks.), i, **170**.
Dinnington, preb. of, *see* York.
Dishforth, i, 87; iii, 162, **163**.
Don, River, iii, 52.
Doncaster, Intr., xv; i, 67, **166**, 167, 181; ii, 150, 151, 212; iv, 226; clerical residents, i, 135, 178; iv,

126; Gr. Sch., ii, 211.
Doncaster, Visitation at, i, 20, 24, 71, 140, 168; ii, 50; iii, 53, 192, 193.
Doncaster, Deanery of, Intr., ix; i, 21, 22, 23, 24, 25, 27, 64, 65, 68, 69, 70, 71, 72, 73, 75, 133, 135, 136, 137, 166, 167, 168, 170, 178, 179, 180, 200, 201, 202, 204, 222; ii, 7, 45, 46, 47, 49, 50, 51, 52, 53, 55, 117, 150, 151, 152, 180, 181, 182, 211, 223; iii, 5, 20, 21, 23, 24, 52, 53, 54, 55, 56, 58, 62, 63, 86, 88, 151, 152, 153, 154, 155, 156, 157, 158, 159, 189, 190, 192, 194, 195, 196, 199, 200, 251; iv, 184.
Doncaster, Deanery of, i, 70.
Dor Hill, iii, 73.
Douai (Douay), iv, 191, 192, 193, 194, 195, 196, 197, 198, 199, 201, 207, 208, 210, 211, 215, 216, 217, 218, 219, 220.
Drax, i, **164**.
Drayton, East; Great Drayton (Notts.), iv, 6, **42**, 149.
Drayton, West (Notts.), iv, **41**, 53, 99, 100, 124.
Driffield, Great, i, **223**; iii, 251, 252.
Driffield, Little, i, 223.
Drighlington Grammar School, i, 61; iii, 189.
Dripool, *see* Drypool.
Drypool, Dripool, i, **176**, 177; ii, 86, 87.
Dublin, iv, 62; Abp. of, Intr., xix; Trinity College, i, 81, 87; iii, 167; iv, 35, 74; *Review*, Intr., xxiii; iv, 205.
Duffield, South, ii, 67.
Dunbar, iv, 240.
Duncombe Park, ii, 59.
Dunham-on-Trent, iv, **42**, 43, 44, 130, 131.
Dunkenhalgh, iv, 214.
Dunnerdale, *see* Seathwaite.
Dunnington, i, **171**, 172; ii, 217; iii, 15, 121.
Dunsforth, i, 221.
Durham, Bp. of, Intr., xv; Dean, Intr., xvi; Preb. 3rd Stall, ii, 221; iii, 36; 10th stall, Intr., xiv; minor Canon, iv, 163; Prior, iv, 204; St. Margaret's, Crossgate, iv, 163; Registry, iii, 246.
Durham County, iv, 195, 238.
Durton, iv, 210.

Eakring, Intr., xvi; iv, **46**, 47, 48.
Ealand, *see* Elland.
Easington (Cleveland), i, **184**, 185.
Easington (Craven), iii, 251.
Easington (Holderness), i, **191**, 192; ii, 79, 135, 136; iii, 125, 126.
Easingwold, Intr., xiii, xvii; i, **183**; iv, 200, 202, 203, 217.
East-Indies, i, 105.
East Acklam, *see* Acklam, East.
East Ardsley, *see* Ardsley, East.
East Ayton, *see* Ayton, East.
East Bainton, *see* Bainton, East.
East Cottingwith, *see* Cottingwith, East.
East Hardwick, *see* Hardwick, East.
East Leake, *see* Leake, East.
East Markham, *see* Markham, East.
East Newton, *see* Newton, East.
East Retford, *see* Retford, East.
East Riding, *see* Yorkshire.
Eastrington, Estrington, i, **193**, 194.
East Rounton, *see* Rounton, East.
East Stoke, *see* Stoke, East.
Eastwood (nr. Rotherham), iv, 226, 228, 230, 231.
Eastwood, Eastwait (Notts.), iv, 63, 151, 175, 176, **177**.
Eaton (Notts.), iv, **55**, 73.
Ebberston, Ebberstone, i, 34, 157, **188**, 211; ii, 135, 153; iii, 177.
Ecclesall, Eccleshall, Ecclesal (Yorks.), i, **180**; iv, 227.
Ecclesfield, i, 23, **179**, 180.
Eccleshill, iv, 240.
Eckington, iii, 192.
Edinburgh, Lord Provost of, i, 22.
Edinburgh, University of, Intr., xx; i, 30; ii, 11, 15, 85, 140, 153, 156; iii, 12, 32, 124, 130, 187, 218; iv, 227, 228, 230.
Edingley, Eddingley, iv, **183**.
Edlington (Yorks.), i, 136, **178**, 179; iii, 68; iv, 184.
Edstone, Edston, Great, i, **184**; iii, 97, 98.
Edwalton, iv, **45**, 134, 182.
Edwinstowe, Edwinstow, iv, 40, **52**, 53, 115, 116, 117, 118, 211.
Egmanton, iv, **50**, 51.
Egton, Eggton (Yorks.), i, **186**, 187; ii, 10, 11, 155; iv, 188, 195, 196, 203, 204, 209, 212, 219.
Egton Bridge, iv, 203.
Egypt, *see* Swinley.
Eire, River, *see* Aire.
Eland, *see* Elland.
Eldroth, Elderoth, iv, 237.
Elkesley, Elksley, iv, **53**, 54, 124.
Elland, Eland, Ealand, Intr., xv; i, 64, **223**; ii, 32; iii, 64; iv, 229, 230.
Elland Park, iv, 228.
Ellerburne, Ellerburn, i, **187**; iii, 7, 8, 211.
Ellerker, i, 118, 119.

Ellerton, i, 36, 157, **190**, 191.
Ellington, Low, iv, 238.
Elloughton, Intr., ix; i, 161, **194**; iv, 233.
Ellslak, *see* Elslack.
Elmire, iii, 162.
Elmley, Emley (Yorks.), i, **177**, 178.
Elmsall, Empsall, iii, 74.
Elslack, Elslake, Ellslak, i, 55, 57.
Elson, *see* Elston Church.
Elsternwick, Elstronwick, i, **192**, 221; ii, 13, 88.
Elston Chapel, iv, 36, **48**, 140, 142.
Elston, Elson, Church, iv, 12, **46**, 154.
Elstronwick, *see* Elsternwick.
Elton-on-the-Hill, iv, 33, **44**, 45.
Elvington, Intr., xii; i, **181**.
Ely, Intr., xxiv; Bp. of, Intr., v, xv; prebend., iii, 7.
Emley, *see* Elmley.
Empsall, *see* Elmsall.
Epperston, Eperston, iv, **49**, 50, 175.
Ergham, Intr., xv, xvii; i, 38, 110, **193**.
Erringden, Errenden, ii, 37, 38.
Escrick, i, **182**, 183; iii, 92.
Eskdale, Eskdailside (Yorks.), i, 157, 189, 211; iii, 177.
Essex, ii, 144.
Eston, ii, 215, **216**.
Estrington, *see* Eastrington.
Eton College, iv, 116.
Eton, preb. of, *see* Southwell.
Etton (Yorks.), Intr., xix; i, **189**, 190; ii, 60, 61, 160; iii, 223.
Everingham, Intr., x, xxiii; i, **189**; ii, 72, 73; iv, 203, 204.
Everton (Notts.), i, 23, 126, 127; iv, **51**, 52, 100, 101.
Exeter, Dean of, Intr., xxiv; Ordination List, i, 87.

Faceby, i, 146, **211**; ii, 219.
Fangfoss, i, 40, 116, **220**; iii, 175.
Farlington (Yorks.), i, **209**, 210; iii, 107, 108.
Farndale, ii, 154.
Farndon (Notts.), iv, 13, **55**.
Farnley-juxta-Leeds, i, 11, **197**, 198; ii, 142.
Farnley-juxta-Otley, i, 223, **224**; ii, 209; iii, 250.
Farnsfield, iv, **58**, 75, 236.
Farnsley, iv, 242.
Featherstone, Featherston, Intr., xviii; i, **199**, 200.
Felixkirk, Felliskirk, i, 88, **208**, 209; iii, 250.
Felkirk, Intr., xvi; i, **201**, 202; iii, 4.
Felliskirk, *see* Felixkirk.
Felton (Northumberland), iv, 213, 219.
Fenay, *see* Finnay.
Fenton (Yorks.), *see* Church Fenton.
Fenton, Preb. of, *see* York.
Ferns, Diocese of, i, 190.
Ferriby, North, i, **212**, 213; ii, 132; iv, 226, 227.
Ferrybridge, iv, 205.
Ferry Fryston, Ferry-Friston, i, 79, **198**, 199; iv, 205, 212.
Fewston, Fuiston, i, **196**; iii, 251.
Field Names, Aislabies Fields, i, 100; Amas, Haemas, Harnas, Acres, iii, 81, 83, 84; Balke; Mill bawkes, iii, 72, 82, 83, 84; Baln-Croft, iii, 74; Bewerley, Buerley, Pasture, iii, 241; Bogard Close, i, 55; Bradley's Pasture, i, 57; Briggs Close, i, 57; Bullcroft, iii, 74; Burntacres, ii, 38; Burthen Crofts, i, 42; Cargarth, iii, 82; Carr, The, iii, 73; Carr, The Far, iii, 77; Church Field, i, 55, 56; Church flat, i, 55, 56; Church Ing, i, 55, 56; Church Lands, Land, i, 204; iv, 43, 59; Church Meadow, ii, 118; Church Staith, i, 138; Clough Yate Ing, i, 57; Common, The, iv, 3; Common Field, iii, 181; Common Meadow, iv, 86; Cow Garth, iii, 77; Dane Pasture, iii, 241; Deheskes, The, iii, 81, 82; Dickeber, i, 55; East Quarter, iii, 246; Emmet Land, i, 110; English moores, iii, 81; Field, The, iii, 9, 83; iv, 170; (East), iii, 69, 72; (South), iii, 77, 79, 82, 84; (West), iii, 69, 79; Fifth Close, iii, 82; Freeman Bull, i, 152; Freeman, freemen's, haggs, iii, 81, 82, 84; Half acres, half acre, flatt, iii, 82, 83; High Cross Close, i, 56; High Cross, Little, i, 55, 56; Hole, The, iii, 77; Ingabridge Close, i, 55; Inglemire, i, 151; Ings, The, iii, 72, 81, 82, 83, 84; Ings, North, iii, 69; Ings, small, iii, 81; Jobson Close, iii, 12; King's Mill, The, iii, 82; Lambeth, The, iii, 226; Learings, ii, 38; Little-Stead Clow, i, 138; Long Croft, i, 55; Long dales, doles, iii, 81, 82, 83, 84; Long Riggs, i, 55; March Closes, iii, 77; Marsh Land, iv, 129; Mildale, The, iii, 77; Mill flatt, iii, 72; Millner Croft, i, 57; Moorber, Moorbar, Moresber, i, 55, 56, 57; Moorbar, Little, i, 57; Netlam Bull, i, 151; Nicholass Smiths

Crofts, i, 57; Nine Acres; Nine Acre flatt; iii, 81, 82, 83, 84; Overlanes, Orlanes, The, iii, 81, 82; Oxney, iii, 73; Oxney, Middle, iii, 82, 83, 84; Oxney, Neither & Upper, iii, 73; Parson Hill, i, 55, 56; Parsonmire, Parsonmyre, i, 55, 56; Parsons, Parson's, lands, iii, 77; Peatmire, i, 55, 56; Pinfold Close, ii, 193; Poor Folks Close, i, 207; Poor Garth, iii, 116; Poor's Close, iv, 162; Poor Widow's Close, iv, 31; Prior, Prior's, flatt, iii, 81, 82, 83; (East), 81, 82, 84; (Middle), 82, 85; (West), 81, 82, 84; (Close), 82; Prior, Priory (garth), iii, 74, 75, 76; (haggs), 81, 82, 84; (mill), 81, 82, 84; (moor), 81, 83; (pighill, pighil), 81, 82, 84; Rawholm, ii, 38; Round Close, ii, 193; Row Close, ii, 118; Saltings, i, 52; Sharp's Close, iv, 31; Spitall, The, iv, 62; Thornton Closes, iii, 73; Three Acres, iv, 170; Tinnale; Tinnale Croft, i, 155; Tinnales Closes, i, 56; Town Fields, ii, 220; Turbridge, i, 55; Tythe Barn (Croft), i, 55; (Garden), i, 56; Vicaridge Croft, i, 55; Waste, Ye, iii, 154; Water lane, iii, 78, 79; Westaby dale, i, 116; Wood dale, i, 116.
Filey, Fyley, i, 216, **217**, 219; ii, 91, 196; iii, 135.
Fillingham, iv, 112.
Fimber, iii, 252.
Finch Mill, iv, 192.
Finnay, Fenay, ii, 44.
Finningley, Finingley, iv, **57**.
Firbeck, i, **204**; ii, 152, 181; iv, 227.
Fishlake, Intr., xviii; i, **200**, 201; iii, 89; iv, 240.
Fiskerton, iv, 104.
Flamborough, Intr., xii; i, 114, **218**; ii, 18; iv, 204.
Flanders, ii, 123; iv, 190, 193.
Flawborough, Flawbrow, Flawburrow, Flawborow, iv, 136, 137, **138**, 185.
Flaxton, i, 85, 86, 207.
Fledborough, Fledborrow, iv, **56**, 57.
Flintham, iv, **183**.
Flixton, Preb. of, *see* Lichfield.
Flockton, i, **205**, 206, 207; iii, 147.
Foggathorpe, Foggerthorpe, i, 100.
Folkton, Intr., xiii; i, **215**, 216, 217, 218, 219; ii, 63, 91, 196; iii, 135.
Fordon, Forden (Yorks.), i, 216, **218**, 219; ii, 91, 196.
Forest of Bowland, iii, 251.
Foston (Bulmer), i, **207**, 208, 222; ii, 215; iii, 158.
Foston-on-the-Wolds, i, **213**, 214; ii, 165, 205; iii, 38.
Fountains Abbey, iv, 200, 212.
Foxholes, i, 114, 115, **214**, 215; iii, 252.
Fraisthorpe, Fraizthorp, i, 39, 111, 112, **216**, 217.
Frederick, Prince (man-of-war), iii, 173.
Frickley-with-Clayton, Intr., x; i, **202**, 203; ii, 52; iv, 205, 221.
Fridaythorpe, i, **219**.
Fridaythorpe, Preb. of, *see* York.
Friesland, Frizeland (Netherlands), Intr., xiii; iv, 2.
Frisby-on-Wreake, super Reak, iv, 132, 133.
Frodingham, North (Yorks.), i, 158, **224**; ii, 86.
Fuiston, *see* Fewston.
Fulford, Fulforth, i, **195**.
Full Sutton, i, **212**; ii, 51; iii, 12.
Fulwood (Yorks.), iv, 227.
Furness, iv, 241.
Fyley, *see* Filey.
Fylingdales, i, 34, 157, 189, **210**, 211; iii, 177.

Gainsborough, iv, 94, 227.
Galmpton, *see* Ganton.
Gameton, iv, 9.
Gamston, Gamstone, Intr., xiv; iv, 31, 32, 53, **63**, 64, 241.
Ganton, Galmpton, (?) Camston, ii, **15**, 16; iii, 220, 221; iv, 239.
Garforth, i, 14; ii, **2**; iii, 43.
Gargrave, Gargreave, i, 55; ii, **4**; iii, 250; iv, 227.
Garton-in-Holderness, i, 192, 221; ii, **12**, 88; iv, 236, 238.
Garton-on-the-Wolds, ii, **16**, 17, 81; iii, 118, 214.
Gate Helmsley, *see* Helmsley, Gate.
Gedling, Godling, Intr., xix; iv, **61**.
Georgia, iv, 60, 240.
Ghent, iv, 193; Bishop of, iv, 7.
Gifford's Hall, Suffolk, iv, 220.
Giggleswick, Gigleswick, ii, **5**, 6, 27, 28; iv, 237, 240.
Gildersome, i, 62; iv, 241, 242.
Gildingwells, Gilldingwells, Gilldinwells, *see* Letwell.
Gillamoor, Gillamore, i, 143; ii, **8**, 125.
Gilling, ii, 59, **221**; iv, 190, 200, 205, 218.
Gill Kirk, Gill Church, i, 54.
Girton (Notts.), iv, **140**, 141.
Gisbrough, *see* Guisbrough.
Gisburn, Gisburne, ii, **3**, 4, 108; iv,

225, 227.
Gisburn Park, iv, 227.
Givendale, Great, i, 120, 121; ii, **18**, 157; iii, 37.
Givendale, Little, ii, 18.
Glaisdale, i, 187; ii, **9**, 11.
Glasgow, University of, Intr. xx; i, 114, 161, 174; ii, 213; iii, 35, 107, 109, 175, 249; iv, 226.
Glenfinnan, iv, 190.
Gloucester, Bishop of, Intr., xiv, xxii; Dean of, Intr., xxiv.
Goadland, *see* Goathland.
Goathland, Goadland, i, 187; ii, **10**, 11.
Godling, *see* Gedling.
Goldsbrough, iii, 73, 80.
Gomersal, Gommersall, i, 61; iv, 226, 240.
Gonalston, Gunalston, Gumalston, iv, **62**.
Goodmanham, Goodmadham, i, 96; ii, **11**, 12.
Goodshaw, iv, 241.
Goole, Gool, Gowle, ii, **54**; iii, 67, 78, 86.
Gosport (man-of-war), ii, 115.
Gotham, iv, **58**, 60.
Goudhurst, iv, 231.
Gowdale, Gowdall, Gowdal, iii, 67, 74, 86.
Gowle, *see* Goole.
Goxhill, Goxhil (Yorks.), ii, **13**, 14, 223; iii, 225, 226, 227.
Granby, Grandby, Intr., xiii; iv, **60**.
Grandby, *see* Granby.
Grange, iii, 173.
Gransmoor, i, 37.
Grantham, The Grange, iv, 211.
Grantham, South, Preb. of, *see* Salisbury.
Grantley (Notts.), *see* Winksley-with-Grantley.
Grasby, Gresby (Lincs.), iii, 218.
Gravelines, iv, 193, 201.
Greasbrough, Greasbrooke, ii, **7**; iii, 21.
Greasley, Greisley, Greisly, iv, **63**, 151, 177, 227.
Great Broughton, *see* Broughton, Great.
Great Drayton, *see* Drayton, East.
Great Driffield, *see* Driffield, Great.
Great Givendale, *see* Givendale, Great.
Great Hatfield, *see* Hatfield, Great.
Great Hopton, *see* Habton, Great.
Great Horton, *see* Horton, Great.
Great Houghton, *see* Houghton, Great.
Great Leake, *see* Leake, East.
Great Moorsome, *see* Moorsome, Great.
Great Preston, see Preston, Great.
Great Sandal, *see* Sandal Magna.
Great Smeaton, *see* Smeaton, Great.
Great Usburn, *see* Ouseburn, Great.
Greenhow, Greenhough, Greenah, Hill, iii, 241; iv, 231.
Greenley-on-the-Hill, *see* Gringley-on-the-Hill.
Greisley, Greisly, *see* Greasley.
Grenofirth, i, 179.
Gresby, *see* Grasby.
Greta Bridge, iv, 192.
Grimston, Grimstone (par. Kirkby Wharfe), ii, 118.
Grimston, North, ii, **19**; iii, 182.
Grimston Garth, iv, 236.
Grindall, Grindale, i, 114, 218; ii, **17**.
Grindall, Preb. of, *see* York.
Grindleton, ii, 176.
Gringley, Greenley-on-the-Hill, iv, **65**, 66, 170.
Groundhill House, iv, 236.
Grove (Notts.), iv, **65**.
Guisbrough, Gisbrough, Intr., xv; ii, **8**, 9, 128, 129, 202; iii, 176, 207; iv, 237, 239.
Guiseley, Guisley, Guisely, ii, **2**, 144; iii, 16; iv, 211, 241.
Gunalston, Gumalston, *see* Gonalston.

Habton, Hopton, Great, ii, 123.
Hackness, ii, **221**, 222.
Hackney, i, 97.
Haisthorpe, Haystrop, i, 37.
Halifax, Hallyfax, Intr., x, xv; i, 59, 64, 131, 132; ii, **31**, 32, 33, 35, 36, 37, 96, 143, 148, 149; iii, 50, 51; iv, 194, 205, 206, 225, 226, 227, 228, 229, 230, 232, 236, 238, 240, 242.
Hallam, West, iv, 98, 147, **183**, 185.
Hallamshire, History of, iii, 153, 251.
Halloughton, iv, 58, **75**.
Hallyfax, *see* Halifax.
Halsham, i, 158, 224; ii, 84, **85**, 86; iii, 219, 220: iv, 206.
Halton Gill, ii, **28**, 29, 30.
Hammersmith, iv, 220.
Hampshire, iv, 194.
Hampsthwaite, ii, **21**, 22; iii, 251.
Handsworth, Hansworth (Yorks.), ii, **53**, 54.
Hardcastle Garth, iv, 238.
Hardwick, East, iii, 4.
Harewood (Yorks.), ii, **23**, 24.
Harlsey, Harsley, East, ii, **71**, 97.
Harome, ii, 60.
Harpham, i, 37, 38; ii, **91**, 92; iii, 123.

Harsley, East, *see* Harlsey, East.
Harswell, i, 189; ii, **72**.
Hartbushes, iv, 195.
Hartfield, i, 200.
Harthill (Yorks.), ii, **47**, 48, 49.
Harthill (Notts.), *see* Hartshill.
Harthill, Deanery of, Intr., ix; i, 35, 39, 93, 95, 96, 97, 98, 100, 101, 102, 103, 105, 115, 116, 118, 119, 120, 148, 149, 150, 156, 161, 175, 176, 189, 190, 193, 194, 212, 220; ii, 11, 18, 72, 73, 74, 75, 79, 80, 92, 131, 132, 133, 137, 158, 159, 160, 161, 194, 205, 207; iii, 11, 30, 111, 112, 113, 114, 116, 117, 118, 136, 174, 211, 212, 213, 221, 222, 229, 251.
Hartshead, Hartishead, ii, **34**, 35.
Hartshill, Harthill (Notts.), iv, 182.
Hartwith, iii, 235.
Harvington Hall, Intr., xvii.
Harwood Dale, ii, 221, **222**.
Harworth, iv, 5, 22, **74**, 102, 147, 148.
Haterskelf, ii, 38.
Hatfield (Yorks.), i, 20, 212; ii, **50**, 51; iii, 52, 226.
Hatfield, Great, iii, 125.
Haughton Park, Houghten Parck, iv, 63.
Hawksworth (Notts.), iii, 155; iv, 31, **68**, 69.
Hawnby, ii, **61**, 62.
Haworth, Hayworth, Intr., xi, xix; i, 58; ii, **39**, 41; iv, 229, 240.
Hawton, Houghton (Notts.), iv, 2, **69**, 80.
Haxby, ii, **70**; iii, 106, 107.
Hayshorne, *see* Heyshaw.
Haystrop, *see* Haisthorpe.
Hayton (Notts.), iv, 39, **73**.
Hayton-with-Beilby, i, 111, **120**, 121; ii, 19; iii, 37.
Hayworth, *see* Haworth.
Hazlewood, iv, 197, 215, 218.
Headingley, Hedingley, i, 128, 129; ii, 24, **25**.
Headon (Notts.), iv, 55, **72**, 73, 171, 173.
Headon (Yorks.), *see* Hedon.
Healaugh, ii, **20**; iii, 144; iv, 229, 232.
Heanley, *see* Hinderley, South.
Heanor, iv, 98.
Heath, iii, 189.
Heck, iii, 67, 74, 86.
Heck, Little, iii, 74.
Heckmondwike, iv, 225, 227.
Hedingley, *see* Headingley.
Hedon, Headon (Yorks.), i, 117; ii, 134, 223; iii, **13**, 14, 36, 178, 179.
Helmsley, Hemsley, Intr., xv; i, 82, 92; ii, **58**, 59, 125, 126; iv, 237.
Helmsley, Hemsley, Gate, Intr., xviii; ii, **68**, 212; iii, 210.
Helmsley, Hemsley, Over or Upper, ii, 68, **212**; iii, 210.
Helperthorpe, ii, **83**, 84; iii, 32, 123.
Hemingborough, i, 93; ii, **66**.
Hemsley, *see* Helmsley.
Hemsworth, Himsworth, ii, **45**, 46; Abp. Holgate's School, i, 73; ii, **45**.
Hencoates, iv, 206.
Hensall, Hensal, iii, 67, 86.
Heptonstall, ii, 33, **35**, 36, 37, 38, 39; iv, 241, 242.
Hereford, Intr., xxiv; Register, i, 68.
Herrnhutt, iv, 240.
Heslerton, East, ii, 82.
Heslerton, West, ii, **81**, 82; iii, 209, 228, 252.
Hesleyside, iv, 207, 209.
Heslington, ii, 56, **65**, 140.
Hessle, Hesle, ii, **75**, 76.
Hethersal, Hethensal, iii, 74.
Hewick, iii, 230.
Hexham, Intr., x, xi, xv; iii, 244, **248**, 249, 250; iv, 191, 202, 206, 207, 208, 209, 217, 220, 229; St. Mary's R.C. Ch., iv, 206.
Hexham, Deanery of, iii, 244, 246, 247, 248, 250.
Hexhamshire, Intr., ix, xv; iii, 244; iv, 192, 193, 236.
Hexhamshire Chapelry, iii, 248, **250**.
Heyshaw, Hayshorne, iii, 241.
Hickleton, Intr., xvii; ii, **52**; iii, 74, 80.
Hickling (Notts.), iv, **66**.
High Hoyland, *see* Hoyland, High.
High Morham, *see* Morham, High.
High Worsall, *see* Worsall, High.
Hilston, Hillston, i, 176, 177; ii, **86**, 87.
Hilton (Yorks.), ii, **65**; iii, 56, 135, 170.
Hinderley, Heanley, South, ii, 46.
Hinderwell, Intr., xiii; i, 216; ii, **62**, 63, 91, 196; iv, 237.
Hipperholme Grammar School, i, 129; ii, 95.
Hippins, ii, 38.
Hirst, *see* Hurst Courtney.
Hockerton, iv, **70**, 71.
Hodsock Park, iv, 21, 199.
Holbeach, iii, 186.
Holbeck (Yorks.), i, 51; ii, **26**, 27; iv, 240.
Holbeck Hall (Notts.), iv, 194, 210, 211.
Holdenby, i, 73.
Holderness, i, 138, 154; ii, 204; iii,

124, 131; iv, 190, 192, 206, 213, 216, 217.
Holderness, Deanery of, Intr., ix; i, 36, 107, 108, 109, 110, 117, 157, 176, 191, 192, 221, 224; ii, 12, 13, 76, 78, 84, 85, 86, 87, 88, 89, 135, 136, 163, 195, 203, 219, 220; iii, 8, 10, 13, 33, 34, 35, 123, 124, 125, 126, 127, 128, 129, 130, 131, 172, 175, 177, 217, 219, 224, 225.
Holland, South (Lincs.), iii, 186.
Hollym-with-Withernsea, Intr., xviii; ii, **87**.
Holmby, ii, 46.
Holme (par. Almondbury), i, 19.
Holme (Notts.), iv, **184**.
HolmeArchiepiscopi,Preb. of, *see* York
Holme Church, *see* Beverley, St. Nicholas.
Holme-Pierrepont, Pierpoint; Holmpierpont, iv, 8, 9, 40, 41, **67**, 68, 182, 184.
Holme, South, ii, 57.
Holme-on-Spalding-Moor, Intr., x, xix; ii, **72**; iii, 78, 153; iv, 200, 207, 213.
Holme-on-the-Wolds, i, 175; ii, **79**, 80.
Holmfirth, ii, **222**.
Holmpierpont, *see* Holme-Pierrepont.
Holmpton, ii, **84**, 86; iii, 219, 220.
Holtby, i, 143; ii, **67**, 68, 212; iii, 209, 210.
Honley, ii, **42**, 43, 44.
Hook, Hooke, i, 27; ii, **54**, 55; iii, 25, 67, 76, 77, 78, 79, 80, 86.
Hooton-Pagnell, Hutton Pannell, Pannel, i, 203; ii, **51**, 52.
Hooton, Hutton Roberts, ii, **46**, 47; iii, 87.
Hopton, Great, *see* Habton, Great.
Horbury, ii, **41**, 42; iii, 187.
Hornby (Yorks.), iii, **234**, 235.
Hornsea, Hornsey, Intr., xii; i, 218; ii, **88**, 89, 90, 147; iii, 36.
Horsforth, Horseforth, ii, **222**.
Horton-in-Craven, ii, 4; iv, 227.
Horton, Great, iv, 240.
Horton-in-Ribblesdale, ii, 6, **27**, 28; iv, 240.
Hose, iv, 60, 132.
Hotham, ii, **74**, 75; iv, 237.
Houghten Parck, *see* Haughton Park.
Houghton (Notts.), *see* Hawton.
Houghton, Great (Yorks.), i, 167; iv, 226.
Houghton Hall, iv, 211, 213.
Houghton, Long, iv, 231.
Hoveringham, iv, **72**, 135, 157.
Hovingham, ii, **57**, 58, 214; iii, 97; iv, 202, 207, 208.
Howden, i, 115, 194; ii, **92**; iii, 77, 78; iv, 226, 229.
Howdenshire, Commissary of, ii, 93; iii, 106.
Howsham, iii, 119, 120.
Hoyland-juxta-Wath; Hoyland Chapel, ii, **55**; iii, 23.
Hoyland, High, ii, **49**; iii, 187.
Hubberholme, Hubberholm, Hubberholmn, i, 12; ii, **29**, 30; iv, 236, 237.
Hucknall Torkard, iv, **71**, 72, 110.
Huddersfield, Intr., x; i, 20, 129, 130; ii, **30**, 31; iv, 242.
Huddlestone Hall, iv, 189, 208, 213, 215, 218.
Huggate, ii, **73**, 74.
Hughflats, iv, 236.
Hull, Bapt. Ch., iv, 242; Bowl-Alley Lane Ch., iv, 228, 229, 233; Central Library, iv, 186; Charterhouse, ii, 78; iii, 114, 115; Dagger Lane Ch., iv, 229; Daily Services, Intr., xv; Dukes of Kingston-on-Hull, iv, 210; Garrison Ch., ii, 77; Henry VIII. Tower, iv, 242; merchants, i, 150, 152; population, Intr., x; Presb. min., i, 98; rents, i, 173; ii, 10; resident clergy, i, 191; ii, 135, 195; iii, 130, 225; residents, i, 154, 155; ii, 75; Trinity Ho., ii, 77; visitation, i, 193; ii, 13, 76, 88; workhouse, ii, 77, 78.
Hull, Holy Trinity, Intr., xvi; ii, **76**; iii, 114, 145; iv, 237.
Hull, St. Mary's, i, 191, 192; ii, **78**, 136; iii, 126; iv, 241, 242.
Humber, River, ii, 137; iii, 10.
Humbleton, i, 192, 221; ii, 13, **88**; iv, 213.
Hunmanby, Intr., xiii; i, 215, 216, 218, 219; ii, 63, **90**, 91, 196; iii, 135.
Hunsingore, i, 123; ii, **222**; iii, 165, 166.
Hunslet, Hunslett, ii, **24**, 25.
Hunsley, iii, 30.
Huntington (Yorks.), ii, **55**, 66, 140.
Hurst Castle, iv, 188.
Hurst Courtney, Hirst, i, 165.
Husthwaite, Husthwait, Intr., xix; i, 143, 147; ii, **68**, 69.
Husthwaite, Preb. of, *see* York.
Hutton Bonville, Bonvile, Bonvill, Bonvil, i, 94; ii, **69**, 70.
Hutton Buscel, Bushell, bushel, Intr., xix; i, 190; ii, **60**.
Hutton Cranswick, ii, 17, **80**, 81; iii, 50, 117, 118, 214.
Hutton-in-the-Hole, ii, 153; iv, 238.
Hutton Pannell, *see* Hooton Pagnell.

Hutton Roberts, *see* Hooton Roberts.
Hutton Rudby, *see* Rudby-in-Cleveland.
Hutton Wannesley, Wanesley, *see* Marston, Long.
Huttons Ambo, i, 141, 142; ii, **56**, 57.

Ickornshaw, School at, ii, 108.
Idle, i, 128, 129; ii, **95**; iv, 226, 229.
Ilkeston, iv, 2, 18.
Ilkley, i, 221; ii, **94**; iv, 194, 208.
Illingworth, ii, 33, **96**; iv, 229.
Indies, West, iv, 228.
Ingerthorpe, iii, 230, 231.
Ingleby Arncliffe, ii, 71, **97**.
Ingleby Greenhow, ii, **97**, 98.
Ipthorne, Preb. of, *see* Chichester.
Ireland, i, 190; iv, 237, 239.
Irthington, iii, 46.
Irton (Yorks.), iii, 132.
Island, The, *see* Sunk Island.

Kayingham, *see* Keyingham.
Keighley, Kighley, ii, 4, **106**, 107, 108; iii, 49; iv, 229, 237, 239.
Kelfield, iii, 91.
Kelham, iv, 69, **80**.
Kellington, ii, **115**.
Kendal (Dr. Rotheram's Academy), iv, 229, 231.
Kensington, i, 2; ii, 62; iv, 81.
Kent, Intr., xiv; i, 162; iv, 64, 231.
Kerby malzerd, *see* Kirkby Malzeard.
Keswick, iv, 229.
Kettlewell, ii, **111**, 112.
Keyingham, Kayingham, i, 118; ii, **136**, 137.
Keyworth, iv, **75**, 134, 160, 183.
Kilburn, Kilburne (Yorks.), i, 120; ii, **121**, 122; iii, 119.
Kildale, i, 30; ii, 9, **128**; iii, 176.
Kildare, Bp. of, i, 190.
Kildwick-in-Craven; Kildwick-near-Skipton, Intr., xi; ii, **108**, 110, 111; iii, 89, 90; iv, 231, 237, 239, 241, 242.
Kildwick Peircy, *see* Kilnwick Percy.
Kilham, Intr., xviii; ii, **138**; iii, 173, 174.
Killala, Bp. of, i, 190.
Killaloe, Bp. of, Intr., xix; iv, 62.
Kilnsea, Kilnsey, i, 191, 192; ii, 79, **135**, 136; iii, 125, 126.
Kilnwick-on-the-Wolds, Kildwick-near-Watton, ii, **132**, 133, 162; iii, 113.
Kilnwick Percy, Kildwick Peircy, perse, ii, 73, **137**, 138, 172, 207.
Kilpin, ii, 93.
Kilvington (Notts.), iv, 34, **79**, 141, 185.
Kilvington, North (Yorks.), iii, 170; iv, 195, 218.
Kilvington, South, ii, **120**, 169; iii, 166, 170; iv, 203, 208, 218, 221, 222.
Kimberworth, iii, 21.
Kinalton, *see* Kinoulton.
Kingerby Old Hall, iv, 221.
Kingston-on-Soar, iv, 76, 134, 60, **183**.
Kingston-upon-Hull, *see* Hull.
Kinoulton, Kinalton, iv, **76**, 77, 78,
Kippax, ii, **105**; iii, 250; iv, 188, 189,
Kirby-in-Cleveland, *see* Kirkby-with-Broughton.
Kirby, Cold, *see* Cold Kirkby.
Kirby-Grindalythe, *see* Kirkby Grindalythe.
Kirby Hill, *see* Kirkby Hill.
Kirby-Misperton, *see* Kirkby Misperton.
Kirby-on-the-Moor, *see* Kirkby Hill
Kirby Underdale, *see* Kirkby Underdale.
Kirk Bramwith, Intr., xiv; i, **65**, 67.
Kirkburn, i, 199; ii, **133**, 161; iii, 136, 223.
Kirkburton, Kirk Burton, Intr., xiii; ii, **116**, 117; iii, 191; iv, 230, 237.
Kirkby-in-Ashfield, Intr., xix; iv, **81**, 240.
Kirkby-with-Broughton, Kirkby-in-Cleveland, ii, 105, **126**, 127; iii, 100, 101.
Kirkby Grindalythe, Grindalyth, Intr., xvii; i, 29, 144, 189; ii, **134**, 135, 153, 155, 190.
Kirkby, Kirby, Hill; Kirby-super-Moram; Kirby-on-the-Moor, iii, 163, 164.
Kirkby Ireleth, Irelyth, ii, **98**, 99, 100, 101, 102.
Kirkby Knowle, Knowl, i, 89; ii, **119**, 120; iii, 166.
Kirkby Malhamdale, Malamdale, ii, **112**, 113.
Kirkby Malzeard, Malzard; Kerby malzerd, iii, **235**, 236, 238; iv, 230, 238.
Kirkby Misperton; Kirkby Overcarr, ii, **122**, 124.
Kirkby Moorside, Intr., xiii, xvi; i, 143; ii, 8, **124**; iv, 237, 238.
Kirkby Overblow, Overblows, Intr., xiii; ii, **104**, 127; iii, 44, 250; iv, 208.
Kirkby Overcarr, *see* Kirkby Misperton.
Kirkby Sigston, iii, **110**; iv, 237, 238.
Kirkby, South, ii, 46; iii, **54**, 195.
Kirkby Underdale, i, 117; ii, **133**, 134; iii, 13, 14.

Kirkby Wharfe, Wharf, ii, **118**, 119; iii, 44.
Kirkdale, ii, 60, **125**, 126.
Kirk Deighton, ii, **103**.
Kirk Ella, i, 212, 213; ii, **131**.
Kirk Fenton, *see* Church Fenton.
Kirkheaton, Kirk Heaton, ii, **113**, 159.
Kirk Leatham, ii, **129**, 130, 155, 156.
Kirk Levington, ii, **130**; iii, 228.
Kirklington (Notts.), iv, **70**, 71.
Kirk Sandall, Sandal Parva, Little Sandall; Sandal, ii, 51; iii, **52**.
Kirk Smeaton, Kirksmeaton, ii, **117**, 118.
Kirkton, *see* Kirton.
Kirton, Kirkton (Notts.), iv, 20, **84**, 85.
Kiveton Park, ii, 49.
Knapton (Yorks.), iii, 252.
Knaresborough, iv, 217, 238.
Knedlington, ii, 93.
Kneesall, Kneesal, -with-Upton, iv, **80**, 114, 115, 230.
Kneeton, iv, 25, **78**, 185.
Knottingley, ii, **222**; iii, 3, 4.

Lambeth, Intr., v, xiv, xxiv; iv, 64.
Lambley (Notts.), iv, **90**, 132, 175.
Lambspring, iv, 191, 193, 197, 203, 204, 205, 209, 218.
Lancashire, Intr., xiii; i, 183; ii, 32, 43, 102, 175; iii, 156; iv, 192, 193, 194, 201, 210, 214, 215, 219, 220, 226, 227, 231, 241.
Landguard Fort, iii, 22.
Lane End (par. Ecclesfield), i, 179.
Laneham, iv, 130, 182, **183**.
Langar-with-Barnston, iv, **87**, 88.
Langcliffe, Longrigg, iv, 237.
Langfield, Lonegfield (par. Halifax), i, 132; ii, 37.
Langford (Notts.), iii, 125; iv, **89**.
Langtoft (Yorks.), i, 162; ii, **165**, 166.
Langtoft prebend, *see* York.
Langton (Yorks.), ii, **162**.
Langwith, iv, 111.
Lastingham, Lestingham, ii, **153**, 154; iv, 237, 238.
Laughton-in-the-Morthing, -en-le-Morthen, Intr., xvi; i, 27, 205; ii, **151**; iii, 159.
Laxton (Notts.), iv, **88**, 89.
Laxton (Yorks.), ii, 93.
Leake (Yorks.), i, 145; ii, **157**, 158; iii, 99, 111; iv, 216.
Leake, Leak, Leke, East; Great Leake (Notts.), Intr., xix; iv, 85, **86**, 87, 242.
Leake, Leke, West (Notts.), Intr., xix; iv, **85**, 86, 87.
Learings (par. Heptonstall), ii, 38.
Leathley, ii, **140**; iii, 194.
Leavening, i, 40, 41.
Leconfield, Leckonfield, Lecconfield, Intr., xvi; i, 190; ii, 133, **160**; iii, 136, 223.
Ledsham, ii, **144**, 145; iii, 143.
Lee, St. John (Northumb.), iii, 246, 247, **248**; iv, 207, 209.
Leeds, Leedes, Intr., x, xv; i, 51, 138, 198; ii, 144; iii, 18, 43; iv, 186, 187, 193, 228, 233, 234, 240, 242.
Leeds, Parish Church, i, 125, 128; ii, 25, 26, 27, **140**, 143.
Leeds, Holy Trinity, i, 46; ii, **145**, 146.
Leeds, St. John's, ii, **142**, 143; iii, 49.
Leeds, Visitation at, i, 48; iii, 144, 178; Grammar School, i, 197; Mill Hill Chapel, iv, 225, 230, 231; Call Lane Chapel, iv, 230.
Leicester, iv, 126, 129.
Leicester Co., iv, 60, 129, 132, 133, 151.
Lenton (Notts.), iv, **92**, 93, 123, 182.
Leppington, Lepington, iii, 119, 120.
Lepton, ii, 113.
Lestingham, *see* Lastingham.
Letwell, Letwells, -with-Gildingwells, Gilldingwells, Gilldinwells, i, 205; ii, **152**, 181.
Leven, i, 97; ii, **163**.
Leverton, North (Notts.), iv, 6, 7, 93, **94**, 95.
Leverton, North, Preb. of, *see* Southwell.
Leverton, South (Notts.), iv, 6, 7, **93**, 94, 95, 238.
Levisham, i, 144, 189; ii, 135, **152**, 153, 154, 155, 189, 190.
Leyden, iv, 233.
Lichfield, Intr., xiii; Bp. of, i, 63; iv, 98.
Lichfield Prebends, Intr., xiv, xix; Curborough, iv, 107; Flixton, ii, 125; Whittington and Berkswych, iv, 64.
Liége, iv, 191, 193, 194, 199.
Lightcliffe, ii, 32, 33, **148**.
Lincoln, ii, 136; Bp. of, Intr., vi, viii; Chanc., ii, 198; Dioc. Intr., viii; i, 101; iv, 154; Preb. Intr., xix; Castor, ii, 220; Coringham, ii, 221; Louth, iv, 107; Record Soc., Intr., viii; Register, i, 26, 210; ii, 136; iii, 18, 23, 62; iv, 89, 155, 184; *Spec. Dioc.*, Intr., viii, xvi.
Lincoln, Co. of, Intr., xii, xvi; ii, 198; iii, 186, 218; iv, 2, 54, 96, 112, 155, 193, 205, 221.

Lindby, *see* Lynby.
Linton-in-Craven, i, 51; ii, 89, 90, **146**.
Linton (par. Howden), ii, 93.
Linton-upon-Ouse, ii, 199; iv, 195, 202, 210, 220, 221.
Linton (par. Spofforth), iii, 142.
Lisbon, iv, 192, 195, 196, 198.
Lismore, *see* Waterford and Lismore.
Lissett, Lisset, ii, **163**, 164.
Littleborough (Notts.), iv, 7, **94**, 95.
Little Driffield, *see* Driffield, Little.
Little Givendale, *see* Givendale, Little.
Little Heck, *see* Heck, Little.
Little Ouseburn, Usburn, *see* Ouseburn, Little.
Little Sandall, *see* Kirk Sandall.
Littlethorpe, Littelthorpe, iii, 230; iv, 213.
Little Weeton, *see* Weeton, Little.
Liverpool, iv, 194, 195, 241; Abp. of, iv, 186, 187, 192.
Liversedge, Intr., xi; i, 61, 62.
Liverton, i, 32, 184, 185, 186; iv, 239.
Llandaff, Intr., xxiv; subs. Bk., ii, 186; iv, 53.
Lockington (Yorks.), ii, **159**.
Lockton, i, 144; ii, 153, **154**, 189, 190.
Lofthouse, ii, **155**; iv, 196, 209.
Lofthouse, North, iv, 211.
Londesborough, Loundsbrough, Intr., xiii; ii, 44, 94, **158**; iv, 185.
Londesborough, Historic, ii, 159.
London, Bp. of, Intr., xiii, xix; ii, 105; Ct. of Chanc., ii, 99; iii, 61, 62; Ct. of Common Pleas, iii, 73; 'Crown' iv, 234; Deaths in, iv, 196, 198, 201, 202; Dioc. of, Intr., xxii; Dioc. Reg., ii, 122; iv, 25, 117, 184; Fire of, ii, 36; Friends' Ho., iv, 234, 235; Lead Mines Co., iii, 245; Ld. Chanc., iii, 168; Preaching, iv, 240; rents, iv, 163; residents, Intr., xiii; i, 43, 96, 143; ii, 8, 36, 37, 124; iii, 5, 9, 58, 59, 60; iv, 12, 95, 242; St. Paul's Preb., iii, 144; Tower of, iv, 204; Dr. William's Library, iv, 223.
Long Houghton, *see* Houghton, Long.
Long Marston (Yorks.), *see* Marston, Long.
Long Preston, *see* Preston, Long.
Long Riston, *see* Riston, Long.
Long Sandall, *see* Sandall, Long.
Longrigg, *see* Langcliffe.
Lorraine, iv, 193.
Lostock (Cheshire) (?), *see* Allostock.
Lothen, *see* Lotherden.
Lotherden, Lothersdale, Lothersden, Lothen, i, 125; iv, 236.
Loudham, *see* Lowdham.
Lound (par. Ecclesfield), i, 179.
Lound (Notts.), iv, 147.
Loundsburgh, *see* Londesborough.
Louth Preb., *see* Lincoln.
Louvain, iv, 193, 202, 206.
Loversall, Lovershal, i, 167; ii, **150**, 151.
Low Bishopside, iii, 239.
Lowdham, Loudham, iv, **91**, 92, 134, 135.
Low Ellington, *see* Ellington, Low.
Lower Silton, *see* Silton, Lower or Nether.
Lowthorpe, Lowthorp, i, 214; ii, **164**, 165, 205; iii, 38.
Luddenden, ii, 33, **149**, 150.
Lund (Yorks.), Intr., xviii; ii, 132, 133, **161**, 162; iii, 113.
Luttons Ambo, iii, 252.
Lynby, Lindby, iv, 4, 5, **90**, 110.
Lythe, Lyth, ii, 19, **157**; iv, 196, 203, 209, 212, 219, 239.

Malla, Bp. of, iv, 187, 192.
Maltby, Maultby, i, 204; ii, 152, **180**.
Malton, New (St. Michael and St. Leonard), ii, **187**, 189; iii, 102; iv, 230.
Malton, New, Visitation at, i, 41, 184; ii, 19, 83, 186, 187; iii, 32, 97, 102, 122, 217, 224.
Malton, Old, ii, **186**, 187, 188, 189.
Manchester, Intr., xiii; i, 183; iv, 241.
Mansfield, Intr., xv; iv, 97, **178**, 179, 230, 238.
Mansfield Woodhouse, iv, **97**, 98, 146, 147.
Maplebeck, Mapplebeck, Intr., xvi; iv, **96**, 97, 166.
Mappleton, ii, 14, 15, **223**; iii, 36, 130, 178, 226, 227.
Marfleet, Intr., xvi; ii, **195**; iii, 130, 225.
Margate, i, 162.
Market Weighton; Weighton, i, 190; ii, 133, 161; iii, 136, **222**, 223.
Markham, East, iv, 41, 42, **99**, 100, 124, 159.
Markham, West, iv, **98**.
Markington, iii, 230; iv, 198.
Marnham, iv, **95**, 105, 106.
Marr, i, 21, 71; ii, **181**, 182.
Marsden (Yorks.), i, 19; ii, **179**.
Marske, Marsk, ii, **191**; iii, 207.
Marston, Long (*alias* Hutton Wannesley), ii, **173**.
Marton-in-Cleveland, ii, **190**, 223.
Marton-in-Craven, ii, **175**.
Marton-in-the-Forest, i, 210; ii, **184**, 185; iii, 107, 108.

Marton-in-Holderness; 'Martin's,' iv, 206, 216, 217, 218.
Marton-on-the-Moor, iii, 162, 163, **164**, 165.
Maryland, iv, 194.
Masham, Massam, iii, 236, **237**, 238; iv, 238.
Mattersey, iv, **101**, 182.
Maultby, *see* Maltby.
Melbourne, Melburn, iii, 174.
Meltham, ii, 43, **179**, 180.
Melton (Harthill), iii, 222.
Melton-on-the-Hill, i, 136, 179; iv, **184**.
Meltonby, iii, 229.
Methley, ii, **177**, 178.
Mexborough, ii, **182**; iii, 23, 193.
Mickleby, ii, 157.
Middlesbrough, Intr., xv, xvii; i, 31; ii, **191**, 192.
Middlesex, i, 97.
Middlesmoor, Midlesmoor, iii, **236**, 237; iv, 195, 210.
Middleton (Cleveland), i, 145, 146; ii, **192**.
Middleton (Ryedale), i, 144; ii, 153, 155, **189**, 190; iii, 8.
Middleton-on-the-Wolds, ii, **194**, 195.
Middleton Hall (nr. Leeds), iv, 193, 213, 219.
Middleton Lodge (nr. Ilkley), ii, 94; iv, 194, 208.
Midhope, Midhop, Middop, i, 73, 76, 179; ii, **223**.
Millington, i, 111, 121; ii, 18, 19.
Mill-town, *see* Milton.
Milton, Mill-town (Notts.), iv, 53, 99.
Mirfield, ii, **178**; iv, 240.
Misne, *see* Misson.
Misson, Missen, Misne, i, 126, 127; iv, 51, 52, **100**, 101.
Misterton (Notts.), iv, 25, **102**, 173, 242.
Mitton (Yorks.), ii, **175**, 176; iv, 194, 210.
Mixenden, ii, 32; iv, 225, 226, 228, 229.
Monk Fryston, ii, 144, **183**; iii, 144.
Moorhouse, iv, 88, 89.
Moor-Monkton, i, 77; ii, **174**.
Moorsholme, Moorsome, Great, iv, 239.
Morham, High, iii, 77.
Morley (Yorks.), i, 62; ii, **223**; iv, 225, 227.
Morton (Notts.), iv, **104**, 105.
Morton (Yorks.), iv, 232.
Moss, i, 134.
Murton (Yorks.), ii, **193**, 217; iii, 15.
Muscoates, Muscoats, ii, 125.
Muskham, North, iv, 183, **184**.
Muskham, North; Preb. of, *see* Southwell.
Muskham, South, iv, **103**.
Muskham, South; Preb. of, *see* Southwell.
Muston (Yorks.), Intr., xiii; i, 216, 218, 219; ii, 90, 91, **196**; iii, 135.
Myton-on-Swale, ii, **185**, 186; iii, 243.

Naburn, Naburne, i, 162, **163**; iii, 105.
Nafferton, i, 214; ii, 165, **204**, 205; iii, 38.
Neepsend, Neapsend, iii, 61.
Ness (par. Hovingham), iv, 202, 207.
Neswick, i, 97.
Nether Poppleton, *see* Poppleton, Nether.
Nether Silton, *see* Silton, Nether.
Netherthong, ii, 44.
Netherton Farm, ii, 43.
Nettlebed, iv, 192.
Newark, Intr., xv, xix; iv, 12, 13, 55, **106**, 107, 165, 174.
Newark, Deanery of, Intr., ix; iv, 2, 12, 31, 32, 33, 34, 35, 46, 48, 55, 56, 69, 70, 79, 80, 88, 89, 95, 96, 105, 106, 122, 136, 138, 139, 140, 141, 142, 153, 154, 164, 165, 174, 184.
Newark, Visitation at, iv, 24, 79, 106.
Newbald, Newbold, North, i, 150; ii, **205**, 206.
Newbald, North; Preb. of, *see* York.
Newbald, South; Preb. of, *see* York.
Newbiggin (Yorks.), iv, 203.
Newburgh, iv, 202, 215.
Newby (Cleveland), iii, 101.
Newcastle-on-Tyne, iv, 12, 193.
Newholm, iii, 209.
New House Farm, Turvin, ii, 38.
New Malton, *see* Malton, New.
Newstead (Notts.), ii, 2.
Newton (par. Howden), ii, 93.
Newton (Lincs.), iv, 155.
Newton, East, ii, 200.
Newton-in-Cleveland, ii, 9, **202**.
Newton Kyme, Kine, ii, **196**.
Newton-on-Ouse, ii, **199**, 213; iv, 195, 202, 210, 220, 221.
Newton-on-Rawcliffe (Ryedale), i, 144, 188; ii, 154, 189; iii, 7, **8**, 211.
Nidderdale, iii, 240.
Norfolk, iii, 189; iv, 205.
Normanby (Lincs.), iv, 129.
Normanby (Yorks.), ii, **201**; iii, 108, 109, 169.
Normanton (Yorks.), ii, **197**, 198;

iii, 187.
Normanton, Preb. of, *see* Southwell.
Normanton-on-Soar, iv, **179**, 180.
Normanton-on-Trent, iv, 96, **105**, (?)130.
Northallerton; Allerton, Intr., xix; i, **34**, 35, 95, 174.
Northampton, ii, 110; iv, 224, 227.
Northampton, Co. of, i, 73; iv, 62.
North Burton, *see* Cherry Burton.
North Cave, *see* Cave, North.
North Cliff, *see* Cliff, North.
North Dalton, *see* Dalton, North.
North Deighton, *see* Deighton, North.
North Ferriby, *see* Ferriby, North.
North Frodingham, *see* Frodingham, North.
North Grimston, *see* Grimston, North.
North Kilvington, *see* Kilvington, North.
North Lofthouse, *see* Lofthouse, North.
North Muskham, *see* Muskham, North.
North Newbald, *see* Newbald, North.
North Otterington, *see* Otterington, North.
North Stainley, *see* Stainley, North.
Northumberland, Intr., ix; iii, 244, 246, 247, 248, 249; iv, 201, 204, 209, 213, 219, 221, 229, 238; Archdn., Intr., xiv.
North Wheatley, *see* Wheatley, North.
Norton (par. Campsall), i, 134.
Norton-Cuckney, iv, **111**, 147, 194, 210.
Norton-juxta-Malton, Intr., xvi; i, 107; ii, **203**.
Norwell, iv, **111**, 112.
Norwell Overhall; Preb. of, *see* Southwell.
Norwell Pallishall; Preb. of, *see* Southwell.
Norwell Tertia Pars; Preb. of, *see* Southwell.
Norwich, Intr., xxiv; iv, 230; Bp. of, Intr., v, xiii; ii, 105; Cathedral Prior, iv, 197.
Nostell Priory, ii, 117.
Nottingham, Intr., x, xv; ii, 49; iv, 2, 15, 18, 63, 116, 201, 211, 223, 230, 231.
Nottingham, Archdn. of, Intr., ix; iv, 16, 60, 67, 119, 121; Bank, iv, 152; Chapels, iv, 224, 230, 242; Clergy residents, 17, 37, 45, 92.
Nottingham, Deanery of, Intr., ix; iv, 2, 3, 4, 13, 14, 15, 16, 17, 18, 26, 36, 49, 61, 62, 63, 71, 72, 81, 90, 91, 92, 97, 107, 109, 110, 116, 122, 142, 143, 144, 146, 155, 156, 166, 177, 178, 179, 180, 184.
Nottingham Grammar Sch., iv, 46, 93, 123, 133; Visitation, iv, 7, 26, 82, 133, 146, 153, 182.
Nottingham, St. Mary's, Intr., xviii, xxii; iv, 26, 41, 68, 93, 117, 123, 134, **180**, 181, 184, 224, 242.
Nottingham, St. Nicholas, iv, **109**, 122, 238, 242.
Nottingham, St. Peter's, iv, 37, **107**, 108, 154, 161, 211.
Nottingham, Co. of, Intr., ix, xiii, xiv, xv, xvi, xix; i, 69, 126, 127, 128; ii, 2, 44, 46, 72, 94, 137, 159; iii, 6, 125, 155; iv, 8, 37, 74, 77, 81, 96, 101, 108, 134, 138, 139, 148, 165, 166, 177, 192, 193, 194, 199, 223.
Nun Appleton, i, 42.
Nunburnholme, Nun-Burnholm, Intr., xx; ii, 138, **207**.
Nuneaton, iv, 225.
Nunkeeling, Nun-Keiling, ii, **203**; iii, 124, 128, 129, 131.
Nun-Monkton, Monckton, ii, **223**; iii, 13, 14, 178, 179.
Nunnington, Nunington, i, 33; ii, **199**, 200; iii, 95.
Nunthorpe (Cleveland), ii, 191, **223**.
Nuthall, Nuttall, iv, 5, 71, 72, 91, **110**.
Nuthill, iv, 206, 216.
Nuttall, *see* Nuthall.

Octon, iii, 173.
Old Byland, *see* Byland, Old.
Old Malton, *see* Malton, Old.
Old Windsor, *see* Windsor, Old.
Ollerton, iv, 40, 52, 53, **115**, 118, 186, 211.
Ompton, *see* Kneesall.
Ordsall, Intr., xvi; i, 138; iii, 6; iv, 22, **113**.
Ormesby (Yorks.), ii, **215**, 216, 217.
Ormskirk, iv, 231.
Orston, Intr., xii; iv, **112**.
Osbaldestone Hall, iv, 221.
Osbaldwick, i, 172; ii, 193, 194, **217**; iii, 15.
Osbaldwick; Preb. of, *see* York.
Oscott College, iv, 186.
Osgodby (Yorks.), ii, 67.
Osmotherley (Yorks.), i, 146, 211; ii, **218**, 219; iv, 211, 215, 216, 217.
Ossett, ii, **209**, 210, 211.
Ossett-Green Chapel, iv, 230.
Ossington, iv, **184**.
Oswaldkirk, i, 208; ii, **214**, 215;

iii, 158.
Otley (Yorks.), i, 223, 224; ii, **208**, 209; iii, 250.
Otterington, Ottrington, North, ii, **217**, 218; iii, 170, 171, 252.
Otterington, South, ii, **213**.
Ottringham, Otteringham, ii, **220**, 221; iii, 218.
Oulston, i, 142; iv, 196, 200, 202.
Ouse, River, iv, 195.
Ouseburn, Usburn, Great, iii, 243.
Ouseburn, Usburn, Little, ii, 186; iii, **242**, 243.
Ousefleet, iii, 200.
Over Helmsley, *see* Helmsley, Over.
Over Silton, *see* Silton, Over.
Overton (Yorks.), ii, 199, **212**, 213.
Owram, North, ii, 32; iv, 226, 228, 230.
Owram, South, *see* Breer's Chapel.
Owston, Ouston (Yorks.), ii, **211**, 212.
Owstwick, iv, 236.
Owthorne, ii, **219**, 220; iii, 175, 176.
Owthorpe, Owthorp, iv, 76, **77**, 78.
Oxford, Bp. of, Intr., v; 'Movement,' Intr., xxiii; Methodists, Intr., xvi; iv, 236; Physique Gdn., ii, 125; Pusey Ho., Intr., xxiv; Reg., ii, 125; University (text only), ii, 125, 173; iv, 178, 216, 240; *Alumn. Oxon.*, Intr., xxiv; iii, 199.
Oxford, Co. of, iv, 192.
Oxton (Notts.), iv, 3, 81, **114**.

Pagula, *see* Paull.
Palethorpe, Palethorp, Perlethorpe, iv, 40, 53, 115, 116, **117**.
Pannal, Pannall, ii, 105; iii, **250**.
Papplewick, Papelwick, iv, 26, **116**, 117, 182.
Paris, ii, 147; iv, 192, 193.
Parlington, iv, 197, 198, 214, 215, 220.
Parson's, Parson, Cross, i, 179.
Pateley Bridge, iii, **238**, 240; iv, 231.
Patrington, Patterington, Intr., xviii; iii, **8**, 9.
Paull, Paul, Pagula (Yorks.), i, 154; iii, **10**, 127, 172, 173; iv, 229.
Pellit-Reid Farm, Crosland, South, ii, 43.
Penistone, Peniston, i, 137, 138, 170, 171; ii, 44; iii, **5**, 6; iv, 113, 114, 231.
Penley, iv, 202.
Perlethorpe, *see* Palethorpe.
Peterborough, iv, 60; Bp. of, Intr., xxiv; Precentor, Intr., xiii; iv, 61; 3rd Stall, Intr., xiv; iv, 64.
Phipping Park, iii, 74.
Pickering, i, 187, 188; iii, **6**, 7, 8, 168, 211; iv, 238.
Pickhill, iii, 163.
Pidsey Burton, *see* Burton Pidsea.
Pilley, iii, 155, 156.
Pleasley, iv, 145, 146
Plompton, Plumpton, Hall, iii, 41; iv, 194, 207, 208, 216, 217.
Plumtree, Plumptree, iv, **116**, 231.
Pocklington, i, 120, 176; iii, **11**, 12, 212, 229; Gr. Sch., i, 212; iii, 118.
Pollington, Pollinton, iii, 67, 74, 86; Carr, iii, 73.
Pontefract, i, 127, 165, 202; ii, 45, 222; iii, **3**, 4, 43; iv, 196, 205, 212, 231.
Pontefract, Deanery of, Intr., ix; i, 13, 14, 15, 26, 58, 60, 62, 63, 126, 127, 128, 129, 130, 131, 132, 139, 165, 177, 198, 199, 205, 223; ii, 30, 31, 34, 35, 39, 41, 42, 54, 95, 96, 113, 115, 116, 148, 149, 177, 178, 179, 197, 209, 222, 223; iii, 3, 4, 16, 18, 19, 25, 46, 48, 49, 50, 51, 67, 147 148, 150, 183, 184, 185, 187, 188, 199, 252.
Ponteland, iv, 201.
Pool, Poole (Yorks.), ii, 209; iii, **250**.
Poppleton, Popleton, Upper and Nether, i, 139; ii, 171; iii, **2**, 3.
Preston, Great, iii, 43.
Preston-in-Holderness, ii, 223; iii, **13**, 14, 178, 179.
Preston Jacklin, Purston Jaglin, i, 199.
Preston, Long, ii, **147**; iii, 45, 46.
Prestwich, Prestwick, iii, 156.
Pudsey, i, 128; ii, 111; iii, **4**, 5; iv, 225, 226, 231, 240.
Purston Jaglin, *see* Preston Jacklin.
Pydsey-Burton, *see* Burton Pidsea.

Quebec, iv, 228.

Radcliffe, Ratcliffe-on-Trent, iv, **120**, 121, 136.
Radford (Notts.), iv, 3, 92, 93, **122**, 123, 182.
Ragby, ii, 46.
Ragnall, Ragnell, iv, 43, 44, **130**.
Rainton (Yorks.), iii, 162.
Rampton (Notts.), iv, 65, 94, **129**, 130.
Rampton, Preb. of, *see* Southwell.
Ranfield, *see* Ravenfield.
Raskelfe, Raskelf, iii, **25**, 26, 161, 162.
Rastrick, Intr., xviii; ii, 33, 37; iii, **18**, 19.
Ratcliffe, *see* Rawcliffe.
Ratcliffe, Ratcliff-on-Soar, iv, 11, 12, **119**.
Ratcliffe-on-Trent, *see* Radcliffe-on-Trent.

Rathmell, Rathmill, ii, 6; iv, 237.
Ravenfield, Ranfield, i, 136, 137; iii, **24**.
Raventofts, iii, 229, 233; iv, 195, 198, 199, 210, 212.
Rawcliffe, Rawcliff, Rocliffe, Roecliffe, Ratcliffe, iii, **25**, 43, 67, 72, 86; iv, 194, 238.
Rawdon, Rawden, Intr., xvi; i, 51; iii, **16**; iv, 238, 241, 242.
Rawholm Farm, ii, 38.
Rawmarsh, Intr., xvii; iii, **20**, 21; iv, 238.
Redmarley, iv, 194.
Reedness, Rednes, iii, 79, 200.
Reighton, iii, **37**, 221.
Rempstone, Rempston, Remston, iv, **118**, 119, 151.
Retford, Redford, Intr., xv; iv, 6, 99, 242.
Retford, East, iv, 8, 42, 100, **123**, 124, 125; Gr. Sch., iv, 53, 54, 124.
Retford, West, iv, 42, 100, **124**, 125, 231.
Retford, Deanery of, Intr., ix; iv, 5, 6, 19, 20, 21, 22, 23, 37, 38, 39, 41, 42, 50, 51, 52, 53, 57, 63, 65, 72, 73, 74, 84, 93, 94, 98, 99, 100, 101, 102, 111, 113, 115, 117, 123, 124, 126, 147, 148, 149, 157, 158, 168, 169, 170, 171, 172, 182, 184, 185.
Ribchester, ii, 175.
Riccall, Riccal, iii, **28**, 29.
Riccall, Preb. of, *see* York.
Rice, *see* Rise.
Richmond (Yorks.), iv, 238; Archdn., Intr., ix; ii, 222, 223.
Richmondshire, iii, 110.
Rillington, ii, 84; iii, **31**, 32, 122, 123.
Rilston, *see* Rylstone
Riplingham, iii, 30.
Ripon, Rippon, iii, 231, 234, 238; iv, 238.
Ripon, Collegiate Church, Intr. ix; iii, 120, **229**, 230, 231, 234, 241, 242; Dean, Intr., xiv, xix; iii, 120, 166, 230, 240; iv, 212; Dean & Ch., Intr., ix; iii, 230; Dean's Verger, iii, 231; gaol, iv, 195, 198; gr. sch., iii, 230, 231, 242; Hospitals, Intr., xiv; iii, 120, 230; Parish clk., iii, 231; Precentor, iii, 244; Preb. 2nd stall, Intr., xiv; ii, 174; iii, 102, 250; 4th stall, iii, 90; 5th stall, i, 32; 6th stall, ii, 173; subdean, ii, 142; iii, 250; Vic. Chor., iii, 232, 233, 243, 244.
Ripon, Memorials of, i, 32; ii, 142, 173, 174; iii, 90, 102, 120, 166, 231, 250.
Ripon, Parish of, iii, 231, 232, 233, 238, 241, 243.
Ripponden, ii, 33, 37; iii, **19**, 20; iv, 238.
Risby (Yorks.), i, 161, 194; iii, 30, 31.
Rise, Rice, i, 36; ii, 89, 90; iii, **35**, 36; iv, 220.
Riseborough, *see* Thornton Riseborough.
Risley, iv, 144.
Riston, Long, Hornsea cum Riston, i, 36; ii, **89**, 90, 147; iii, 36.
Robin Hood's, Robin's hood's, Bay, i, 34.
Rocliffe, Roecliffe, *see* Rawcliffe.
Rolleston (Notts.), iv, 110, **122**.
Rome, ii, 147; iv, 193; Engl. Coll., iv, 192, 196, 197, 206, 216, 217.
Roos, Ross (Yorks.), iii, **33**; iv, 236, 238.
Rosedale, i, 174; iii, **26**, 27.
Ross, *see* Roos.
Rossendale, iv, 241.
Rossington, Intr., xix; iv, **126**, 127.
Rothbury, Intr., xiv.
Rotherham, ii, 7, 55, 183; iii, 20, **21**, 22, 193; iv, 224, 230, 231.
Rothwell (Yorks.), iii, **16**; iv, 206, 213, 219, 225, 227, 228, 232.
Rotterdam, iii, 222.
Rouen, iv, 201.
Roundhay, i, 44; iv, 195, 198.
Rounton, Rownton, Rouneton, East, ii, 65; iii, **27**, 28, 110 (?), 206.
Rounton, West, Intr., xvi; i, 32; iii, **29**, 30, 110 (?); iv, 237, 238.
Routh, Intr., xv; iii, **34**, 35; iv, 239.
Rowley, iii, **30**, 31.
Rowsby, ii, 62, 63.
Roxby (Yorks.), iv, 237.
Royston (Yorks.), iii, **23**, 195; iv, 238.
Rudby-in-Cleveland; Hutton Rudby, ii, **63**, 64; iii, 28, 206; iv, 208.
Ruddington, iv, **121**, 152, 238.
Rudstone, Rudston, i, 111, 121; ii, 19, 138; iii, **36**, 37.
Rufford, iv, 211.
Rufforth, i, 172; ii, 217; iii, **14**, 15.
Ruston Parva; Ruiston, i, 214; ii, 165, 205; iii, **38**.
Rutland, iv, 193.
Ryedale, Rydall, Rydale, Deanery of, Intr., ix, xv; i, 28, 33, 34, 89, 90, 91, 143, 184, 187, 188; ii, 8, 10, 57, 58, 60, 61, 122, 124, 125, 152, 153, 154, 186, 187, 189, 199, 201, 214, 221; iii, 6, 8, 26, 94, 95, 96, 97, 98, 108, 168, 203, 211.
Rylstone, Rilston, i, 50, 51, 52.
Ryther, ii, 105; iii, **250**.

Sacrista (al. Segeston), Preb., *see* Southwell.
St. Asaph, Intr., xxiv.
St. David's, Bp. of, Intr., v; Reg., Intr., xxiv.
St. John Lee, *see* Lee, St. John of Beverley.
St. John Thropham, Throapham, *see* Thorpe St. John.
St. Michael, Residence of, iv, 212.
St. Nevis, iii, 17.
St. Omer, iv, 199.
Salendine Nook, iv, 242.
Salisbury, Intr., xxiv; Preb. Grantham, South, i, 35; Reg., iii, 46.
Salterforth, i, 76.
Saltmarshe, ii, 93.
Salton, ii, 201; iii, **108**.
Sancton, ii, 78; iii, **113**, 114, 115; iv, 213, 219.
Sandal Magna; Great Sandall, i, 132; iii, **46**, 47, 48; iv, 214.
Sandal Parva, *see* Kirk Sandall.
Sandall, Long, iii, 52.
Sand-Hutton-juxta-Thirsk, ii, 121; iii, **250**.
Sand-Hutton (York), i, 85, 86.
Sandiacre, iv, 2, 18.
Saundby, iv, **184**.
Sawley (Yorks.), iii, **241**.
Saxton, iii, **43**, 65; iv, 214.
Scagglethorpe, iii, 120.
Scalby, Scawby, i, 160; iii, **132**, 169, 228; iv, 239.
Scammonden, Scamuden (al. Deanhead), iii, **51**.
Scampston, ii, 84; iii, 32, **122**, 123.
Scarborough, Intr., x, xv, xviii; ii, 65; iii, 56, 109, 121, 122, **133**, 135, 170; iv, 231, 238.
Scarborough, Hist. of, iv, 231, 238.
Scarcliffe, Scardeclive, iv, 8.
Scarcroft, iv, 218.
Scarle, South, iv, **140**, 141, 239.
Scarrington, iv, 113.
Scawby, *see* Scalby.
Scawton, iii, **94**, 95.
Scholes, i, 44.
Scorborough, i, 104, 106; ii, 133, 162; iii, **112**, 113.
Scotland, iii, 35; iv, 180, 193, 223, 224, 230, 237, 239.
Scrayingham, Intr., xiv; iii, **119**, 120, 230.
Screveton, iv, 72, 92, **134**, 157.
Scrooby, Intr., xv; iv, 5, 74, **148**.
Scruton, iii, 30.
Sculcoates, i, 191; ii, 78; iii, **114**, 115.
Seamer-in-Cleveland, ii, 127; iii, **100**.
Seamer (Dickering), i, 39, 159, 160; iii, **132**.
Seasey, *see* Sessay.
Seathwaite, Seathwait, ii, 99, 102.
Seaton Ross, iii, **118**.
Selby, Selbye, Intr., xviii; i, 81; iii, **65**, 66; iv, 214, 231.
Selby Abbey (old), iii, 69, 74, 82.
Selby, Hist. of, iv, 215.
Selston, iv, **184**.
Sessay, Seasey, iii, **90**.
Settle, iv, 236, 237.
Settrington, i, 171, 172; iii, **120**, 121, 172.
Sewerby, i, 114.
Sharlston, i, 127.
Sharow, iii, 230.
Sheffield, Intr., x; i, 167; iii, 57, 58, 59, 61, 251; iv, 201, 215, 226, 227, 233, 239.
Sheffield, Hospital, iii, 59, 60, 61, 62; Meth. Circuit, iv, 240; Nether Hall Ch., iv, 224, 231; Parish (Old) Church, i, 180; iii, **56**, 57; St. Paul's (New) Church, iii, 57, **58**, 59, 60; Upper Ch., iv, 224, 227, 231; Visitation, i, 204; ii, 54, 152; iii, 21; iv, 113.
Shelford (Notts.), iv, 120, 121, **135**, 136.
Shelton (Notts.), iv, **138**, 139.
Sherburn, Shereburn, Shereburne, Sherborn-in-Elmet, i, 204; iii, 43, 44, **64**, 65; iv, 213, 215, 218.
Sherburn-in-Harford Lythe (Buckrose), iii, **121**, 135.
Sheriff, Sheriffe, Hutton, i, 83; iii, **92**.
Sherwood, iv, 223.
Shewbroad, iv, 236.
Shipley, iv, 242.
Shipton (Harthill), iii, **136**, 222, 223.
Shipton (par. Overton), i, 25; ii, 212, 213.
Shire Green, i, 179.
Shitlington, Nether, iii, 148.
Shore (Halifax), iv, 236.
Sibthorpe, iv, **184**.
Sicklinghall, ii, 104.
Sierston, *see* Syerston.
Sigglesthorne, iii, **124**; iv, 90.
Sikehouse, *see* Sykehouse.
Silkstone, Silkston, iii, **62**, 63.
Silsden, ii, 108, 109, 111; iii, **89**; iv, 231.
Silton, Over, Upper, i, 145; ii, 158; iii, **99**, 111; iv, 211, 212, 215, 216, 217.
Silton, Nether, Lower, i, 145; ii, 158; iii, 99, **111**; iv, 211, 212, 215, 216, 217.
Sinnington, Sinington, i, 184; iii, **97**, 98.

Skeckling-cum-Burstwick, iii, 10, **126**, 172, 173; iv, 206, 216.
Skeffling, Skefling, i, 192; ii, 79, 135, 136; iii, **125**.
Skegby, iv, 98, **146**, 147.
Skelbrooke, Skelbrook, Intr., xvi; i, 64, 223; iii, **63**, 64.
Skelton (Bulmer), iii, **109**.
Skelton (par. Howden), ii, 93.
Skelton (Ripon), iii, 230, **241**, 242.
Skelton-cum-Brotton, *see* Skelton-in-Cleveland.
Skelton-in-Cleveland, Intr., xviii; i, 92, 93; iii, **103**, 104; iv, 216, 236, 239.
Skerne, ii, 17, 81; iii, **117**, 118, 214.
Skidby, i, 154, 155, 156; iii, **116**.
Skipsea, Skipsey, ii, 14, 223; iii, 36, **129**, 178; iv, 239.
Skipton-in-Craven, Intr., xvi; i, 51, 55, 57; ii, 111, 147; iii, **45**; iv, 237, 239; Visitation, ii, 175; iii, 146.
Skipton (Bulmer), iii, 162.
Skipwith, iii, **105**, 116.
Skirlaugh, Skirley, i, 138; iii, 124, 127, 128, 129, **131**.
Skirpenbeck, i, 119, 120; ii, 121, 122; iii, **118**, 119.
Slackthwaite, *see* Slaithwaite.
Slaidburn, Slaidburne, ii, 5, 113; iii, **250**.
Slaithwaite, Slaighwaith, Slackthwaite, ii, 143; iii, **48**.
Sledmere, i, 223; iii, **251**, 252.
Sleningford, Slemmingford, iii, 230.
Slingsby, ii, 58; iii, **96**, 97.
Smeaton, Great, i, 31, 32.
Snainton, i, 90, 91; iii, **98**, 99.
Snaith, i, 140, 165; ii, 54, 55; iii, 25, **67**, 68, 69, 71, 72, 73, 74, 75, 76, 80, 81, 83, 84, 85.
Snape, iii, 237; iv, 238.
Sneaton, Sneton, iii, **102**.
Sneinton, iv, **184**.
Sneton, *see* Sneaton.
Soham (Cambs.), iv, 229.
Somerset, iv, 69.
South Crosland, *see* Crosland, South.
South Duffield, *see* Duffield, South.
South Holme, *see* Holme, South.
South Kilvington, *see* Kilvington, South.
South Kirkby, *see* Kirkby, South.
South Newbald, *see* Newbald, South.
South Otterington, *see* Otterington, South.
Southowram, *see* Breer's Chapel.
South Scarle, *see* Scarle, South.
Southwell, Southwel, Intr., ix; iv, 8, 20, 25, 75, 79, 104, 159, 176, **185**.
Southwell, Chapter of, Intr., ix; iv, 8, 25, 26, 41, 43, 55, 58, 71, 95, 104, 105, 110, 112, 115, 130, 159, 160, 173, 175, 177, 183, 184; Gr. Sch., iv, 24, 25; Liberty, iv, 177; Vic-Chor., iv, 58, 159.
Southwell, Peculiars of, iv, 24, 25, 40, 42, 43, 55, 58, 75, 94, 103, 104, 111, 114, 129, 130, 159, 173, 174, 176, 183, 185.
Southwell, Prebends at; Beckington, iv, 156; Eton, iv, 110; Leverton, North, iv, 88; Muskham, North, Intr., xiii; ii, 105; Muskham, South, iii, 36; Normanton, iv, 33; Norwell Overhall, Intr., xiv; Norwell Pallishall, iv, 119; Norwell Tertia Pars, iv, 163; Rampton, Intr., xiv; iii, 102; Sacrista (al. Segeston), iv, 110; Woodborough, i, 69; iv, 158.
South Wheatley, *see* Wheatley, South.
Sowerby, Sowersby, -juxta-Halifax, ii, 32, 33, 38, 81; iii, **49**; iv, 228, 229.
Sowerby-juxta-Thirsk (Bulmer), iii, **93**, 94, 166.
Sowerby Bridge, ii, 33; iii, **50**, 51; iv, 232.
Soyland, iv, 238.
Spalding, iv, 107.
Spaldington, Sparrington, iii, 78; iv, 200.
Spargrove, iv, 69.
Sparrington, *see* Spaldington.
Speeton, Intr., xv; i, 216, 218, 219; ii, 91, 196; iii, **135**.
Spink Hill, Spinkill, Spinkett, iv, 111, 194, 201, 210.
Spofforth, Intr., xix; ii, 19; iii, **41**, 176, 181; iv, 194, 208, 216.
Sproatley, Intr., xvi; ii, 204; iii, **123**, 124, 127, 128, 129, 131.
Sprotborough, Sprottbrough, iii, **53**.
Stableford, *see* Stapleford.
Stafford, iv, 230; Co. of, iv, 10, 11.
Stainburn, Stainburne, ii, 118, 119; iii, **44**.
Stainley, North, iii, 230.
Stainton-in-Cleveland, ii, 65; iii, **56**, 135, 170.
Stainton-juxta-Tickhill, iii, **55**
Stainton (Westmoreland), iv, 227.
Staithes, ii, 63.
Stamford Gr. Sch., iv, 96.
Standish (Lancs.), iv, 192.
Stanford-on-Soar, Intr., xiii; iv, 90, **131**, 132.
Stannington (Yorks.), i, 73, 74; iv, 225; Grange, iv, 199.

Stannington Chapel, i, 73; iii, **251**.
Stansfield (par. Halifax), i, 132; ii, 32, 37, 38; iv, 229, 236.
Stanton, Staunton-on-the-Wolds, Intr., xiii; iv, 24, 46, 76, **133**, 134, 160, 182, 183.
Stapleford, Stableford (Notts.), iv, **143**, 144.
Starbotton, Starboton, iv, 236, 237.
Starfits, ii, 125.
Staunton Chapel (Notts.), iv, 34, 79, 137, 138, 141, **185**.
Staunton Church (Notts.), iv, **163**, 138, 185.
Staunton-on-the-Wolds, *see* Stanton-on-the-Wolds.
Stay House, iv, 211.
Stillingfleet, iii, **91**.
Stillington (Yorks.), i, 209, 210; ii, 184, 185; iii, **107**, 108.
Stoakam, *see* Stokeham.
Stoake, *see* Stoke, East.
Stockeld Park, iv, 208.
Stockholm, ii, 75.
Stockton-on-the-Forest (Bulmer), ii, 168; iii, **104**.
Stockwith, West (Notts.), iv, 102, **149**, 150, 151.
Stoke Ash (Suffolk), iv, 196.
Stoke, Stoake, East (Notts.), iv, 36, 48, **139**, 140, 142.
Stokeham, Stoakam, iv, 6, 42, **148**.
Stokesley, Stoxley, Stoaxley, Intr., xiii, xvi; i, 91, 146; ii, 129; iii, **101**; iv, 188, 202, 211, 217.
Stokesley, Visitation at, i, 29; ii, 9, 63, 65, 127, 128, 190, 215; iii, 56, 100, 169, 176.
Stonecroft, iv, 206, 207.
Stoneferry, ii, 75.
Stonegrave, Intr., xviii; ii, 200; iii, **95**.
Stonor Park, iv, 192.
Stonyhurst, ii, 175; iv, 194, 210.
Storriths, Storrithes, iii, 45.
Stourton-on-the-Clay, *see* Sturton-on-the-Clay.
Stourton Lodge (par. Aberford), iv, 197, 213, 219.
Stoxley, *see* Stokesley.
Strelley, iv, 13, 14, **142**, 143.
Strensall, ii, 70, 71; iii, **106**, 107.
Strensall, Preb. of, *see* York.
Studley Royal, iii, 231; iv, 197.
Sturton, Stourton-in-the-Clay, Intr., xiii; ii, 44, 94, 159; iv, 158, 182, **185**.
Suffolk, iv, 196, 205, 220, 221.
Sunk Island; 'Ye Island,' i, 118; ii, 136.
Sussex, i, 200.
Sutton Bonington, iv, 242; St. Ann's, iv, **132**; St. Michael's, iv, **132**.
Sutton (par. Brotherton), iv, 205, 212.
Sutton (par. Campsall), i, 134.
Sutton-in-Ashfield, iv, **144**, 232.
Sutton-in-Craven, iv, 241, 242.
Sutton-on-Derwent, Darwent (Harthill), iii, **111**, 112, 213.
Sutton Grange (Ripon), iii, 238; iv, 238.
Sutton-on-the-Forest, Intr., xvi, xix; iii, **92**; iv, 239.
Sutton-in-Holderness, ii, 75, 196; iii, **130**, 225.
Sutton-on-Lound, Lown, iv, 5, 21, 22, 111, **147**, 148.
Sutton-on-Trent, iv, 32, 34, 79, **141**, 185.
Sutton-under-Whitestone Cliff, i, 208.
Swanland, iv, 225, 226, 227.
Swarkstone, iv, 144.
Swillington, Intr., xiii; iii, **42**, 43, 222.
Swinburne, iv, 207.
Swine, ii, 204; iii, 124, **127**, 128, 129, 131; iv, 205, 206, 216, 217.
Swinefleet, Swinfleet, iii, 79, 200.
Swinley (al. Egypt), iv, 226.
Swinton (Yorks.), iii, **86**, 87, 88.
Syerston, Sierston, Syrestone, Syreston, iv, 36, 48, 140, **142**.
Sykehouse, Sikehouse, i, 200, 201; iii, 68, 73, 83, 85, **88**, 89; iv, 240.

Tadcaster, ii, 21, 184; iii, **143**; iv, 215, 218, 229, 232.
Tankersley, Tankersly, iii, **155**, 156.
Temple Newsam, iv, 189.
Terrington (Yorks.), i, 82, 83, 84; iii, **160**, 161.
Teversall, Teversal, i, 127, 128; iv, **156**.
Thirkleby, Thirtleby, i, 89; ii, 119, 120, 222; iii, 94, **165**.
Thirsk, i, 222; iii, 123, **166**, 167; iv, 208, 218, 237, 239; Visitation at, i, 86; ii, 61; iii, 26, 161.
Thirtleby, *see* Thirkleby.
Thorganby (Yorks.), Intr., xv; iii, **167**.
Thorgumbald, *see* Thorngumbald.
Thormanby, iii, 26, **161**, 162.
Thornaby (par. Stainton-in-Cleveland), ii, 65; iii, 56, 135, **169**, 170.
Thorne, i, 208; ii, 215; iii, **157**, 184, 185; iv, 239.
Thorner, iii, **144**, 145; iv, 218.
Thorney (Notts.), iv, **154**.
Thorngumbald, Thorgumbald, iii, 127, **172**, 173.
Thornhill, i, 15, 205, 206; ii, 37; iii,

147, 148, 188.
Thornholme, Thurnholm, i, 37.
Thornthwaite (Yorks.), ii, 22; iii, **251**.
Thornton-juxta-Bradford, i, 58; iii, **148**, 149; iv, 232, 236.
Thornton-in-Craven, iii, **145**, 146.
Thornton Dale, i, 160, ii, 201; iii, 132, 133, **168**, 228.
Thornton-le-Moor, ii, 218.
Thornton Riseborough, ii, 201.
Thornton-on-Spalding-Moor (Harthill) i, 40, 116, 220; iii, **174**.
Thornton-le-Street, ii, 218; iii, **170**, 171, 252; iv, 208, 218.
Thoroton, iv, 113.
Thorp (par. Howden), ii, 93.
Thorp-Arch, iii, **142**, 143.
Thorpe-Bassett; Thorp-Basset, i, 173; iii, 121, **171**.
Thorpe Buzzard, Bozard, *see* Thorpe-in-the-Glebes.
Thorpe-in-the-Clotts, Clods, *see* Thorpe-in-the-Glebes.
Thorpe-in-the-Glebes, iv, 63, **151**, 177.
Thorpe, Thorp-by-Newark, iv, 12, 46, 108, **153**, 154.
Thorpe St. John; St. John's, Thropham, i, 27; ii, 151; iii, **158**.
Thorpe, Thorp, Salvin, iii, **159**, 160, 201.
Thribergh, *see* Thrybergh.
Thropham, *see* Thorpe St. John.
Thrumpton, iv, **153**.
Thrybergh, Thribergh, Thriburg, iii, 68, **151**.
Thurgarton (Notts.), iv, 72, 134, 135, **156**.
Thurnholm, *see* Thornholme.
Thurnscoe, iii, **151**.
Thwing, ii, 139; iii, **173**, 174.
Tickhill, Tickel, iii, 61, **156**, 157, 192.
Tinsley, Intr., xi, xviii; iii, **152**, 153.
Tithby, Tythby-with-Cropwell, iv, **152**, 158, 162.
Tockerington, Preb. of, *see* York.
Tockholes, iv, 227.
Todmorden, i, 132.
Todwick, iii, **154**; iv, 68, 69.
Tollerton (Notts.), iv, 121, **152**.
Tong (Yorks.), iii, **150**; iv, 186, 218, 219.
Topcliffe, Topcliff, iii, **162**, 163, 164, 165; iv, 225, 232, 239.
Tosside, Tossit, Tossett, iii, **146**.
Toton, iv, 2.
Tottlebank, iv, 241.
Towneley, iv, 194, 205, 206.
Treeton, Intr., xix; ii, 72; iii, **153**, 154.
Treswell, i, 69; iv, 153, **157**, 162, 182, 185.
Tristhorp, iii, 52.
Trowell, iv, **155**, 168.
Trumfleet, Trumphlet, iii, 52.
Truro, Bp. of, Intr., vi, viii.
Tunstall-in-Holderness, Intr., xix; ii, 219, 220; iii, 42, **175**.
Turvin, ii, 38.
Tuxford, iv, 99, 100, **158**, 159.
Tythby, *see* Tithby.

Uffington (Lincs.), Intr., xvi.
Ugglebarnby, i, 34, 157, 189, 211; iii, **177**.
Ughill, iv, 225.
Ugthorpe, Ugthorp, ii, 157; iv, 196, 203, 204, 209, 239.
Ulleskelf, Ullerskelf, ii, 118.
Ulrome, Ulrom, Ulroom, i, 109; ii, 14, 223; iii, 36, 129, 130, **177**.
Upleatham, ii, 9, 129; iii, **176**.
Upper Hemsley, *see* Helmsley, Over or Upper.
Upper Poppleton, *see* Poppleton, Upper.
Upper Silton, *see* Silton, Upper.
Upton (Pec. of Southwell), iv, **159**, 160, 185.
Upton, *see* Headon-with-Upton, and Kneesall-with-Upton (Ompton).
Ushaw, iv, 186.

Valladolid, Engl. Coll., iv, 192, 202.

Waddington (Yorks.), Intr., xviii; iii, **182**.
Wadworth, Wadsworth, ii, 37, 38; iii, **199**.
Waghen, *see* Wawne.
Wailsby, *see* Walesby.
Wakefield, Intr., x, xv; ii, 42, 49, 50, 198; iii, 18, **185**, 187, 202, 203; iv, 230, 240; Gr. Sch., Intr., xi, xix; iii, 185, 187; Lecturer, ii, 41; Presby. Ch., iv, 232; Visitation at, i, 15, 133, 169, 205; ii, 35, 36, 39, 44; iii, 148, 252.
Wales (Principality), Intr., xx; Church in, Intr., xxiv.
Wales (Parish), iii, 159, 160, **200**, 201.
Walesby, Wailsby (Notts.), iv, 73, **170**, 171, 172, 173, 239.
Walkeringham, Walkringham, Walkingham, iv, 66, **170**.
Walkington, iii, **251**.
Wallerthwaite, iii, 230.
Walmgate, *see* York, St. Denys.
Walsoken, Intr., v.
Walton (Yorks.), i, 223; iii, **180**.
Walton Hall, iii, 46; iv, 214.

Warley (Yorks.), ii, 32, 150; iv, 226, 228, 229, 232.
Warmfield, ii, 197; iii, **183**.
Warmsworth, Warmsfourth, iii, 68, **189**, 190; iv, 239.
Warrington, iv, 241.
Warsop, iv, **168**.
Warter, i, 176; iii, **212**.
Warthill, ii, 68, 212; iii, **209**.
Waterford and Lismore, Dioc. of, Intr., xix; iv, 62.
Wath-on-Dearne, i, 24; ii, 183; iii, 23, 86, 87, **192**, 193; iv, 239.
Watten (Belgium), iv, 191, 193, 194, 208, 214, 222.
Watton (Yorks.), ii, 17, 81; iii, 118, **213**, 214.
Wawne, Wawn, Waghen, ii, 196; iii, 130, **224**, 225.
Weather Coat, *see* Wether Cote.
Weaverthorpe, i, 115, 215; iii, **252**.
Weeton (par. Harwood), ii, 23, 118.
Weeton, Little, iii, 30.
Weighton, *see* Market Weighton.
Weighton, Preb. of, *see* York.
Welbeck Abbey, iv, 111.
Welbury, Wellbury, iii, **204**, 205.
Wellow, Welley (Notts.), iv, 73, 171, **172**, 173.
Wells, Dean of, Intr., xxiv; Preb. of Yatton, iii, 144.
Welton (Yorks.), iii, 43, **221**, 222.
Welwick, ii, 84, 85, 86; iii, **219**; iv, 239.
Wem, iv, 230.
Wenlakesbarn, Preb. of, *see* London, St. Paul's.
Wentworth (Yorks.), ii, 140; iii, **194**.
West Acklam, *see* Acklam, West.
West Ayton, *see* Ayton, West.
Westerdale, iii, 101, 102.
West Hallam, *see* Hallam, West.
West Indies, *see* Indies, West.
West Markham, *see* Markham, West.
Westminster, Card. Abp. of, iv, 186; Prebend of, Intr., xiii, xix; ii, 105; iii, 41, 42.
Westmoreland, iv, 227; scholar, i, 209.
West Ness, ii, 200.
Weston (Notts.), iv, 103, 104, **174**.
Weston (Yorks.), i, 49; iii, **179**; iv, 239.
Westow, iii, **214**, 215, 216.
Westphalia, iv, 193.
West Retford, *see* Retford, West.
West Rounton, *see* Rounton, West.
West Stockwith, *see* Stockwith, West.
Wetherby (par. Spofforth), ii, 19, 20; iii, 41, **181**, 182.
Wether Cote; Weather Coat, ii, 125.
Wetwang, i, 223; iii, 251, **252**.
Wharfe, iv, 237.
Wharram Percy, Peircy, perse; Wharam-Peircy, i, 41; iii, **216**, 217, 224.
Wharram, Wharam-le-Street, i, 41; iii, 217, **223**.
Whatton (Bingham), iv, 153, 158, **162**.
Wheatley, Whealey, Hall (Doncaster), i, 70.
Wheatley, North (Notts.), Intr., xii; iv, 23, 24, **169**, 173.
Wheatley, South (Notts.), iv, 25, 103, **173**.
Wheldrake, iii, 187, **202**.
Whenby, iii, **203**.
Wherwell, Preb. of, iv, 129.
Whiston (Yorks.), i, 68, 69; iii, **192**.
Whitby, ii, 82, 168; iii, 102, **207**, 208, 209, 252; iv, 203, 209, 219, 232, 239.
Whitcliffe, Whitecliffe, iii, 230; iv, 213.
Whitgift, iii, **199**, 200.
Whitkirk, iii, **252**.
Whitley (par. Kellington), iii, 67, 74, 75.
Whitley Hall (Dewsbury), ii, 44.
Whittington (Lancs.), iv, 210.
Whittington and Berkswych, Preb. of, *see* Lichfield.
Whitwell (Yorks.), i, 142.
Whorlton (Yorks.), ii, 65; iii, 28, **205**, 206.
Wibsey, i, 58; iii, **188**; iv, 228, 232.
Wickersley, Intr., xiii; ii, 117; iii, **190**.
Widmerpool, iv, 39, 161, **162**, 232.
Wigginton, Wiggington (Yorks.), iii, 39, 40, 141, 142, **210**.
Wighill, Wighil, ii, 223; iii, 13, 14, **178**, 179.
Wigston, iv, 129.
Wilberfoss, iii, 112, **213**.
Wilford, iv, 27, **163**, 164, 232.
Willerby, Intr., xvii; ii, 16; iii, **220**, 221.
Willitofts, iv, 200.
Willoughby-in-the-Wolds (Notts.), iv, 37, 108, 151, **161**.
Wilsden, iii, 150.
Wilton-in-Cleveland, ii, 9, 191; iii, **207**.
Wilton (Ryedale), Intr., xv; i, 188; iii, 7, 8, **211**.
Winchester, Intr., xxiv; i, 63.
Winckesley, *see* Winksley.
Windmoor Side, Winmoreside, i, 44.
Windsor, Intr., xiii; ii, 116; iii, 191.
Winestead, ii, 220, 221; iii, **217**, 218.
Winkburn, iv, 97, **165**, 166.

Winksley, Winckesley, iii, 235, **243**.
Winmoreside, *see* Windmoor Side.
Winterburn, Winterburne (Yorks.), ii, 4; iv, 227.
Winthorpe (Notts.), Intr., xix; iv, 107, **164**.
Wintringham, Winteringham (Yorks.), iii, 209, **252**.
Wisbech, Intr., v.
Wistow (Yorks.), i, 138; iii, **197**, 198.
Withernwick, Intr., xviii; ii, 14, 15, 223; iii, **225**.
Wittering, Preb. of, *see* Chichester.
Wold Newton (Yorks.), iii, 38, **221**.
Wollaton-with-Cossall, iv, 156, **166**, 167, 168, 232.
Wombwell, i, 168.
Womersley, iii, 158, **184**, 185.
Woodborough, Woodborrow (Notts.), iv, **174**, 175, 176, 177, 232.
Woodborough, Preb. of, *see* Southwell.
Woodchurch, *see* Woodhouse, and Woodkirk.
Woodhouse, Wentworth Woodhouse, iii, 73, 80 'Woodchurch.'
Woodkirk, Woodchurch, i, 15; iii, 148, **187**, 188; iv, 226, 232.
Woodland (Lancs.), ii, 99, 100, 101.
Woodsetts, Woodseats, iii, 61.
Woodsome Hall, i, 206.
Woolley, Wooley (Yorks.), iii, **195**, 196.
Worcester, Dioc. of, i, 63; Preb. 2nd stall, Intr., xix; iv, 107; Co. of, Intr., xvii.
Worksop, Worksopp, iv, **171**, 172, 219.
Worsall, High, ii, 218; iii, 171, **252**.
Worsborough, iii, 54, **194**, 195.
Wortley-juxta-Tankersley, iii, 155, **196**, 197.
Wragby (Yorks.), iii, **252**.
Wressell, Wressle, iii, **211**.
Wycliffe, Wyclif-on-Tees, iv, 189, 192, 195, 215.
Wykeham (Yorks.), i, 91; iii, 99, **203**, 204.
Wysall, iv, 76, 134, 151, **160**, 183.
Wyton (Holderness), iv, 205, 218.

Yapham-with-Meltonby, iii, **229**.
Yardhill, iv, 209.
Yarm, ii, 130, 131; iii, **227**; iv, 219.
Yatton, Preb. of, *see* Wells.
Yeddingham, i, 160; iii, 133, 169, **228**.
Yokefleet, Yoakfleet, ii, 93.
York, Abps. of, Intr., viii, xix; i, 1, 103, 104, 109, 126, 155, 188; iii, 60, 62, 143; iv, 187 (*see* sub Blackburn, Dawes, Herring, Holgate, Hutton, Matthew, Sharp); Abp. Holgate's Sch., ii, 199, 213; iii, 138; Archdn., Intr., ix, xiii, xix; ii, 105, 118, 183; iii, 144, 153, 156, 246; iv, 234 (*see* sub. Chetwood, Hayter); Act Bk., i, 114; iii, 106; iv, 64; Bar Convent, iv, 195; Call Bk., Intr., vii, ix; i, 48, 94, 145, 164; iii, 58, 106, 250, 251; iv, 134, 151, 179; Castle, iv, 196, 198, 202, 204; Chanc., i, 114, 172, 218; ii, 48, 57; iv, 12.
York, Churches of, All Saints', North St., i, **4**, 5; ii, 171; All Saints', Pavement ('Al hallowes'), i, **4**; ii, 208; iii, 68; Holy Trinity, Goodramgate, iii, **136**, 137-140; Holy Trinity, King's Ct; Christ Ch., Intr., xvi; i, 122; iii, **140**, 141; Holy Trinity, Micklegate, iii, 40, **141**, 211; iv, 220-222; St. Crux, i, **121**; ii, 20; St. Cuthbert, i, **122**; iii, 141; St. Denys, Dennis, i, **162**, 163, 164; ii, 168; iii, 104, 105; St. George, i, **163**; ii, 168; iii, 105; St. Helen's, Hellens, Stonegate, i, 121; ii, **20**, St. John, ii, 44, **93**, 94, 159; iv, 185; St. John-del-Pyke, pike, iii, 137, **138**, 139, 140; St. Lawrence, ii, 56 66, **139**; St. Margaret, i, 163, 164; ii, **167**, 168; iii, 104, 105; St. Martin, Coney, Cony, St., ii, 137, 138, **172**; St. Martin, Micklegate; St. Martin's-cum-Gregory, ii, 120, 121, **169**; St. Mary Bishophill Junior, the Younger, i, 39; ii, **171**; iii, 2, 3; Senior, the Elder, i, 5; ii, **170**; St. Mary, Castlegate, ii, 166, **167**; iii, 106; St. Maurice, iii, 137, 138, **139**, 140; St. Michael-le-Belfrey, iii, **253**; St. Michael, Ousebridge, ii, **166**, 167; St. Olave's & St. Giles', Intr., xvi; i, 4; ii, **207**; St. Peter the little, i, 4; St. Sampson, Samson, iii, **40**; St. Saviour, iii, **39**, 141, 142, 211; St. Wilfrid (R.C.), iv, 221.
York, Colliergate, iv, 99, 211; Colton Hosp., iv, 233; Corporation, ii, 56, 167, 170; iii, 141; County Hosp., iii, 139; Court of Yk., i, 99, 156; iii, 227; iv, 33; Daily Serv., Intr., xv; Dean, i, 34, 61, 121, 189, 215; ii, 11, 62, 63, 90, 91, 94, 137, 138, 139, 151, 158, 196, 207, 208; iii, 143 (*see* sub Osbaldeston).
York, Dean & Ch., Intr., ix; i, 25, 26, 33, 41, 78, 79, 80, 99, 101, 104, 117, 118, 120, 138, 147, 161, 162, 195, 196, 204, 220, 221, 222, 223;

ii, 19, 20, 54, 69, 83, 84, 99, 102, 118, 119, 140, 166, 171, 172, 183, 206, 217-223; iii, 13, 14, 29, 40, 64, 65, 105, 108, 197, 198, 210, 223, 224, 225, 227, 233, 235, 238, 243, 252, 253; iv, 7, 23, 24, 103, 150, 151, 185; Dean & Ch. Peculiars, iv, 183, 184

York, Deanery of, Intr., ix; i, 4, 121, 122, 162, 163, 195; ii, 20, 93, 139, 166, 167, 169-172, 207; iii, 39, 40, 136, 138-141, 253.

York, Diocese of, Intr., vi, ix, xvi; i, 31, 56, 210, 213, 216, 218, 219; ii, 35, 101, 136; iii, 246; iv, 81, 179, 191, 210, 234.

York, '*Eboracum*,' Intr., xix; iii, 153; Executions, iv, 188, 204; Exhibits Bk., Intr., vii; i, 48, 54; ii, 115; iv, 57, 122, 179; Foss Bridge Gr. Sch., i, 163; Horse Fair Gr. Sch., i, 196; Institution Bk., i, 145; Lop Lane, iv, 220; Methodists, iv, 240; Micklegate, iv, 222; Micklegate Bar, iv, 200; Minster, Intr., ix; i, 208; ii, 19, 51; iii, 121; Minster Library, iii, 246; Nunnery, iii, 141; iv, 209, 220, 221, 222.

York, Prebs. of, Alne & Tollerton, iii, 109, 211; Ampleforth, iii, 102; Bole, iii, 156; Dinnington, ii, 221; Fenton, i, 99, 204; iii, 113; Fridaythorpe, iii, 120; Givendale, i, 4; Grindall, i, 190; Holme Episcopi, ii, 114; Husthwaite, iii, 63; Knaresborough, i, 43; Langtoft, ii, 19; iii, 42; Newbald, North, iii, 93; Newbald, South, i, 167; Osbaldwick, ii, 198; Riccall, ii, 215; Strensall, Intr., xiii; ii, 105; Weighton, i, 159; Wistow, Intr., xiv.

York, Parishes, Intr., xii; Pop., Intr., x; Precentor, ii, 208; iii, 36; iv, 220; Presbyterians, i, 194; Quakers, iv, 237.

York, Registry of, Intr., vii, xxi; i, 128, 221; ii, 35, 85, 87, 98, 101, 103, 191, 211; iii, 7, 80, 102, 104, 168, 192, 240, 249; iv, 50, 54, 182.

York, Residents at, i, 20, 97, 99, 208; ii, 56; iii, 79, 96; iv, 225; clerical, i, 42, 122, 163, 165, 171, 181, 195; ii, 12, 56, 62, 65, 113, 139, 193, 217; iii, 15, 35, 40, 109; iv, 124, 125.

York, Roman Catholics, iv, 188, 191, 192, 195, 206, 208, 210, 212, 216, 220, 221.

York, Sinners, i, 173; iii, 187; St. Saviourgate Congr. Ch., iv, 229, 230, 232, 233; Stonegate, iii, 40; Sub-dean, Intr., xiii; ii, 105; Succent. Canon, iii, 42, 176; Vic-Chor., Intr., xiii; ii, 44, 138, 159, 172; iii, 138, 253; Visitation, i, 180; iii, 144, 198, 202; York, i, 162.

Yorkshire, Intr., ix, x; i, 118; ii, 36, 137; iii, 80; iv, 68, 90, 158.

Yorkshire, Archaeol. Journal, iv, 214; Baptists, iv, 241; clergy, ii, 102; Congreg., iv, 223; Friends, iv, 235-239; High Sheriff, iii, 123; largest par., ii, 23; Methodists, iv, 240; moors and Dales, iii, 102; iv, 196, 203, 204, 237; 'nettles,' Intr., xiii; villages, Intr., xi.

Yorkshire (Riding, East), iv, 238, 239; *Archae. Soc. Trs.*, iv, 205; Archdeacon, Intr., ix, xiv; i, 159; iii, 31, 36, 120 (*see* sub Dering, and Jaques Sterne); '*Worthies*,' iv, 238; (*Riding Records, North*), iv, 237; (Riding, West), Intr., x; Meth., iv, 234; Friends, iv, 237.

Yorkshire, Roman Catholics, iv, 188, 189, 190, 192, 193, 194, 195, 199, 214, 222.

INDEX OF PERSONS.

(B)—Baptist Minister; (cl)—Clerk in Holy Orders; (I)—Independent Minister; (L)—Lawton's *Collectio*; (M)—Methodist Teacher; (MH)—Meeting House; (Mor)—Moravian Teacher; (P)—Presbyterian Minister; (Q)—Quaker Teacher; (R)—Roman Priest; (*)—Chapel or Meeting House. Names in square brackets are not in the text.

Abbat, Samuel, iii, 107.
Abbott, Mark, iii, 15; Samuel, v, 56; Thomas, iv, 69.
Abram, John, i, 160.
Abson, John (cl), iv,, 109, 110, 122; Samuel (cl), iv, 183.
Acklam, Thomas, ii, 204.
Ackroyd, William (cl) (1518), ii, 173.
Acomb, Philip, ii, 21; Quint: ii, 173.
Adams, *see* Watson, Peter (R).
Adams, Henry, iv, 18; John, iii, 43, 86; Margaret, iii, 43; Robert, i, 170.
Adamson, T. (R), iv, 186; William, ii, 11.
Adcock, John, iii, 40.
Addey, William, iii, 24.
Addiman, Thomas, i, 10.
Addinall, John, ii, 119.
Addison, George, ii, 32; iv, 205, 206; Henry, i, 79; John (cl), i, 183; Robert, iii, 216; Robert (cl), iii, 43, 44, 45; William, ii, 67, 105.
Addy, George, i, 71.
Addye, Thomas, ii, 117.
Adkin, John, iv, 50.
Agar, Christopher, iii, 132; John, i, 142; ii, 68; Lawrence, ii, 73; William, ii, 66; iii, 66.
Ager, Ralph, ii, 191.
Airton, Richard, i, 11.
Aiscough, *see* Ayscough.
Aked, Richard, ii, 34.
Akers, —, iii, 235; iv, 230.
Akid, David, i, 43.
Albemarle, Duke of, iii, 111.
Alcock, John (cl), i, 51; ii, 146, 147.
Alderson, Jo: iii, 51; Thomas (cl), i, 64, 223, 224; iii, 64.
Aldred, Alred, Jeremiah, iv, 232; John (P), iv, 232; Timothy (P), i, 62; iii, 185; iv, 225, 232.
Aldridge, Thomas, ii, 142.
Alforth, John, iii, 251.
Alland, John, iv, 39.
Allanson, John, ii, 222.
Allen, Joseph, i, 187; Richard, iv, 72; William, iii, 154; iv, 184.
Allerston, Mr. Henry, ii, 122.
Allet, Allert, Bryan (cl), ii, 44, 94, 159; iv, 185.
Alleyne, Richard (cl), iv, 132.
Allinson, Cowper, i, 156; John, iv, 43.
Allison, John, ii, 68; Joseph, iii, 132.
Allon, William, iv, 237.
Allyn, Mr. [L. 'Thomas'], i, 200.
Almond, Anthony (cl), i, 150; ii, 206; iii, 114; George (cl), ii, 115; Jonathan, i, 8; Rowland, ii, 214.
Alred, *see* Aldred.
Alston, Sir Rowland, Bart., i, 144.
Altham, George, iii, 183.
Anabaptists, *see* Baptists.
Anderson, Sir Edmund, Bart., ii, 73, 138; Henry, i, 33; Ignatius (P), *al.* Sheffield, iv, 221, 222; William (P), later, Sir William, of Penley, iv, 192, 194, 202.
Andrew, Joseph, ii, 156; Mark, ii, 189; Thomas, ii, 222; iii, 4; William, iii, 13.
Andrews, Thomas (cl), iii, 249; William, ii, 67.
Angier, Anger, Mr. John (I) i, 212; iv, 226, 227.
Anne of Frickley, iv, 190, 200, 202, 205; Marmaduke, iv, 221.
Anne, Queen, i, 22; iii, 21; Bounty, i, 54, 74, 193; ii, 46, 47, 69, 70, 95, 149, 186, 210; iii, 50, 86, 144, 189, 241, 246, 247, 248; iv, 45, 134.
Antinomians, ii, 30.
Antipedobaptists, *see* Baptists.
Apley, Robert, ii, 151; William, iii, 159.
Appleby, Family of, ii, 199; iv, 210; Michael, iii, 121.
Appleton, Robert, gent., i, 102; Mr. Rob: i, 116; Samuel, i, 35; Timothy, ii, 12.
Appleyard, Francis Esq., i, 103, 105; John, ii, 41; Joseph, i, 135; Philip, i, 165, 166; William, ii, 197.
Archer, Joseph, ii, 117; Thomas, iv, 96
Arderon, Francis, i, 163.
Arianism, iv, 129, 224, 225, 226, 228, 235.

Armatedge, Richard, iii, 154.
Armitage, Joseph, ii, 31; William, iii, 190.
Arnet, George (cl), iii, 187, 202, 203.
Arthington, Arthinton, Family of, i, 6; Henry, iii, 81, 82, 84.
Arthur, Charles (cl), iii, 199; William, i, 63.
Artrum, William, iii, 154.
Ascough, Marmaduke, iii, 238.
Ash, Leonard (cl), ii, 12.
Ashton, William, iv, 185.
Ashwell, Edward, iv, 136.
Askew, Henry, iv, 147.
Askham, William, iii, 40.
Assheton, Family of, iv, 227.
Atkinson, Charles, ii, 5; Mr. Franc: iv, 172; George, ii, 163; Henry, iii, 130, 183; Isaac, ii, 163; James, i, 11; John, ii, 95; iii, 180; John (cl) (Vic. of Brompton), i, 91; iii, 99, 204; John (cl) (A.C. Kellington), ii, 115; Luke, iii, 251; Paul, ii, 61; Paul (P), iv, 188; Roger, iii, 169; Thomas, i, 33; ii, 113, 212; William, ii, 163, 222; iii, 4, 194, 220.
Attersly, Joseph, i, 20.
Attorney General, The, iii, 62.
Audas, Joshua, ii, 130.
Audley, Dr. John, i, 201.
Audun, Robert, i, 168.
Audus, James, iii, 209.
Aukland, William, i, 64.
Ault, Benjamin, iv, 93.
Avison, William, iii, 7.
Awdin, John, iii, 197.
Ayde, Robert (cl), i, 69; iv, 158, 182.
Ayer, John, i, 172.
Ayeton, senior; William, ii, 5.
Ayscough, Aiscough, Henry (cl) (1640), iii, 68, 69, 70, 71, 72.

Bache, Sharington (cl), i, 23, 24.
Backus, Richard, i, 167.
Badger, James (cl), iv, 179.
Bagguley, F.L.A., Mr. W. H., iv, 186.
Bagshaw, Robert, i, 181.
Bailey, Mrs. Eleanor, *see* Bayley.
Baily, Thomas, i, 23.
Bainbridge, Edward (cl), ii, 22; iii, 251; Francis (Bainbrigg, Bainbrigge) (cl), iv, 36, 48, 140, 142; Philip (cl), i, 184; iii, 98.
Bainbrigge, Richard (cl), i, 125 (*see also* Bainbridge, Francis).
Baine, John (cl), iii, 58.
Baines, Thomas, ii, 173.
Bainton, Thomas, i, 158.
Bairstow, Mr. John, ii, 96.
Baiston, Peter, i, 222.
Baker, Arthur Pacificus (R), iv, 207; George, iv, 238; Mr. John, iv, 186; J. Brogden, iv, 231, 238; Jonathan, i, 75; Robert, iv, 154; Samuel (cl), i, 172; iii, 121.
Balby, John, i, 26.
Baldock, Edward, i, 4.
Balguy, John (cl), Intr. xix; i, 35, 95, 174.
Balgy, Matthew, i, 200.
Ball, Mr., iii, 154; John, i, 22; iv, 182; Peter, iii, 46.
Banks, Barnard, ii, 209; Joseph (cl), ii, 47; iii, 87.
Bannister, Canon, Intr., xxiv.
Baptists, Anabaptists, Antipedobaptists; Intr., x, xi, xxiii; i, 37, 52, 53, 58*, 60*, 61*, 62*, 76*, 98*, 101, 109, 111, 112*, 125*, 131*, 193, 200, 215; ii, 2*, 17, 21, 30*, 32, 35*, 36, 39, 78*, 80, 90, 95, 108*, 140, 149, 161, 187, 208; iii, 16*, 114, 145, 199, 220, 233; iv, 10, 16, 17, 18*, 28, 29, 32, 33, 34*, 53, 54, 55, 63*, 76*, 107, 109*, 110, 114, 119, 135, 153, 161, 164, 179, 180, 181*, 232, 234, 235, 236, 241*, 242*; General, iv, 102*, 235, 242; Handbook, iv, 236, 241; *History of*, iv, 236, 242; Particular, iv, 235.
Barber, Gervas, ii, 182; John, iii, 240; Thomas, i, 81; ii, 199.
Barf, Henry, i, 87.
Barke, John (cl), iii, 86.
Barker, Mrs., ii, 73; George, iii, 90; Isaac (P), iii, 208; iv, 232; John, ii, 62, 184; iii, 90, 223; iv, 48; Richard, iv, 121; Thomas (cl), i, 97; ii, 163; Thomas, ii, 115; iii, 108, 171; William, iii, 233.
Barlow, Family of, iv, 201; Anthony, Esqre., iv, 201; Elizabeth, 'Sister Frances Clare,' iv, 201; Robert, iv, 73; Samuel, iv, 184.
Barmby, John, iii, 66.
Barnard, Henry, iii, 80; Ramsden, Esqre., ii, 73; Thomas (cl), iii, 43.
Barnby, Matthew, i, 44.
Barnett, Abel, iv, 79; John, iii, 30.
Barney, John, gent., iv, 212.
Barns, William, iv, 41.
Barr, Bryan, ii, 62; Richard, i, 92.
Barraclough, William, i, 65.
Barratt, Joseph, iv, 5; William, ii, 220.
Barrett, James, i, 93; William (cl), i, 9.
Barritt, Thomas, ii, 115.
Barron, William, i, 222.
Barstow, Thomas, ii, 166.
Bartindale, Christopher, ii, 190.

Barton, Richard, gent. [?=Mr. Richard Burton, *q.v.*], i, 103; Stephen, ii, 148.
Barwick, Sir Robert, ii, 197; Thomas, ii, 69; Lady Ursula, ii, 197.
Bashall, Richard, iii, 183; Robert, iii, 183.
Bass, Thomas, iv, 30.
Bateman, Jeremiah, iii, 65; Jonathan, iii, 86; William, iii, 65.
Bates, Henry, ii, 34.
Bathurst, 1st Earl of, iv, 111.
Batty, John, ii, 117; Lawrence (M), ii, 6, 27; iv, 240; Reuben, ii, 52; William, iii, 187.
Baxter, John, ii, 67; William, iii, 228.
Bayles, John, iii, 52, 66.
Bayley, Benjamin (cl), iii, 5; Mrs. [L. Eleanor], i, 195; Thomas, iii, 108.
Baynes, Robert (cl), ii, 25.
Beacroft, Henry, ii, 5.
Beafser, John, iii, 236.
Beakly, Mrs., iv, 32.
Beal, Edward, i, 86.
Bealby, Matthew, iii, 231.
Bealey, Edmund, iv, 73.
Beane, George, ii, 58.
Beanland, Joseph, i, 60.
Beanlands, Thomas, ii, 95.
Bearde, John, iv, 166.
Beardlsey, John, iv, 18.
Beardshaw, John, i, 201.
Bearpark, John, i, 82, 83.
Beatson, William, iii, 187.
Beaumont, Barony of, iv, 201; 8th Baron, iv, 201; Mr. [L. George or Thomas], i, 169, 205; Mr., ii, 113; Godfrey, ii, 43; John (cl), iii, 120; John, i, 202; Joseph, i, 20; Mary, iii, 154; Richard, ii, 44; Samuel, ii, 31; Thomas (cl), iv, 15, 18; Thomas, ii, 44.
Beavers, Joseph, i, 202.
Beckett, Joseph (cl), i, 172; ii, 194, 217; iii, 15; Thomas (cl), ii, 70.
Beckwith, Thomas, iii, 128.
Bedford, Mary, iii, 18; Oswald, i, 221; Richard, i, 207.
Beecroft, John, iii, 240; Thomas, i, 197.
Been, Anthony, i, 83.
Beetham, Samuel, iii, 44.
Beetson, Mr. William, i, 165.
Beevers, Mr. (cl), iii, 87.
Belamy, John, iii, 142.
Belasyse, Family of, iv, 202.
Belcher, John (cl), iii, 189.
Belk, Belke, Charles, iii, 154, 155.
Bell, Alexander (cl), iii, 37, 38, 221; Canon, Intr., xxiv; Guy, iii, 26; John, i, 43; iii, 35, 167; Thomas (cl), ii, 75; Thomas, ii, 192; William, i, 214; iii, 214.
Bellamy, William, iii, 195.
Bellay [Bellon], Richard, ii, 93.
Bellerby, William, ii, 135.
Bellinger, John Edward (cl), iv, 55, 73.
Bellwood, Roger, i, 211; ii, 185.
Belt, Thomas, i, 91.
Belwood, John, ii, 115; iii, 99.
Benedict XIII, Pope, iv, 196, 213; Benedict XIV, iv, 193.
Benedictines, i, 183; iii, 248; iv, 192, 197, 202, 203, 204, 205, 207, 208, 214, 216, 218, 222.
Bennett, Mr. Thomas, Notary-Public, iv, 77.
Bennington, Thomas, i, 116.
Bennison, Marmaduke, ii, 16; Richard, iii, 56; William, i, 93.
Benson, John (cl), ii, 144, 145; Martin, Bp. of Gloucester, (*see Places*, Gloucester); Thomas, ii, 102; William, elder and younger, iv, 212.
Bentham, Benjamin, iii, 18; Ed: ii, 169; Thomas (cl), i, 10.
Bentley, Daniel (cl), ii, 96; Frans: iii, 20; John, ii, 60; iii, 92; William, ii, 213.
Berdmore, Scrope (cl), iv, 41, 68, 181, 182, 184; Thomas (cl), iv, 26; William (cl), i, 7, 46.
Berket, Thomas, iii, 95.
Berks, Brian (cl), iv, 159; Richard (cl), iv, 20.
Bernard, John, iii, 61.
Berriman, John, i, 211; Thomas, gent., i, 102.
Berryman, William, ii, 222.
Bertie, C. M. (cl), Intr., xvi.
Bestall, Joseph, iv, 140, 142.
Beswick, — (a Black), i, 105; Richard, iii, 92; William, iii, 99.
Bettinson, George (cl), iv, 144.
Bettison, Joseph, iv, 183.
Beulay, Robert, iii, 142.
Beverley, John, iii, 211; Stephen, i, 163.
Bewlay, Henry, i, 5.
Billiard, Robert, iv, 22.
Billings, John, iv, 9.
Bilton, Francis, iii, 141; William, iii, 43.
Bingham, Joshua, iv, 100; Thomas, iv, 123.
Bingley, Rt. Honble. Lord, i, 55; Henry, iv, 57; John, ii, 114; Richard, i, 73; Thomas, iii, 148; William, ii, 183; iii, 88.

Binnington, John, i, 119; Robert, ii, 91; Thomas, ii, 165.
Binns, John, i, 56; Joseph, i, 57; Thomas, ii, 117.
Bintine, John, iii, 23.
Birbeck, Edward (cl), i, 181; John (cl), ii, 159.
Birch, William, iv, 184.
Bird, Henry (cl), i, 82; John (cl), i, 68; Richard (cl), ii, 118; Samuel, (cl), iv, 58, 75.
Birdsall, John, iii, 65.
Birkby, Richard, iii, 142.
Birket, William, ii, 7.
Birkhead, Isaac, i, 63.
Birkit, James, i, 65.
Birkitt, John, i, 61.
Birks, John, i, 73; Miles, iii, 73; Thomas, i, 135; William, i, 135.
Birley, Birly, Mr. William, iii, 58, 60, 61.
Birt, O.S.B., Dom. H. N. (R), *Obit Book*, iv, 187, 194, 197, 203, 205, 207, 208, 209, 214, 217, 218, 222.
Bishop, Henry, iii, 73.
Blacheller, Mr., i, 190.
Blackbird, Mrs. Ann, iii, 12.
Blackburn, Launcelot, Abp. of York ['His late Grace' &c.], Intr., xiv, xxii; i, 39, 68, 89, 96, 109, 126, 128, 158, 161, 165, 176, 178, 183, 190, 193, 212; ii, 2, 12, 14, 17, 32, 35, 82, 84, 85, 104, 119, 128, 137, 155, 158, 177, 185, 198, 202, 207; iii, 31, 34, 35, 54, 109, 113, 125, 171, 183, 184, 212, 219, 220, 221, 246, 247; iv, 10, 12, 15, 17, 23, 28, 32, 53, 62, 68, 69, 75, 96, 98, 100, 103, 108, 120, 122, 126, 134, 136, 137, 141, 147, 152, 154, 157, 161, 162, 177, 178, 188, 189, 212, 213, 234.
Blackburn, Mr., *see* Blakehurst; John, iii, 55.
Blackburne, Nicholas, i, 51; Peter, iii, 242; Tho: i, 26; iii, 42.
Blackett, Walter, Esqre., iii, 246, 247, 248.
Blackmore, Matthew, iv, 48.
Blacksmith, William, iii, 21.
Blackwell, John, iv, 177.
Blake, Zachariah (cl), i, 195, 196.
Blakehurst (? Blackburn) Mr., iv, 199.
Blakeley, John, iii, 156.
Blakeston, George, i, 223.
Blakey, Thomas (Q), ii, 106; iv, 237; William, ii, 108.
Blanshard, James, i, 98; Robert (*al.* Blandshard), ii, 93; William, i, 194.
Blansharde, Robert, i, 105.
Blashall, Francis, iii, 34; John, iii, 131.
Blashell, William, ii, 88.
Blatherwick, Benjamin, iv, 16; Thomas, iv, 115.
Blenkan, Edward, iii, 161.
Blenkhorn, Thomas, iii, 111.
Blenkin, John, ii, 131; Matthew, iv, 169.
Bley, Mr. John, iv, 86.
Bloome, Thomas, i, 68.
Blythe, George ('Georgh'), i, 222.
Boawre, William (cl), iv, 20, 85.
Boggit, Edward, iii, 244.
Bokin, William, iv, 185.
Boley, Joseph, iv, 132.
Bolland, Edmund, i, 13; William, i, 140.
Bolton, Edward, i, 60; Thomas, i, 82, 83; William, ii, 198.
Bonnell, William, ii, 58.
Bontham, Francis, ii, 34.
Boocock, —, *see* Bowcock.
Booker, George, iii, 157; John, iv, 34.
Booth, Boote; Bryan, Brian, Brion, iii, 72, 81.
Booth, John, i, 61; iii, 185; Peter, iv, 55; Richard, ii, 117; Thomas, ii, 63.
Boott, Thomas, iv, 84.
Borwick, James (cl), ii, 82; iii, 209, 252; iv, 209.
Bosomworth, George, ii, 122.
Bosvile, John, i, 71; Thomas, Esqre., iii, 68, 69, 70, 71, 72.
Boswell, Thomas, iv, 79.
Botham, Richard, ii, 114.
Bott, Luke, iv, 43.
Botterell, Thomas, i, 21.
Botterill, Thomas, iii, 224; Milburne, iii, 224.
Bourne, Richard, iv, 177.
Bowbank, Israel, ii, 131.
Bowcock, Boocock [L. 'Isaac'], ii, 107, 108.
Bower, Chris: iii, 191; John, i, 168; iii, 14, 154; Joshua, i, 180; Robert, iv, 95.
Bowes, Frank, i, 184; Richard, i, 143; Thomas, ii, 62.
Bowley, William, iv, 119.
Bowman, A. N., Intr., xxiv; John (cl), i, 223; iii, 180, 192; Robert, iv, 48; William (cl), i, 221, 222, 223; William, iii, 230.
Bowser [L. 'Edward'], i, 134; James, i, 41.
Bowzer, Mr. Francis, i, 167.
Boy, Robert, ii, 215.
Boyes, John, i, 224; ii, 8, 60; iii, 209; Joseph (cl), iii, 40; Robert, ii, 154.

Boyn, John, i, 135.
Boynton, Family of, iii, 25; Mrs. Elizabeth, i, 37; Sir Francis, i, 99; Sir Griffith, 3rd Bart., i, 109; 5th Bart., i, 99, 109; John Wood, Esqre., ii, 132; Mrs. [L. 'Judith'], ii, 201; Witham, iii, 209.
Brabbs, Henry, ii, 67.
Brabiner, Thomas, iii, 93.
Brackon, Edward (cl), i, 121; ii, 20; John (*al.* 'Bracken') (cl), iv, 97, 166.
Bradfield, Thomas (cl), iv, 60, 61.
Bradford, James, iii, 158; Matthew (cl), iv, 33, 34, 45; Samuel, Bp. of Carlisle, Intr., v.
Bradley, Francis, i, 160; John (cl), ii, 68(2), 212; iii, 210; Jonathan, i, 14; Richard, iv, 46.
Bradshaw, Ellerker, Esqr., i, 194; iii, 30; Henry, iv, 123.
Brady, Dr. W. M., iv, 187, 189, 192.
Brailsford, John (cl), Intr., xix; iv, 81, 83.
Bramall, Joseph, i, 168.
Brame, Joseph, ii, 142.
Bramley, Robert, iv, 132.
Brand, William, iii, 121.
Brandling, Ralph, Esqr., iv, 213, 219.
Brandram, Samuel, iv, 168.
Brandrith, John, iv, 146.
Branfoot, John (cl), i, 85.
Brantam, Francis, i, 192.
Brasier, John, ii, 113.
Brathwaite, Marmaduke, iii, 136.
Breares, William, i, 68.
Brearey, Christopher Spencer (cl), ii, 195.
Breerton, Henry, i, 124.
Breighton, John, iii, 223.
Brenand, Nic: i, 49; Thomas, iii, 251.
Breton, John (cl), iv, 61.
Brett, George, iv, 141; John, iv, 11; Thomas, iv, 11.
Brewer, John, ii, 176.
Brewster, Thomas, ii, 190; iii, 52.
Bricknall, Jonathan, iv, 30.
Bridges, —, Mr. (cl), iv, 188, 189; Joseph (cl), iii, 253; Michael (cl), i, 141, 142; ii, 57; [William], senr., (cl) (1674), iv, 58, 59; William, junior (cl), iv, 60.
Briggs, John (cl), i, 14; Jon: iii, 187; Thomas, ii, 53; iv, 5.
Brigham, Family of, iv, 218.
Bright, —, Mrs., ii, 190; Thomas, i, 180.
Britch, Joseph, iii, 237.
Brittain, Christopher, ii, 122; John, ii, 121.
Broadbelt, Bernard, ii, 140.
Broadhead, John, i, 76.
Brock, Thomas, iv, 53.
Brockbank, William (cl), ii, 62.
Brocklebank, William, ii, 75.
Brodhurst, William (cl), iv, 13, 56.
Brogden, Richard, ii, 4.
Bromhead, Thomas, iii, 4.
Bromley, Andrew, i, 81; John, i, 165; ii, 115; Richard, i, 21.
Brook, John (P), iv, 233; John, ii, 52; Joseph, ii, 116; Samuel (cl), i, 19, 205, 207; William, ii, 212.
Brooke, George, ii, 44; John, i, 15; ii, 31; John (P), i, 150; iv, 226; Joshua (cl), iii, 150; Richard, iii, 19; William (cl), i, 61; William (*al.* Brookes), i, 90.
Brookes, William, *see* Brooke, William.
Brooks, S.J.; Father (R), iv, 199; German, iv, 153; John, i, 70; Richard, iv, 10.
Brooksbank, Family of, iv, 228; Mr. John, iv, 228; Joseph (cl), iii, 252.
Brough, George Stanton (Staunton), (cl), iv, 156, 166, 168.
Brough, John, i, 127; 'ye Younger,' ii, 75.
Broughton, Edward (cl), iv, 12, 106, 107; Mr. John, i, 167; William, i, 23.
Brown, Antho: iii, 15; Christopher, gent., ii, 108; George, i, 83; Isaac, i, 63; James, ii, 111; James (R) (1), ii, 32; iv, 194, 205; James (R) (2), iv, 194; John (cl), iv, 168; John, iii, 146; Marmaduke, ii, 137; Martin, i, 43; Nathaniel, i, 116; Richard, ii, 5; iii, 44, 99; Robert, ii, 105, 124; Stephen, ii, 148; Thomas, iii, 168; William (cl), iii, 17, 18; William (Q), iii, 166; iv, 239; William, ii, 161; iii, 154.
Browne, Mr. Charles, iv, 182; Henry, (cl), i, 69; John (cl), i, 192; ii, 13, 88; Mr. [L. 'Obadiah'], i, 68; Robert (cl), i, 27; ii, 151; iii, 159.
Bruce, Stephen, iii, 143; Thomas, iii, 230.
Bruen, Joseph (cl), iv, 92, 135.
Bruerton, Thomas, iv, 52.
Bryan, Mrs., iv, 6.
Buck, John, iii, 10; Marmaduke (cl), ii, 173; Matthew (cl), i, 21, 71; ii, 182.
Buckle, Marmaduke, iii, 138.
Buckles, Robert, iii, 173.
Buckloe, John, iv, 20.
Bugg, Henry (cl), iv, 25, 79, 185.
Bughs, Thomas, iii, 111.
Bugtrout, George, iii, 187.

Bullcock, James, i, 77.
Bullivant, John, iv, 183; Samuel, iv, 6.
Bullock, John, iv, 98.
Bulmer, Daniel, ii, 167; Franc: i, 93; Peter, i, 4; Rowland, ii, 191; Thomas, ii, 221; iii, 18.
Bunyan, John, Intr., xxiii; iv, 241.
Burdett, — Mrs., iii, 62.
Burges, William (cl), iii, 212.
Burgess, Sam., iii, 86.
Burghope, George (cl), iv, 139.
Burke's *Peerage*, iii, 43; iv, 210.
Burkitt, William (cl) (1703), ii, 113, 144.
Burland, Joseph, iii, 4.
Burlington, 3rd Earl of, i, 96; ii, 158.
Burn, Mr. Henry, iii, 157; Richard, *Eccl. Law*, Intr., xxi.
Burnet, Thomas, iii, 141.
Burnham, Francis, iii, 116.
Burnitt, John, iii, 162.
Burril, Mr., Junr., i, 152; William, senior, i, 152.
Burroughs, William, iv, 82, 240.
Burrow, Robert (cl), i, 166.
Burrows, Barnaby, iv, 84; Jonathan, iv, 90.
Burton, Clement, ii, 142; Dr. E. H., iv, 187, 192, 193; Edmund, iii, 15; George, i, 169; John (cl) (V. Bubwith), i, 100, 101; John (cl) (A.C. High Hoyland), ii, 50; John, iv, 25; Mr. Richard, i, 103, 151, 152, 155; Robert, gent., i, 40; Robert, ii, 199; Thomas (cl), i, 197.
Busby, Dr. (cl), iv, 54; Thomas (P) (*al.* Roberts), iv, 29, 194, 201.
Busfield, Anne, iii, 43; William, iii, 43.
Butcher, Mr. John, iv, 182.
Butler of Rawcliffe, iv, 194; Mr. (R) (*al.* Peter Seel), ii, 175; iv, 194, 210; Benjamin (cl), i, 60; Francis, iv, 22; James (cl), ii, 221; iii, 218; John, i, 167; iii, 65; iv, 120, 121; Thomas, i, 190; iv, 65.
Butterfield, Christopher (cl), i, 75, 179; John, i, 223; Richard, i, 49; Thomas, i, 41.
Butterill, Richard, iv, 129.
Butterwood, Robert (cl), iv, 129.
Butterworth, John, iv, 146; Matthew, iii, 63, 194.
Buttery, Roger, iii, 163, 164.
Buttle, John, i, 36.
Butts, Robert, Bp. of Norwich, Intr., v.
Byrne, O.S.B., Dom. H.K. (R), iv, 186.
Byron, William, Lord, iv, 72.
Bywater, William, i, 199.

Cade, Robert, ii, 212; Thomas, iv, 85.
Calverley, Sir Walter (*al.* Calverly), iii, 16; William, iv, 143.
Calvert, Thomas (cl), ii, 58; iii, 97; Thomas, ii, 174; William, i, 126.
Calvin, John, iv, 224.
Calvinistic Baptists, iv, 241.
Camb, Stephen, iv, 44.
Campion, John, iv, 96; Robert, ii, 191.
Cant, Marmaduke, i, 122.
Canterbury, Abp. of, *see* Places (Canterbury).
Cape, Brian, iii, 209.
Capes, John, iii, 176.
Capp, Ralph, iv, 80.
Cappe, Joseph (P), iv, 230, 233; Newcome (I), iv, 233.
Capps, John, iv, 184.
Capuchin Friar, iv, 201.
Caradas, John, ii, 108.
Carlile, William, i, 195.
Carlill, Jeremiah, i, 161; Thomas, iii, 177.
Carlin, Thomas, iv, 177.
Carling, John, i, 186.
Carlisle, Diocese of, *see* Places (Carlisle).
Carlisle, Earldom of, iv, 189; 3rd Earl, ii, 219, 220; 4th Earl, iii, 171.
Carlton, Richard, i, 120.
Carmelites, iv, 192, 194.
Carnaby, James, iv, 238; Priscilla, iv, 237.
Carnson, Cranson, John (P), iii, 239; iv, 231.
Carr, —, (R), iv, 213; Benjamin, i, 29; Mr. Bonomi, iv, 206; George, i, 24; ii, 7; James (cl), i, 12, 53, 58; John (cl), ii, 28; John, ii, 6; iii, 102; Richard, i, 169; Thomas, i, 73; Thomas (Q), ii, 6; iv, 237; William (cl), i, 51; ii, 27; William, i, 38; ii, 66.
Carrett, George, ii, 86.
Carritt, William, ii, 142.
Carter, — (cl), iv, 163; Jeremiah (cl), ii, 154; John Segar (cl), ii, 13, 15, 223; iii, 225, 227; Moses, iv, 42; Mr. Richard, i, 205, 206; Robert, i, 218, 223; Thomas (cl), iv, 72, 110.
Cartwright, Mr., iv, 105; John, iii, 15.
Carver, John, iv, 86; Marmaduke, iii, 192; Thomas, iv, 87; William, iii, 94.
Case, John, iv, 28.
Cass, David, iii, 108; Eustace (cl),

iii, 41, 42; Joseph, ii, 93; William, ii, 61, 157.
Cassen, William, iii, 81.
Casson, George, iii, 168; Nicholas (cl), iv, 35.
Castley, Thomas (cl), i, 93; iii, 104.
Catholic Rec. Soc., Intr., xvii; App. A. *passim*.
Catley, Robert, i, 80.
Catterton, Henry, iii, 250; Silvester, i, 12.
Caudwell, William, iv, 51.
Cave, Andrew (cl), iv, 43, 44, 131.
Cawood, John, i, 8.
Cawthorne, Mary, i, 199; Thomas, i, 135.
Cawton, William, ii, 167.
Cayley, Arthur (cl), i, 34, 157, 188, 189, 211; iii, 177; John (cl), ii, 61.
Cecil, William, iv, 137.
Ceikell, John, i, 62.
Chadwick, John, ii, 179; Joseph (cl), iv, 4; Thomas, iv, 84.
Challoner, Bp., iv, 187, 192.
Challoner Catholics, iv, 191.
Chaloner, Mr., ii, 9.
Chamberlain, Mr. [L. 'Leonard'], ii, 75.
Chamberlaine, Mr. Thomas, iii, 46.
Chamberlayne, Leonard (P), iv, 229.
Chambers, Mr., ii, 78; John, ii, 24.
Champney, Thomas, gent., iv, 216.
Chandler, William, iii, 96.
Chantrill, Darcy, gent., iv, 206; William (R), iv, 206.
Chaplin, William, ii, 67.
Chapman, George, iii, 142; John (cl), i, 13; John, ii, 184; Jonathan, iv, 111; Joseph, i, 119; Richard, iii, 2; Thomas (cl), i, 198; ii, 142; Thomas, i, 9; ii, 62.
Chappell, Edward (cl), iv, 37, 108, 154; George (cl), iv, 12, 46, 154.
Charles I, King, ii, 36, 37; iii, 68; iv, 201.
Charles Edward, Prince, iv, 188, 190, 198.
Charlesworth, George, i, 20; John, i, 62.
Charleton, Mr. John, *see* Charlton.
Charlsworth, Robert (cl), i, 44.
Charlton, Mr., iv, 136, 167; of Hesley-side, iv, 207; John, O.S.B., Dom. (R), iv, 208, 209.
Charnley, William, i, 80, 81; iii, 66.
Charnock, James, ii, 96.
Charworth, William, iv, 71.
Chenevix, Richard (cl), Intr., xix; iv, 62.
Chester, Diocese of, *see* Places (Chester).
Chester, Penelope, iii, 4; Robert, ii' 198; Thomas, ii, 184; Sir William, iii, 4.
Chesterfield, Philip, 2nd Earl, iv, 10; 4th Earl, Intr., xix; iv, 62.
Chetham, John (cl), iii, 46.
Chetwood, Archdn., Knightley, ii, 183.
Chibchase, William, iii, 196.
Chilton, John, iii, 65.
Chippindale, Thomas, iii, 46; Thomas, junior, iii, 46; William, i, 224.
Cholmeley of Brandsby, iv, 190, 199.
Cholmley, Chumley, Chombley, Chomondley, Mr., i, 84; [L. 'Francis'], Esqr., i, 82, 83; Hugh, Esqr., ii, 168; Lady, iii, 178.
Chowler, Jos., ii, 140.
Chumley, *see* Cholmley.
Church, Henry, iii, 26.
Cinna, Bp. of., iv, 195.
Claggett, Nicholas, Bp. of St. David's, Intr., v.
Clapham, Henry (B), i, 59; iv, 241; Jeremiah, i, 223; Thomas, ii, 108; iii, 144; Mr. Thomas, ii, 7.
Clapison, Enoch, iii, 34.
Clare, Earl of, iv, 53; Sister Frances, *see* Barlow.
Clares, Poor, iv, 201.
Clarges, Sir Thomas, iii, 111.
Clark, Abraham, *see* Clarke; George, iii, 24; H. W., iv, 235; John (cl), *see* Clarke; John (Q), i, 209; Robert, i, 165; Samuel, iv, 171; Thomas (cl), ii, 114; William (cl), i, 96; ii, 12.
Clarke, Abraham (Clark) (cl), ii, 65; iii, 56, 135, 170; Charles (cl), iv, 62; Francis, iii, 184; Henry (cl), iv, 104; Henry, iv, 78, 132; John (senior) (cl), i, 191; ii, 78; iii, 114, 115; John (junior) (cl), i, 192; ii, 79, 136; iii, 125, 126; John (*al.* Clark) (cl), Intr., xi, xix; i, 104; ii, 124; Joseph, i, 222; Matthew, ii, 93; Richard, ii, 147; Dr. Samuel (cl) (1729), iii, 7; iv, 129; Stephen (cl), i, 107; ii, 203; Thomas (cl), iv, 15, 18; Thomas, i, 36, 54; iv, 68; William (*al.* Clerk) (cl), iv, 98, 146, 147; William, i, 222; iii, 97.
Clarkson, John (cl), iii, 63; John, ii, 91; Michael, i, 62; Mrs. Ruth, iv, 97, 178; William, ii, 93.
Clay, Benjamin (cl), iv, 51; Mr. John, iv, 185.
Clayton, Col., ii, 123; Mr. James, iv, 110; Joseph, ii, 35.
Cleator, John (cl), ii, 183; iii, 23, 193.

Cleaver, Solomon, iv, 107.
Clemenge, Marmaduke, iii, 107.
Clement, Henry (cl), iii, 111.
Clerk, William (cl), *see* Clarke.
Cleworth, Thomas (cl), Intr., xxiii; i, 135.
Cliff, Jos: ii, 142.
Clifford, Thomas, i, 189.
Clifton, Family of, iv, 201; George, iv, 201; Gervase, iv, 201; John, i, 135; Sir Robert, iv, 28; William (cl), iv, 27, 28; William, iv, 201.
Clint, Samuel (cl), ii, 198.
Clipp, Samuel, iv, 183.
Clough, Hugh, ii, 111; John, i, 124; iii, 81; ('Hough'); 82, 84; William, i, 124.
Coale, Benjamin, *see* Cole.
Coates, Family of, iv, 211; James, i, 35; John (cl), i, 25, 26; John, ii, 131, 153; iii, 232; Nicholas, iii, 223; Richard, iii, 140; Thomas, ii, 113; William, iii, 253.
Cobb, Roger, i, 212; William, i, 208.
Cockayne, Benjamin (cl), iv, 3, 19.
Cockayne's *Compl. Baronetage*, iv, 201, 214.
Cockburn, William (cl), iii, 105, 106.
Cockerill, Henry, ii, 222; John, i, 192.
Cockin, William, i, 167.
Cockram, Edward, i, 221.
Cockroft, Caleb, ii, 37; Mr. Henry, ii, 37.
Cockshutt, Thomas (cl), i, 138; iii, 6; iv, 113, 114.
Coggrave, Robert, i, 194.
Colbatch, George (cl), i, 223; iii, 251, 252.
Coldwell, Joseph, i, 138.
Cole, Benjamin (*al.* 'Coale'), i, 94; Gervas, iv, 129; Jervas, iv, 34; John, iii, 252; Canon R.E.G., Intr., viii; Thomas, ii, 69; William, iii, 104.
Colebeck, Thomas, iii, 230.
Coleby, James, iii, 121; Thomas (cl), i, 61.
Coleridge, S.J., H. J. (R), iv, 220.
Colishaw, John, iv, 67.
Colley, John, i, 91; William, ii, 60.
Collier, C. V. (cl), ii, 162; Rubin, ii, 8; William, i, 179.
Collingridge, O.S.F., Matthew (R), ii, 218; iii, 99, 111; iv, 211, 215, 216, 217.
Collins, Mr., iv, 109; Mr. Marmaduke, ii, 78.
Collinson, C. B. (cl), iv, 151; William, i, 37; ii, 223.
Collison, John, i, 61.
Colton, John, ii, 112; iii, 46, 80; Thomas (*al.* Coulton), M.D. (P), i, 194; iv, 233.
Comber, Thomas, Esqr., ii, 200.
Coney, George, ii, 125.
Congill, Richard, iv, 173.
Coniston, Thomas, ii, 87.
Conn, William, ii, 52.
Consett, George, i, 208; William (cl), ii, 215, 216, 217.
Constable, of Burton Constable, iv, 206, 213, 216, 217, 218; of Flamborough, iv, 204; of Halsham, ii, 85; Mr. (Ld. Par. of Holderness), iv, 190; Mr., i, 103; Catherine, iv, 211; Mr. Cuthbert (*al.* Tunstal), ii, 85; iv, 206, 215, 217; Sir Marmaduke, iv, 190, 204; Philip, iv, 211; Robert, S.J. (R), iv, 222; Robert, i, 97; William, Visc. Dunbar, iv, 217; William, Esqr., iv, 217.
Constantine, Jonathan, i, 51; Robert, i, 51.
Conyers, Mother Esther, iv, 220.
Cook, Dr., *see* Cooke, William (cl); Margaret, i, 185; Thomas, ii, 200.
Cooke, Emanuel, iii, 209; George, iii, 82, 83, 84; Henry (cl), Intr., xiii; iii, 101, 102; John (cl), iv, 172; John, i, 119; Richard, iii, 168; Samuel, i, 159; Thomas, i, 157, 183; [William] (cl), D.D., i, 134; William, ii, 56, 93; iv, 76.
Cookson, Edward (cl), ii, 142; Joseph (cl), ii, 141, 142; Miles (cl), iii, 237.
Coope, John, ii, 42.
Cooper of Thurgarton, iv, 72; George, ii, 212; John (cl), iv, 63, 151, 177; John, iv, 140; Joseph, i, 199; Richard, iii, 74; Thomas (cl) (v. Riccall), iii, 29; Thomas (cl) (v. Kneesall), iv, 81, 114, 115; Thomas, i, 168; ii, 24, 168; William, iii, 203.
Coops, Thomas, i, 168.
Coor, Henry, ii, 4.
Cope, Benjamin, ii, 42.
Copendale, George, iv, 88.
Cordingley, Joseph, ii, 96.
Cordley, John, i, 223.
Cordukes, Richard (cl), i, 5; ii, 170, 171.
Cordwell, Adam, iv, 112.
Corner, Jno: iii, 61; Robert, i, 186.
Cornforth, John, i, 95.
Corps, James, i, 146.
Cosin, James, iv, 187, 199, 216.
Cossens, Richard, i, 33.
Cotham, William, i, 30.
Cottam, John, iv, 183.
Cotton, Jonathan, iii, 46.

Coulson, Mrs. Ann, iv, 211; Christopher (cl), iii, 35; John, ii, 62; iii, 204; Ralph, iii, 144; Richard, iii, 216.
Coultass, John, i, 212; Richard, ii, 135; Robert, iii, 37.
Coulton, Brian, ii, 168; Thomas, *see* Colton.
Coupland, Robert, iii, 65.
Coverdale, William, i, 211.
Coverley, William, i, 114.
Cow, William, iv, 174.
Cowburn, James, iii, 144.
Cowgill, Francis, ii, 209.
Cowley, Daniel, iv, 40; Richard, iv, 148.
Cowling, Edmond, iii, 18; Joshua, iii, 90.
Cowper, Charles (cl), i, 208; ii, 215; iii, 158; Mr. John, ii, 97.
Cowton, Henry, i, 113.
Cox, John, iv, 19; Thomas, ii, 47; William, ii, 53.
Crabtree, John, ii, 150; Robert, i, 70; Samuel, ii, 150.
Cradock, H. C., iv, 186.
Craft, Thomas, iv, 119.
Crampton, John, iv, 33.
Cranson, *see* Carnson.
Crathorne, Family of, iv, 190, 202, 207; Mary, iv, 202; Mr. Ralph, iv, 202; Richard, i, 183; Thomas, iv, 202.
Craven, Jos: i, 117.
Crawshaw, Francis, ii, 151; George, i, 75.
Cream, Christopher, ii, 11.
Cresey, John, iii, 216.
Croe, Christopher (cl), ii, 162.
Croesdale, Stephen, i, 54.
Croft, Edward (cl), i, 95; John, i, 12; William (cl), ii, 42, 44.
Crompton, Abraham, i, 160.
Cromwell, Oliver, iv, 231, 232; Robert, iv, 147.
Crosby, David (*see* Crosley); George, i, 46; John, i, 143; iii, 92; Thomas, i, 34.
Crosfield, George, i, 127.
Crosier, Philip, ii, 82; Thomas, i, 121.
Crosland, James, i, 19; John, ii, 31; Joshua, i, 20.
Crosley, Mr., ii, 149; David (*al.* Crossley, Crosly, Crosby) (B), Intr., xxiii; ii, 35, 108, 'Hossley'; iv, 241, 242; Thomas, ii, 34; Tindale, iii, 167.
Cross, Lat: (cl), iv, 152; Richard, iii, 12; Robert, ii, 138; Thomas, iv, 17.
Crosse, Gordon, Intr., xxiv.
Crossley, David, (*see* Crosley); E.W., F.S.A., Esqr., Intr., xxiv.
Crowle, Mr., ii, 144; Thomas (cl), ii, 78.
Crowther, John, i, 51; Johes, iii, 19; Thomas, iii, 198.
Cubit, Jacob, iv, 105.
Cudworth, John, i, 133; Timothy, i, 138.
Culverson, John, ii, 97.
Cummins, O.S.B., Abbot, iv, 186.
Cuncliffe, Ellis, ii, 95.
Cundall, Richard, ii, 221.
Cunningham, James (I), iv, 229.
Currer, John (cl), ii, 112.
Cussons, Thomas, ii, 62.
Cutforthay, John, iii, 23.
Cuthbert, John, i, 164.
Cuttle, Thomas, iv, 23.

Dade, Thomas (cl), Intr., xix; i, 38, 110, 193; ii, 92.
Dagget, Mic: iii, 141.
Daggett, Christopher, iii, 230; Richard, iii, 232.
Dalby, James, iii, 42; Peter, iii, 42; Richard, i, 124.
Dale, George, ii, 10; James, iii, 252; John (cl), iii, 238; John, i, 174; iii, 180; Richard, iii, 170; Robert W. (C), iv, 235.
Dalgarno [Arthur] (cl) (1731), i, 190.
Dalton, David, i, 214; John (cl), iv, 140, 141; John, ii, 169; Joseph, iii, 227; Richard, iii, 211, 222; Robert, ii, 190.
Danby, William, ii, 120.
Daniel, John, iv, 210; Joshua, ii, 134; Robert, i, 78; Thomas (R), iv, 195, 210, 220, 221, 222.
Daniell, Mark, i, 196.
Dannyel, Thomas, iii, 81.
Danvers, Sir John, ii, 125.
Darby, William, i, 87.
Darell, *see* Westbrooke.
Darley, Stephen, iii, 38; William, ii, 196.
Darns, John, iv, 14.
Daubuz, Charles (cl) (1717), ii, 31; Claudius (cl), Intr., xix; ii, 31.
Davis, Mrs. Parnel, iv, 85, 86; Peter, S.J. (R), i, 54; iv, 194, 200; Robert Ambrose, O.S.B. (R), iv, 222.
Davison, John, i, 44; Robert, i, 38; William, i, 44.
Dawes, Daws, Sir William; Abp. of York, Intr., vi; i, 57, 62; ii, 14, 36, 69, 199, 213; iii, 102; iv, 100, 110; William, i, 33.
Dawf, Ralph, iii, 107.
Dawnay, Christopher, Esqr., iii, 68, 69, 70, 71, 72; Sir Thomas, knt.,

iii, 73, 80, 81, 82, 83, 84, 85.
Dawney, Benjamin (cl), ii, 199, 213.
Dawson, Eli (senior) (P), ii, 32; iv, 227, 228, 232; Eli (junior) (cl), iv, 228; George (Q), ii, 175; Isaac, ii, 3; John (cl), iv, 11; John, i, 114, 139; ii, 209; Joseph (P), iv, 227, 228, 229; Joseph, iv, 228; Kettlewell, i, 33; Miles, iii, 179; Richard, ii, 2; Richard, Esqr., ii, 171; Robert, i, 45; Samuel (P later cl), iii, 188; iv, 227, 228, 232; Samuel, ii, 51; Thomas (cl), ii, 49, 50; iii, 187; Thomas, ii, 51, 105; William (cl), i, 209, 210.
Dawtry, —, i, 126.
Day, Edward, ii, 122; Francis (cl), iii, 163, 165; Rt. Rev. Monsignor, O.B.E., D.S.O., iv, 186; Thomas, iv, 72; William, i, 168; ii, 208.
Dealtary, Henry (cl), iii, 216; John (cl) (*al.* Dealtry), i, 120; ii, 122; iii, 119.
Dean, Mr., ii, 149; Mr. John, i, 223; John (cl), iv, 62; Samuel, iii, 200.
Deane, Thomas, i, 189.
Deason, Thomas (cl), i, 144; ii, 135, 153, 155, 190; iii, 8; William (cl), i, 146, 211; ii, 219.
Deeping, John, iv, 69.
Degge, Staunton (cl), iv, 138 (2), 185.
De Hayne, John (cl), ii, 111; iii, 90.
Deighton, Richard, iii, 142; Robert, i, 15.
Delamotte, Mr. Charles, iii, 116.
Demaine, Joseph, ii, 113; William, i, 197.
Denby, Thomas, iii, 81.
Denham, Mr. Thomas, i, 60.
Dennis, Samuel (cl), i, 108; ii, 164; Samuel, iv, 168.
Dennison, Thomas (cl), i, 222; Thomas, iii, 187.
Dent, Robert (cl), ii, 218; iii, 171, 252; Robert, iii, 62.
Denton, John, iii, 184; Peter, gent., i, 103; Richard, i, 168; Robert (cl), iii, 96; Samuel, iv, 53; Thomas (cl), i, 67, 68.
Depledge, John, i, 169.
Derby, William, i, 8.
Dering, Heneage, *see* Ripon, Dean of.
Devonshire, Countess of (1663), iii, 197; Duke of, iv, 145.
Dewsberry, William, i, 40.
Dibb, Robert, i, 60; Thomas, i, 124.
Dicconson, Edward, Bp. of Malla (R), iv, 187, 195, 215, 220; his Letters, iv, 192; *List of Clergy*, App. A. *passim.*
Dickinson, Charles, i, 197; Elihu (*al.* Dickenson) (Q), i, 170; ii, 116; iv, 236, 237; George, ii, 184; iii, 98; Mr. Joc: iii, 91; John, iii, 157; Luke, iii, 143; Ralph, i, 221; Simeon, i, 29; Thomas (P), ii, 32; iv, 228, 230; William, i, 201.
Dickson, Francis, iii, 187; Henry, i, 12; ii, 184.
Didsbury, Robert, iii, 191.
Digges, S.J., Francis (R), ii, 120; iv, 208.
Dindley, Edward, ii, 140.
Dinsdale, Thomas, iii, 141, 230; William, ii, 209.
Disney, James, ii, 169.
Dixon, Mr. John, ii, 73; John, ii, 142; iv, 226; Joseph, i, 58; iii, 46; Mr. Nathan, i, 59; Stephen (M), iv, 82, 240; William (cl), i, 90; William, i, 60; Mr. William, iii, 46.
Dobson, Mr. Alderman, ii, 75; Bartholomew, i, 26; Elizabeth, i, 123; John, ii, 157; iii, 86; William, i, 33; iv, 94.
Doddridge, D.D. [Philip], (I), ii, 110; iv, 224, 227, 230.
Dodge, William (P), ii, 32; iii, 49; iv, 228, 229.
Dodgson, Christopher (*al.* Dodson) (cl), i, 27; ii, 54, 55; Edmund, ii, 4; Jo: iii, 144; Samuel (cl), i, 129; ii, 26; Thomas, i, 45; William, i, 4, 33.
Dodsley, John, iv, 2.
Dodson, Christopher (*see* Dodgson); Thomas, iv, 152.
Dodsworth, George (cl), iii, 133; John, ii, 154; Marmaduke, i, 111; William (cl), i, 4; ii, 208; William, iii, 98.
Dominicans, iv, 192, 193, 197, 206, 207, 218, 219.
Doncaster, George, iv, 97; Stephen, i, 173; William, iv, 89.
Donkin, Thomas, iii, 177.
Donn, Richard (cl), iii, 118.
Donohough, John (R), iv, 207.
Dossie, John (cl), iii, 57.
Dove, Samuel, i, 150; William, iii, 122.
Dowbiggin, Thomas (cl), ii, 17, 81; iii, 118, 214.
Dowe, Henry, i, 143; William, iii, 232.
Dowker, John, iii, 109; Philip (cl), ii, 201; iii, 109.
Down, Lord, *see* Downe, 3rd Viscount.
Downam, William, ii, 22.
Downe, Robert, iii, 101; Henry

Pleydell, 3rd Viscount, iii, 67, 73, 165.
Downes, George, i, 110; John (cl), iii, 58, 60, 61, 62; Robert, ii, 131.
Downham, John, iii, 251; William (cl), iii, 241.
Downing, John, iii, 63.
Dowsland, Ralph, iii, 204.
Dowson, Edward, iii, 27; John, iii, 102; Thomas, iii, 102.
Dowthwaite, John, i, 183; Joseph (cl), i, 88, 209.
D'Oyly, Doyly, Doyley, Robert (cl), Intr., xiii; ii, 116, 117; iii, 191.
Drabble, Joseph, iii, 251.
Drabwell, John, iv, 101.
Drake, Capt., i, 56; Francis, *see* York *Eboracum*; Robert, ii, 167; Samuel (cl), Intr., xix; ii, 72; iii, 153; William (cl), i, 212; ii, 51.
Dransfield, Charles, ii, 31; Samuel (cl), i, 203; ii, 52.
Draper, William, Esqr., i, 105; Mr. William, i, 105.
Drewry, Mr. William, iv, 182.
Driffeild, Christopher (cl), i, 200.
Dring, Francis, ii, 196; Richard, ii, 187; William, iv, 183.
Drinkrow, Henry, i, 223.
Drinkwater, Thomas, ii, 176.
Drummond, Honble. Robert Hay; Abp. of York, Intr. viii.
Dubourdieu [Jean], ii, 124; [Jean Armand], ii, 124; Peter (cl), ii, 124.
Duck, Daniel, iii, 102; Mich: i, 43; Richard, ii, 129; William, iii, 104.
Ducke, William, ii, 164.
Ducker, Christopher, iii, 150.
Ducket, Charles, i, 13.
Duckworth, Christopher, iii, 149; Isaac, i, 60.
Duffield, Parker, i, 196.
Duffin, Richard, i, 79.
Dugdale, John, ii, 6.
Duggleby, Peter, ii, 133.
Duglas, John, ii, 171.
Dunbar, Lady, iv, 214; William, 4th Viscount, iv, 217.
Duncombe, Duncomb, Honble. Edward, iii, 117; William, Intr. xiv.
Dunford, Robert, iii, 148.
Dunhill, Richard, iii, 4.
Dunn, John, ii, 93; Thomas, i, 107; iii, 40; William, ii, 218.
Dunwell, John, ii, 103.
Dupeer, Mr. Solomon, i, 165.
Duty, John, iii, 220.
Dyson, Abra: i, 130; George, iii, 58; Henry, iii, 187; John, i, 178, 223; ii, 31.
Ealam, John, iv, 53.
Eaglehard, Dan: iii, 49.
Earle, Richard, i, 71.
Earnshaw, John, iii, 154; Thomas, i, 65.
Earwaker, John (*see Places*, Cheshire).
Easterby, Thomas, i, 222.
Eastwood, John, ii, 211; Jones, ii, 222.
Eaton, Mr., *see* Dicconson; George (B), iv, 109, 230, 242; Joseph, M.D. (B), iv, 242; Joseph, iii, 197; Samuel, D.D. (P), iv, 180, 224, 230.
Eccles, John, iii, 51.
Eckels, John, iv, 241.
Ecton [John], iv, 189.
Eden (? Eddins) William (P), ii, 116; iv, 230.
Eddins, *see* Eden.
Edge, Mr., iv, 167; Mr. William, iv, 108.
Edmonds, Robert, i, 54.
Edmonson, Henry, ii, 4.
Edmund, John, iii, 221.
Edmunds, Mr., ii, 183.
Edwards, Thomas (cl), iv, 7, 93, 94 (2), 95; Thomas, iii, 80.
Eggleston, Richard, iii, 253; Mr. Richard, iii, 10.
Elam, John (cl), iii, 157.
Elcott, Richard, iii, 28.
Elibank, 4th Baron, ii, 221; 5th Baron, Patrick Murray, ii, 221.
Eling, Mr. [L. 'Benjamin Eland'], i, 190.
Elizabeth, Queen, ii, 198; iii, 186; iv, 218.
Elizabeth Grammar Schools, Queen; Halifax, ii, 32, 34; Hexham, iii, 249; Mansfield, iv, 178; Wakefield, iii, 185.
Elkington, John, i, 104.
Ella, Samuel, i, 145.
Ellard, Thomas, iv, 22.
Ellat, John, iii, 154.
Eller, Michael, ii, 120.
Elleray, John (cl), i, 114.
Ellerby, George, ii, 60.
Ellerker, Thomas, i, 97.
Ellerton, William, iii, 127.
Elliot, John, iii, 24.
Ellis, Mr., iii, 87; George, iii, 107, 154; James, i, 13; ii, 24; John, ii, 42, 208; iii, 24, 252; Joshua, iii, 6; Robert, i, 24; Thomas, iii, 185.
Ellison, Job, ii, 5; Mr. John, iii, 61; Robert, ii, 105.
Elmire, John, i, 28.
Elmsall, Henry (cl), i, 15; iii, 148, 188.

Else, Mr. John, iv, 110.
Elsley, William (cl), iii, 250.
Elstob, Lewis, Esqr., iii, 160.
Elston, Hananiah (P), iv, 230; William, iv, 135.
Elsworth, Henry, i, 78.
Elwood, John, iii, 200.
Emerson, Richard, ii, 60.
Emmerson, Robert, iii, 55.
Empson, Amaziah, ii, 93; John (cl), iii, 193; William, i, 165.
Engal, Widow, iii, 154.
Errington, Family of, iii, 248; iv, 207, 209.
Estill, George, i, 160.
Etherington, John, iii, 5, 138.
Etty, Lewis (cl), ii, 166, 167; Robert, ii, 125.
Evans, Thomas (cl), iv, 162.
Evers, William, iii, 43.
Ewood, William, i, 179.
Exeter, Earl of, iv, 55, 73, 171.
Exley, Matthew, ii, 50.
Eyles, —, *see* Isles, and Jackson, S.J., Ambrose.
Eyre, Family of, iv, 129; Anthony, Esqr., iv, 129; Benjamin, iv, 57; Mr. Gervas, iv, 129.

Fairbourne, Thomas, iii, 112.
Fairbrother, Mr. Isaac, iv, 172.
Fairburn, William, ii, 140.
Fairburne, William, i, 7.
Fairfax, of Emley, iv, 205; Charles Gregory, 9th Viscount, iv, 205; of Gilling, iv, 190, 205.
Faith, William, iii, 56.
Falkner, Job (cl), iv, 121, 152; William, iv, 121.
Fall, Edward, ii, 173; Thomas, iii, 230.
Farley, Fabian, ii, 208.
Farmary, Farmery, Mrs. [L. 'Jane'], iii, 156, 157.
Farnley, Richard, ii, 198.
Farrand, Mr. John, iii, 222.
Farrar, Family of, iv, 228; Thomas (P), ii, 32; iv, 228.
Farrer, Mr. Elkanah, ii, 96; Jere: i, 198; John (cl), i, 202; John (M), iii, 18; Robert, iii, 180.
Farside, Thomas [L. Robert], Esqr., ii, 60.
Farthing, Thomas, i, 217.
Fauconberg, Family of, iv, 202, 215; Lady, iv, 196, 202; Thomas, Viscount, iv, 190, 196.
Faussett, Simon, iii, 253.
Favell, Charles, iv, 32; George (cl), iv, 57.
Fawcet, James, D.D. (cl), ii, 142; Richard (cl), Intr., xix; ii, 142, 143.
Fawcett, John (cl), ii, 72; John, ii, 60; Thomas, ii, 60.
Fawkes, Francis, Esqr., of Farnley, ii, 209; Francis (cl), iii, 190; Jeremiah (cl), Intr., xix; iii, 190; John, iv, 160.
Fearnley, Ben., i, 223; Joseph, i, 61; William, i, 15.
Fell, Thomas (cl), iv, 5, 74, 148.
Fellows, Thomas (cl), iv, 105.
Fenton, Family of, iv, 205; Robert, ii, 198; William, ii, 142.
Ferrand, Mr. Thomas, i, 59.
Ferrard, Samuel (cl), iii, 191.
Fetherston, Thomas, ii, 20.
Fewsdale, John, i, 183.
Fewster, John, iii, 109.
Fieldhouse, John, i, 12.
Fife, Stephen, ii, 75.
Fillingham, Bartholomew, iv, 152; William, iv, 153.
Finney, William, iii, 23.
Firrey, Mr., ii, 10.
Firth, Abraham, i, 61; Joseph, i, 64; Phineas, ii, 149.
Fish, Thomas, i, 201; iii, 89.
Fisher, —, iv, 32; Francis, iv, 211; George, ii, 31; John, O.S.B. (R), ii, 72; iv, 207; John (Q), iii, 158; iv, 239; Octavia, iv, 211; Philip, i, 175; Richard (cl), ii, 32, 148, 149; Thomas, iii, 82, 84, 'Fish'; 86, 116; William, iv, 79.
Flaccus, Q. Horatius, iii, 66.
Flamstead, Mr., iv, 167.
Flaworth, John, iii, 135.
Fleetwood, William, Bp. of Ely, Intr., v, xv.
Fleming, John (cl), iii, 145; William, ii, 20.
Fletcher, Mr., iv, 217; John, ii, 2, 67; Joseph, i, 43; Thomas, i, 135; iv, 217.
Fligg, Nathaniel, ii, 67.
Flinders, Richard, iv, 68.
Flint, Richard, i, 40.
Flintoft, Christopher, ii, 65.
Flockton, John, ii, 142.
Floggan, Dame Cecily, iv, 178.
Foley, S.J., Henry (R), *Records, &c.*, App. A, *passim*.
Foljambe, Mr., iii, 20; iv, 231.
Foord, William (cl), i, 115, 215; iii, 252.
Footitt, George, iv, 35; John, iv, 32.
Forrest, Jer: iii, 4.
Fort, Richard, i, 77.
Foss, John (cl), i, 127; iv, 52, 101.
Foster (*see Places*, Oxford); Caleb, iii, 143; Canon Charles, F.S.A., Intr.,

xxiv; Christopher, i, 218; Edward, ii, 71; James, iii, 198; John, i, 14, 78, 221; ii, 39; iv, 151; Mary, ii, 162; Richard, ii, 86; Thomas, i, 70, 142; ii, 20; William (cl), iii, 137, 138, 139, 140; William, ii, 39; iv, 4.
Fotherby, Mr. Robert, i, 103.
Fothergill, Francis (cl), iv, 184; Mr. John, iii, 46; Joshua, i, 133; Timothy, iii, 230.
Foulds, Samuel, iv, 156.
Foulstone, Richard, iii, 194.
Fountain, Mr. Richard (senior), ii, 147; Thomas, ii, 186.
Fowin, *Lord*, ii, 208.
Fowler, *see* Ripon; Chappell (cl), iv, 160, 185; John, iii, 221; Richard, i, 7.
Fowlis, Richard, ii, 114, 115 'Thowlis.'
Fox, Anthony, iii, 154, 155; George, Esqr. (*see* Lane Fox); George (Q), iv, 238; Henry, iii, 218; John (cl), i, 136, 179; iv, 184; Richard, i, 107; Thomas, i, 121; Mrs. [L. 'Thwaites Fox'], i, 103.
Foxcroft, John (cl) (1619), iv, 58; Moses (cl) (1619), iv, 58.
Foxe, *see* Pool, S.J., James.
France, Mr. John, i, 167.
Francelin, Hugho, *see* Frankland, O.S.B., Hugh.
Franceys, Francis, Henry (cl), iv, 155, 156, 168.
Francis, William, iv, 4.
Franciscans, ii, 218; iii, 249; iv, 188, 192, 193, 203, 206, 207, 211, 215, 217.
Frane, Christopher, iii, 116.
Frank, Robert, i, 64; ii, 154; William, iii, 27.
Frankland, O.S.B., Hugh (R); 'Hugho Francelin,' iv, 208; Richard (P), iv, 225, 227, 228, 232; Sir Thomas, iii, 165; William, iii, 183.
Franks, Thomas (cl), iii, 106.
Frederick, Prince of Wales, iv, 230.
Freeman, Capt., iv, 231; James, iii, 225; Richard, iv, 58.
Freer, Samuel, ii, 217.
Frere, Walter; Bp. of Truro, Intr., vi.
Fretwell, James, Intr., xxiii; William, i, 62.
Friends; 'Quakers' Intr., x, xi, xxiii; i, 4, 10, 11*, 12*, 14, 15, 16*, 17*, 20, 21, 28, 29*, 30, 31, 33*, 34*, 42, 43, 44, 46, 49*, 50*, 54, 58*, 59*, 60*, 61, 62*, 63, 66*, 69, 70, 75, 76*, 77, 79, 80, 81, 85, 86, 88, 91, 93, 95, 103*, 105, 112*, 116, 118, 121, 124, 125*, 130, 131*, 133, 136, 140, 142, 143, 145, 149*, 156*, 160*, 161, 162, 164, 166*, 168, 170*, 171, 172, 173*, 177, 183, 184, 187, 191, 193-196, 200*, 207*, 209*, 216, 217; ii, 2*, 3, 4, 5***, 6, 8*, 12*, 20, 21, 23, 24, 26, 27, 29*, 30, 32***, 39*, 49, 53*, 55-58*, 61, 62*, 63, 66, 69, 71, 77*, 80*, 86, 87*, 88*, 92*, 93-6, 100, 106*, 108*, 111*, 112*, 116**, 121, 122, 124*, 125*, 126, 130, 139, 140*, 146-149, 153*, 155, 157, 158*, 166, 167*, 169, 173, 175*, 177, 183*, 189, 192, 193, 201, 203, 205, 208, 212-214, 217, 218*, 219; iii, 3*, 6, 7*, 8, 9*, 16*, 18*, 19*, 20*, 23*, 25*, 26, 27, 29*, 30, 33*, 41, 45, 46, 50, 54, 57*, 62, 64*, 65, 67, 88, 91, 92*, 93, 94, 97, 101, 102, 103*, 105, 106, 108, 110*, 114, 116, 117, 119, 124, 126*, 129*, 132*, 133*, 138, 140, 142, 143, 145, 146, 148, 150, 151, 156, 157, 162*, 165, 166*, 167, 168, 170, 175, 176, 179, 185*, 187, 188, 189*, 190, 193*, 199, 204, 205, 207, 208*, 210, 219*, 221, 227*, 233, 235-237*, 239, 244-246, 249; iv, 7, 9, 12, 21*, 22, 33, 39*, 42, 47, 49-51, 58*, 74, 76, 80*, 81, 89, 90, 92, 93*, 96, 99, 101, 102, 105-107, 109*, 110, 111*, 'Quaquers'; 113, 114, 119, 121*, 123, 124, 140*, 141, 144, 146, 148*, 155, 'Qukers'; 167, 170, 171*, 174, 176-178*; 'Almshouse', 180, 191, 213, 216, 232, 234-9; Friends' House, *see* London.
Froggott, John (cl), ii, 103.
Frost, Henry E., Intr., xxiii; John, i, 137; Thomas, i, 39.
Fryer, Cornelius, ii, 5.
Fuester, Richard, ii, 122.
Fuller, John (cl), i, 139; ii, 171; iii, 2, 3.
Furniss, John, ii, 35.

Gabbitas, John, iv, 42.
Gains, John, iii, 163.
Gale, Thomas (cl) (R. Linton), i, 36, 37; ii, 89, 90, 146; Thomas (cl) (R. West Rounton), iii, 30.
Gamble, George, ii, 122; Thomas, i, 8.
Gant, Benjamin, iii, 5.
Garbut, George, i, 92; William (*al.* Garbutt), ii, 126.
Gardam, Robert, iii, 114.
Garden, James (cl), ii, 58; iii, 97; Thomas, i, 150.
Garencières, Theophilus (senior),

M.D., iii, 135; Theophilus (junior) (cl), iii, 56, 135, 170.
Garforth, Mr., i, 20.
Garland, Richard, iii, 139.
Garnet, John (cl) (1699), iii, 168.
Garrick, David, ii, 159.
Garrit, Jeoffrey, i, 32.
Garside, John, ii, 31.
Garthwait, James, ii, 4.
Garton, Henry, iv, 180; William, gent., i, 102.
Gascoigne, Sir Edward, iv, 189, 190, 197, 198, 214, 215; Sir Thomas, iv, 220.
Gaskings, Thomas, iii, 253.
Gaunt, Richard, i, 60.
Gawthorpe, John, iii, 184.
Gaythorn, Ann, iii, 77, 79, 80.
Gearey, James, ii, 180.
Gee, Mrs. Elizabeth, i, 99; Elizabeth (midwife), iv, 161; James, Esqr., i, 99; Thomas, Esqr., i, 99.
Geen, Joseph (?=Green), i, 178.
George, H.M. King; First, i, 22; iii, 21; Second, i, 168; ii, 145; iii, 42, 43, 151; iv, 2, 62, 67, 188, 189, 235; Third, i, 63.
Gibson, Edmund; Bp. of Lincoln, Intr., vi, viii, xiv; James (cl), iv, 70, 71; John (cl), iii, 89; John, i, 201; ii, 39; iii, 175; Joseph, iv, 13; Mr. Richard, iv, 108; Robert, iii, 188; Thomas, iii, 65; William, iv, 129.
Gilbert, John; Abp. of York, Intr., xv; Mary, iv, 83, 84.
Gilby, Mr., ii, 136, 137.
Gilderson, Anthony, iii, 158.
Gill, Mrs., iii, 156; Daniel, iii, 19; Ebenezer (I), iv, 229; Fran: i, 13; George, iii, 154; Jeremiah (senior) (P), iv, 227; Jeremiah (junior) (P), i, 180; iv, 227; John, i, 78; ii, 112; Stephen, i, 197; Thomas, i, 149; iv, 203; William (cl), i, 204; iii, 65; William, ii, 31.
Gillam, Thomas, iii, 44.
Gilliott, Joseph, i, 194.
Gillow, Joseph; *Cath. Dic.*, iv, 187, 197, 200, 208, 210, 220.
Gilmore, O.S.B., Robert Paul (R), iv, 197.
Ginnings, George, i, 41.
Girling, *see* Gyrling.
Glaedall, *see* Glendall.
Gleadal, John [L. 'Glendall'], i, 72.
Gleadall, William, ii, 45.
Gleadhill, David, iii, 51.
Gleadow, Richard, iii, 73.
Glendall, John (*see* Gleadal); Thomas (*al.* Glaedall), iii, 81.
Gloucester, Bp. of (*see Places*, Gloucester).
Glover, Thomas, ii, 151.
Goakman, John, i, 98.
Godard, Samuel, ii, 184.
Godbourne, Thomas, iv, 90.
Goddard, Richard, i, 24.
Godfrey, John, i, 14; iii, 79; iv, 122; Peter, iv, 183; William (P), iv, 186; William, iii, 77.
Godley, John (cl), ii, 210, 211; William (*al.* Godly) (cl), ii, 159, 160.
Godson, Robert, ii, 66.
Goe, John, i, 14.
Golding, Sir Charles (1667); iv, 201; Sir Edward, 1st Bart., iv, 201; Sir Edward, 3rd Bart., iv, 29, 201; Edward, Esqr. (1642), iv, 201; John, iv, 201; Magdalen, iv, 201.
Good [L. 'William', 1641] (cl), i, 66.
Goodall, Benjamin, iii, 86; Joshua, i, 62.
Goodday, William (cl), iv, 14, 143.
Goodill, John, iii, 161.
Goodman, Canon, Intr., xxiv.
Goodrick, Philip, ii, 208.
Goodwin, George (cl), ii, 178; Richard (cl), iii, 156.
Gorbutt, William, ii, 221.
Gordon, — (R), iv, 212; Charles, ii, 94.
Gote, William, i, 108.
Gott, Joseph, i, 53.
Gouge, Nicholas (cl), ii, 221.
Gouthwait, Joseph, iii, 250.
Gowndril, George (cl), ii, 204; iii, 124, 128, 129, 131.
Gradell, Christopher, iv, 215; Christopher (R) (*al.* Gradwell), iii, 57; iv, 215.
Graham of Esk, Honble. Catherine, ii, 200; Charles, 3rd Viscount Preston, ii, 200; Honble. Mary Susan, ii, 200; Mr. Ranald (*al.* Grahame), ii, 200.
Graham, James, ii, 211; Martin, ii, 22; Thomas, ii, 22; William (cl), iii, 249, 250; William (P) (*al.* Greame, Gream), ii, 32; iii, 50; iv, 226, 229, 232.
Grainge, Mich., iii, 240.
Granger, Thomas, iii, 135.
Granville, Dennis, Dean of Durham, Intr., xvi.
Gravell, Robert, iii, 81.
Graves [John] (*see Places*, Cleveland); William, iii, 86; iv, 104.
Gray, Edward, iv, 136; Mrs. Edwin, ii, 138; James, i, 218; John, iii, 194; Robert, i, 176; Robert (M.D.),

iv, 13; Thomas, ii, 60.
Gream, Greame, *see* Graham, William.
Greaves, Mr., i, 155; Edward, iii, 203; George, iii, 58; John, iv, 76; Joshua, iii, 184; William, iii, 63.
Green, John (cl), iv, 145, 146; John, ii, 51, 218; iii, 48, 151; Joseph (*al.* Geen), i, 178, 202; Joshua, iii, 194; Thomas, iii, 148; William, iv, 179.
Greene, John, iv, 182.
Greenhalgh, Elias, ii, 176.
Greenup, John, iii, 142.
Greenwood, Charles (cl) (1642), ii, 37; Christopher, ii, 5; Mr. Henry, i, 165; John, ii, 36, 38 (2), 148; Luke, iii, 20; Paul, ii, 37; Thomas (cl), ii, 39; Thomas, iv, 183.
Greg, John, iii, 236.
Gregory, Mr., iv, 181; Edward (cl), iv, 39, 163.
Grenside, John (cl), i, 31; ii, 192.
Grey, Richard, iv, 163.
Griffith, John (cl) (senior), iii, 192; John (cl) (junior), ii, 140; iii, 194.
Grimeston, Robert, Esqr., i, 97.
Grimshaw, John (cl), ii, 150; John (Q) (*al.* Grimshay), iii, 16; iv, 238; William (cl), Intr., xix, xxii; ii, 39, 41.
Grimshay, *see* Grimshaw.
Grindred, John, iii, 50.
Grundall, Richard, iii, 125; Thomas, ii, 154.
Guest, Jonathan, i, 137.
Guilford, 1st Earl of, i, 63; 2nd Earl (Lord North), i, 63.
Gumbley, O.P., F.R.Hist.Soc., Walter (R), iv, 186.
Gunby, Christopher (cl), ii, 81; iii, 49, 50.
Gunthorp, Robert (cl), iv, 32, 141.
Gurnell, John, iv, 42.
Guy, Edward (cl), i, 57.
Gylby, Thomas (cl), iv, 42, 100, 124, 125.
Gyrling, Girling, Nicholas (cl), ii, 197.

Haggerston, Sir Carnaby, iv, 204; William, iv, 204.
Hagyard, William, ii, 207.
Haigh, Mrs., ii, 44; Francis (cl) (*al.* Haigue), i, 73, 76, 179; ii, 223; George, iii, 148; Mr. James, ii, 44 (2); John, i, 68; ii, 179; Joseph (cl), iii, 148, 149; Joseph, i, 63; ii, 211; Mr. Joseph (senior), ii, 43; Mr. Joseph (junior), ii, 44; William, iii, 63.
Haighton, Richard (cl), i, 49; iii, 180.
Haigue, *see* Haigh, Francis.
Hainsworth, Thomas, iv, 26.
Hakesley, James, iii, 154.
Haldenby, John, i, 14; ii, 55.
Haley, John, i, 62.
Halfpenny, Joseph, ii, 159.
Haliday, Jane [L. Helen Holliday], iii, 242.
Hall, Daniel (cl), ii, 163; David (Q), ii, 108; iii, 45; iv, 237, 239; Edward, iii, 98; George (cl), i, 32; John (cl), i, 62; ii, 166; John, ii, 171; iv, 14, 157; John George (*see Places*, Cave, South); Jo., iii, 42; Joseph (cl), iii, 155, 197; Leonard, i, 33; Robert, i, 194; ii, 108; Samuel, iii, 120; Thomas, i, 186; iii, 24; iv, 72; William, i, 33, 221; ii, 51; iv, 42.
Halliday, John, iii, 113.
Hallily, John, i, 223.
Halstead, George, ii, 38.
Hamer, William, ii, 114.
Hammond (D.D.) (cl), Henry (1660), iii, 7.
Hamshaw, Daniel (*al.* Hampshaw), iii, 253; George, i, 128; John, i, 128.
Hamsworth, Hemsworth, David, i, 44.
Hanley, William, i, 71.
Hanna, Thomas, iv, 159.
Hansell, John, ii, 217.
Hansom, J. S., iv, 195, 204.
Hanson, George, i, 64; Joseph, iii, 46; Thomas, ii, 209.
Harborough, Philip, 2nd Earl of, iv, 88.
Hardacre, Richard, ii, 3; iii, 16.
Hardcastle, Joshua (P), i, 59; iv, 225.
Hardesty, O.S.B., William Laurence (R), i, 183; iv, 203.
Hardey, John, iv, 170.
Harding, Richard, i, 33.
Hardwick, John, ii, 58; Thomas, ii, 20, 124; iv, 141.
Hardwicke, 1st Earl of, iv, 188.
Hardy, James, iii, 128; John [*al.* Thomas] (cl), ii, 116, 117; John, i, 98; iii, 125, 218; Matthew, i, 114; Richard (cl), iv, 76, 77, 78; Richard, ii, 17; Thomas, *see* John (cl); William, ii, 11, 151.
Hare, Laurence, iii, 185.
Hargreaves, Robert (cl), ii, 19, 20.
Harker, John, ii, 122; William, iii, 206.
Harland, Nicholas, i, 186; William, ii, 153.
Harney, James, ii, 51.
Harper, Christopher, i, 220; George, i, 120; James, i, 120; John, i, 86; Robart, i, 83; Thomas, iii, 251;

William (cl), i, 45.
Harrington, Earl of, iii, 31; John, ii, 166.
Harris, Christian, iii, 154; John (P), i, 103; iv, 225; Robert, iii, 154.
Harrison, Daniel, ii, 118; Edward, iii, 32; Elias (cl), ii, 107, 108; Franc., iii, 27; George, i, 144; iii, 26, 81; Hugh, iii, 13; Isaac, i, 60; John, ii, 13, 166, 191; iii, 92; Jeremiah (cl), ii, 147; iii, 46; John (R), iv, 194; John, iii, 97; Jos., i, 221; Ralph, ii, 59; Richard, ii, 22, 111; Robert, ii, 62; iii, 3; Roger, iii, 10; Stephen, ii, 24; Thomas (cl), ii, 121, 169; Thomas, ii, 68; iii, 46, 253; iv, 155; William (cl), iii, 203; William, iii, 4, 29.
Harrop, John (cl), ii, 222; Richard, ii, 183; Thomas (P) (*al.* Harropp), iv, 180, 230; Samuel (P), iv, 230.
Harsnett, Harsnet, Samuel; Abp. of York, i, 138.
Hart, Mr., iv, 32, 34; John, i, 144, 187; Mr. Matthew, iv, 108; Robert, iii, 103; William, iv, 121.
Hartley, Richard (cl), i, 50; Samuel, ii, 105, 140; Thomas, ii, 54.
Harwood, Charles, ii, 20; John, i, 70; Robert, i, 91.
Harworth, Richard, iii, 236.
Hascard, Henry (cl), iv, 132.
Hasletine, *see* Hesletine.
Hasleton, iv, 239.
Hassard, Thomas, iii, 74.
Hassell, Samuel (cl), ii, 98.
Hassleton, *see* Hesleton.
Hastings, Lady Elizabeth, i, 9, 124; ii, 144; iii, 142, 143, 144, 145; Lady Margaret, iv, 240.
Hastwell, Philip (cl), i, 12.
Hatfield, George (cl), i, 21; Joseph, iii, 153.
Hattersley, John, i, 65; Nicholas, i, 168; Robert, i, 14.
Hatton, O.B., D.D., Edward Antoninus (R), iv, 213, 218, 219.
Hautene, *see* Hawtene.
Hawkesworth, George, ii, 67.
Hawkins, John, iii, 91; Thomas, iii, 3.
Hawksby, Francis, iii, 241.
Hawksley, Richard, iv, 183.
Hawkswell, Rt. Rev. Monsgr., iv, 186; Richard (cl), iii, 92.
Haworth, Mr. Francis, ii, 79.
Hawtene, Hautene, [Lautene,] gent., Nicholas, Nichols, iii, 68, 69, 70, 71, 72, 73; Robert, iii, 74, 80, 81, 82, 83, 84, 85.
Hay, Joseph, i, 20.
Haydock, Cuthbert (R), iv, 219; William, Esqr., iv, 219.
Hayes, Ralph, iii, 103.
Hayne, Edward, iv, 10.
Hayson, Thomas, ii, 155.
Hayter, Haytor, *see Places* (York, Archdeaconry).
Hayton, James (cl), iii, 235; Samuel, i, 166.
Hayward, John, i, 173.
Haywood, John, i, 147.
Hazzard, William, iv, 89.
Head, John, ii, 92.
Headon, *see* Heddon, William.
Headley, Martin, iii, 73.
Heald, Thomas (cl), iv, 23, 113, 114.
Healey, George, iii, 75; William, i, 130.
Heath, Mrs., iv, 178.
Heaton, —, i, 165; John, i, 13, 70; Robert, ii, 111.
Hebblethwaite, Edward, iii, 230; John (cl), iv, 158; Thomas (cl), iv, 153, 158, 162.
Hebden, James, i, 90.
Heber, —, Esqr., i, 56; John (cl), ii, 175.
Heberon, George, iii, 102.
Hebleston, John, i, 128.
Heddon, George Henry (R), iv, 215, 218; William (*al.* Headon), ii, 93.
Heelhouse, John, i, 197.
Heighton, Thomas, ii, 176.
Heild, William, ii, 174.
Hell, Joseph, ii, 108.
Hemingway, Thomas, i, 138.
Hemsley, John, i, 159; Thomas, iii, 44.
Hemsworth, David (*al.* Hamsworth), i, 44; Stephen, iv, 114.
Henchman, Charles (cl), iv, 23, 24, 134.
Henlock, John, i, 221.
Henry, H.M. King; Eighth, Intr., vii; iv, 178.
Henson, John (cl), iv, 46, 133, 134, 182.
Hepton, John, iii, 7; William, iii, 2.
Heptonstall, John, iii, 4; Mark, i, 168.
Hepwell, William, i, 70.
Hepwood, *see* Hopwood, Thomas.
Hepworth, John, i, 200; iii, 154; Richard, iii, 188; Robert, iii, 154.
Herbert, Dr. A., iv, 186.
Herd, Henry (cl), ii, 186; iii, 243.
Herdsman, William (cl), iii, 102, 103.
Heron, Mr. Francis, ii, 88; Jo: i, 4.
Herries, 9th Baron, iv, 204.
Herring, John, Intr., v; Martha, Intr., v; Thomas, Abp. of York, Intr., v, vi, vii, viii, xiv, xv, xix,

xxii; i, 1, 2; iii, 190; iv, 188, 191, 193, 195, 212; v, 1-30 ['Your Grace', *passim*].
Hervey, Henry, iv, 196; John, *Lord*, iv, 235; Monox (R) (*al.* John Moxon; *al.* John Rivett), ii, 155, 157; iv, 192, 195, 196, 203, 209, 211, 216.
Hesketh, Robert (P), i, 131; ii, 32; iii, 187; iv, 225, 226, 228, 229, 232.
Hesletine, Hasletine, Thomas, iii, 4.
Hesleton, Hassleton, Philip (senior) (Q), iii, 103; iv, 239; Philip (junior), iv, 239.
Heslewood, Matthew, ii, 151.
Hesslegrave, John, ii, 45.
Hewett, Robert (cl), i, 40, 116, 220; iii, 175.
Hewit, James, ii, 147; John (cl), i, 56.
Hewitt, Mm., i, 103; Richard, iv, 148; Robert (cl), i, 101, 102.
Hewood, John, i, 72.
Hewytt, John (cl), ii, 49.
Hey, Robert, iii, 18.
Heywood, Oliver (P), iv, 228.
Hick, William, i, 121.
Hickington, Peter (cl), i, 161, 195.
Hickman, John, iv, 138.
Hide, William (cl), ii, 9, 128, 129; iii, 176.
Hilden, John, i, 51.
Hildyard, Christopher, Esqr., ii, 164; Christopher (cl), iii, 218.
Hill, Francis, iv, 81; John, ii, 173; iv, 162; John Samuel (cl), i, 188; iii, 7, 8, 211; Michael, ii, 194, 217; Richard, i, 83; Thomas, iii, 142; William, i, 52; iii, 40.
Hilton, James, iv, 56; Joseph, iv, 158.
Himsworth, Jo: iii, 48.
Hinch, Joseph, iv, 183.
Hinchcliffe, Edward, i, 63; James, ii, 222.
Hind, John, iv, 33.
Hindson, Joseph, iv, 139; William, iv, 112.
Hineley, John, iv, 101.
Hird, Sam., i, 50.
Hiron, Mrs., iv, 21.
Hirst, George, i, 19; ii, 31; James, i, 223; Margaret, ii, 116; Robert, ii, 44.
Hitch, Henry, Esqr., ii, 140; Robert (cl), i, 222.
Hoadly, Benjamin, Bp. of Bangor, Intr., xix; i, 35; iv, 129.
Hobkirk, John, iii, 56.
Hobson, John, i, 20; Robert, i, 9.
Hodgkinson, *see* Hopkinson, S.J., Charles (R).
Hodgson, George, iii, 130; H. R., iv, 236, 237; Hugh (cl), ii, 119; iii, 44; James, iii, 252; John, iii, 232; Nathaniel (cl), i, 208, 222; Richard, i, 83, 119; Thomas, i, 186; ii, 56; William (cl), i, 97; William, ii, 209; iii, 123, 133.
Hodson, Francis (cl), i, 92; ii, 59, 60, 126.
Hoggard, Richard, iv, 158.
Hoggart, Christopher, i, 214; William, i, 213.
Holden, Laurence (P), iv, 226.
Holder, John, iii, 48.
Holderness, Holdernesse, Earl of, i, 21; iii, 234.
Holdroyd, John, i, 63.
Holdsworth, Benjamin, ii, 142; James (cl), iii, 196; John (cl), ii, 32, 33, 34; Thomas (cl) (*al.* Houldsworth), i, 64.
Holey, Joseph, iv, 168.
Holgate, John, ii, 148; Robert, Abp. of York, Grammar Schools (Hemsworth), i, 73; ii, 45; (Malton), ii, 186; (York), ii, 199, 213 (*see Places*, York).
Holland, James, iv, 15; John (cl), iv, 184; John, iv, 31; Joseph, iv, 17; William, iii, 221.
Holliday, Helen, *see* Haliday; John, i, 216.
Hollings, Mr. Joseph, [L. 'Hollis'], i, 60; Mark, iii, 81, 82, 83, 85; Martin, iii, 81.
Holloway, John, iv, 50.
Holme, John (cl) (R. Kirk Sandall), ii, 51; iii, 52; John (cl) (A.C. Doncaster), i, 167; ii, 151; John (cl) (A.C. Barmston), i, 110.
Holmes, Mrs., ii, 32; Abr., ii, 105; John, iii, 172; Joseph, ii, 72; Joshua, iii, 152; Mary, iii, 154; Richard, ii, 95; Thomas, i, 58; iii, 46 (3); William, iii, 77, 78, 79, 80; iv, 16, 62.
Holt, Luke, iii, 148.
Honywood, Colonel, ii, 123.
Hood, William, ii, 186.
Hook, Daniel, iv, 46.
Hooke, Thomas (cl), i, 140.
Hooton, Jervas, iv, 98.
Hopetoun, Charles, Earl of, i, 223.
Hopkins, Daniel (cl), iii, 252.
Hopkinson, S.J., Charles (R) (*al.* Mr. Siddal, Sydal, Siddle), iii, 227; 'Hodgkinson', iv, 220; Jo: iii, 189; John (cl), ii, 131; iii, 228.
Hopper, Christopher, iii, 37; John, i, 91; Richard, i, 111.

Hopperton, William, iii, 93.
Hops, Thomas, ii, 174.
Hopton, James, ii, 181.
Hopwood, Mark, iii, 112; Robert, i, 10; Thomas (*al.* Hepwood), iii, 144.
Horace, *see* Flaccus.
Horbry, Thomas, iv, 170.
Hore, A. H. (cl), *Church in England*, iv, 235.
Horn, Timothy, ii, 133.
Hornby, George, iii, 14; John, i, 138; Matthew, ii, 221.
Horncastle, Thomas, iii, 86.
Horne, Mr., ii, 182; Caleb, i, 222.
Horner, Thomas, i, 12.
Horsefall, Timothy, ii, 40.
Horsfall, Abra., ii, 31; Henry, ii, 150; Michael, ii, 41; Thomas, iii, 149, 150.
Horsfield, John, ii, 115.
Horsley, John, iii, 213; iv, 37.
Horton, Thomas, Esqr., iii, 49.
Hossley, *see* Crosley, David.
Hotham, Henry, i, 100; John (P), iii, 39; iv, 232, 233.
Hothersall, John, iii, 73.
Hough, John, *see* Clough; Thomas (cl), iii, 151.
Houldsworth, *see* Holdsworth, Thomas.
Houle, Thomas, i, 24.
Hounshill, Martin (R), iv, 195, 198.
Houseley, Samuel, iv, 4.
Houseman, Henry, i, 43.
Howard, Dr. Charles (R), iv, 217; Mr. John (R), *see* William; Joseph, iii, 158; William, S.J. (R) (*al.* Mr. John), iv, 213, 214.
Howe, Juliana, *Lady*, iv, 49; Sir Scrope, 1st Viscount, iv, 49; Emanuel Scrope, 2nd Viscount, iv, 49.
Howit, John, iv, 161.
Howlet, Nicholas (cl), iv, 94, 130.
Howson, James, ii, 133; Ralph, iii, 154; Richard, iii, 18.
Hoyes, John, iv, 36.
Hoyland, Edward (cl), i, 168.
Hoyle, Jacob, iii, 52.
Hoyles, John, iv, 12.
Hubbock, James, iii, 206.
Huby, John 'the elder', i, 93.
Huddleston, E., Esqr., iv, 225; Francis, ii, 201.
Hudson, A. V., Esq., Intr., xxiii; Christopher, ii, 19; Franc: i, 208; George, ii, 61; Henry (cl), i, 7; Henry, i, 116; ii, 19; James, ii, 81; John (cl), ii, 71, 97; John, iii, 120; Samuel, iii, 130; Thomas (cl) (R. Scawton), iii, 95; Thomas (cl) (C. Idle), ii, 95; Thomas (cl) (A.C. Hexhamshire Chapel), iii, 249, 250; Thomas, i, 126, 129.
Hughs, William, ii, 197.
Hugill, Robert, ii, 191; Thomas, ii, 62; William, ii, 154.
Hullam, *see* Hulme.
Hulley, William, ii, 119.
Hulme, Hullam, Samuel (P), iii, 148; iv, 232.
Humble, Benjamin, ii, 3.
Humfrey, Henry (cl), i, 224; ii, 209; iii, 250.
Humpton, William (cl), i, 180.
Hungate, Family of, iv, 214, 215; Sir Charles Carrington, iv, 214; Robert (Grammar Sch., Sherburn-in-Elmet), iii, 65.
Hunt, Robert, i, 21; Thomas, i, 72.
Hunter [Joseph] (P), i, 70, 168; ii, 45; iii, 153, 251; iv, 199, 200; Thomas, iii, 231.
Huntingdon, Countess of, iv, 240.
Huntington, William (cl), i, 213; ii, 131, 132; William, iv, 150.
Hurst, John, iii, 63; Samuel (cl), iv, 38; Thomas, iii, 23.
Hurt, John, iv, 156.
Husband, George, iv, 95; William (cl), ii, 9, 202.
Huscroft, Roger, ii, 118.
Hussay, David, i, 25.
Hutch, John, iii, 25.
Hutchinson, Family of, iv, 78; Anthony, iii, 18; Anthony Cuthbert, O.S.B. (R), iii, 41; iv, 194, 216; Charles (cl), iv, 37, 108, 161; Edward, iv, 116; Eliza, iii, 79; John, ii, 98; iv, 94; Mr. [John], iii, 136; Colonel John (1664) and Mrs., iv, 78; Jonathan, iii, 77, 78, 79; Joseph, ii, 117; Robert, i, 219; Thomas, iii, 127; William, i, 223; iii, 148; iv, 164.
Huthwaite, Huthwait, James (I), i, 128; iv, 226, 229.
Huton [L. Hutton, *q.v.*], Mrs. Eleanor.
Hutt (R. D.), R. H. M. (cl), iv, 10.
Hutton, Mrs. Eleanor (*al.* Huton); iii, 2; Mr. George, iv, 112; Matthew (II), Bp. Elect of Bangor; Abp. of York; Intr., xix; i, 1; ii, 19; iii, 41, 42, 175, 176; Sir Richard (1617), iii, 73, 80, 81, 82, 83, 84, 85.
Hyde, George (cl), iii, 230, 242; Robert (cl), ii, 7; William (cl), iii, 160, 201.
Hyndford, John, Earl of, iv, 64.

Ibberson, John, i, 180.

Ibbotson, Robert, iii, 194.
Ideson, Humphrey, i, 58; iii, 46.
Illingworth, John, ii, 96.
Independents, Intr., x, xi; i, 15, 62, 176; ii, 26, 32, 43, 77*; iii, 46, 57*, 77, 114, 130, 235; iv, 21, 26, 45, 67, 92, 107, 142, 163, 223, 227, 230, 231 (or Presbyterians), iv, 17, 26, 76, 81, 109, 116*, 122, 144*, 167, 180, 224, 225, 232.
Ingham, Benjamin (M), i, 9, 49, 61; ii, 32, 210, 211; iv, 107, 240; Jonathan, iii, 50; Roger, iii, 63; William, iv, 240.
Ingle, Matthew, ii, 2.
Ingilby, William, gent., iv, 198.
Ingleby, John, iii, 240.
Ingleson, John, iii, 230.
Ingleton, Franc: iii, 56.
Ingram, Goodrick (cl), iii, 236, 238.
Inman, John, i, 51; Robert, iii, 55.
Ireland, John, i, 7.
Irish, John, i, 197.
Irwin, Arthur, 6th Lord, iv, 189.
Isaac, Thomas, ii, 85.
Isles, Family of (*al.* Eyles), iv, 205; William, i, 221.
Ismay, Joseph (cl), ii, 179.

Jackson, Ambrose [Eyles], S.J., (R), iv, 205, 212; Christopher (cl), ii, 199, 213; Edward, iii, 161; Francis, iii, 167; Hartley, i, 114; Henry (cl), i, 94, 148; John (cl) (R. Rossington), Intr., xix; iv, 127, 129; John (cl) (V. Sherburn-in-Harford-Lythe), iii, 122, 135; John, ii, 140; iii, 156, 207, 227; Sir John, Knt. (1617), iii, 74, 80, 81, 82, 83, 84, 85; Jonathan (cl), iii, 90; Michael, ii, 70; Ralph (cl), i, 30 (*al.* Randolph); ii, 128, 129; Richard (cl), iv, 73, 171, 173; Richard, iii, 92; iv, 138; Robert, iii, 126, 209; Roger, iv, 177; Thomas (cl), i, 117; ii, 134; iii, 13, 14; Thomas, i, 114; ii, 206; iii, 114; iv, 73, 236; William (cl), i, 6; William (B), ii, 108; iv, 242; William, iii, 88, 194 [*see* Johnson, Paul].
Jacobites, ii, 123, 200; iv, 190, 195, 196, 198, 203, 212.
Jacques, John, i, 167; Richard, iii, 236.
Jagger, William, ii, 44.
James, H. M. King; First, i, 16; ii, 38; iii, 73, 80; iv, 204.
James, Richard, iv, 87; William (cl), i, 138; iii, 10; William, iv, 103.
Jarratt, John, i, 114; Mr. John, ii, 75.
Jarrett, O.P., Bede (R), iv, 187, 213.
Jefferson, Abigail, iii, 79; Anthony, gent., iv, 213; David, iii, 79, 80; Emanuel, iii, 79; Mr. Francis, ii, 166; Henry (cl), i, 175; ii, 80; Mr. Joshua, ii, 54; iii, 76, 80; Robert (R), iv, 213; Robert, iii, 77, 79; Stephen, iii, 38.
Jefferys, Joseph (B), iv, 63, 241.
Jeffreys, Henry, ii, 22.
Jeney, Richard, i, 34.
Jenkins, D.D., Claude (cl), Intr., xxiv.
Jenkinson, Paul (cl), iv, 174; Thomas, iii, 24.
Jennett, John, ii, 45.
Jennings, Hugh, iii, 46; Jonathan, iii, 46.
Jennison, John, iv, 68.
Jephson, Alexander (cl), i, 222.
Jepson, John, iv, 5.
Jerdison, Robert, iii, 101.
Jerman, Thomas, i, 210.
Jesuit (Missions), i, 54, 64, 75, 142, 202; ii, 120; iii, 227; iv, 192, 195, 196, 198, 200, 201, 205, 208, 210, 211, 213, 214, 215, 218, 222; College of Immaculate Conception, iv, 193, 194; College of St. John Evangelist, iv, 193; Residence of St. Michael, iv, 193, 212.
Jewett, Thomas, ii, 93.
Jibson, Paul, i, 173.
Jinnings, Leonard, iii, 119.
Johnson, Elizabeth, iii, 154; George, iv, 61; Henry, iv, 156; John, i, 104; ii, 27, 106; iii, 251; iv, 141; Dr. [L. John], i, 116; Matthew, iii, 118; Paul, iii, 81, 83; 'Jackson', 84; 'Jackson', Richard, ii, 118, 119; iii, 125; Dr. [Samuel], iii, 51; Thomas, ii, 145; iii, 5, 12, 93; Timothy, i, 114; William (cl), ii, 176; William, i, 208; ii, 223; iii, 86, 92; iv, 66, 99.
Johnston, James, iii, 120; Samuel (cl), i, 102, 103; Thomas, i, 215; ii, 88.
Jollie, Timothy (P), iv, 227, 233; *Academy*, iv, 224, 232.
Jones, Isaac, ii, 218; John (senior), S.J. (R), i, 202; iv, 205.
Jowsey, William, iii, 211.
Joy, John, ii, 57; Seth, ii, 140.
Jubb, Mr. [Robert], ii, 98; Thomas, iv, 102.
Jugland, Matthew, i, 200.
Julian, John, i, 224.
Juman, Thomas, ii, 214; William, ii, 68.
Justice, David, ii, 171.

Kailey, John, i, 195.
Kay, John, i, 28; ii, 25; iii, 194; Richard (cl) (R. Moor Monkton), i, 77; ii, 174; Richard (cl) (V. Bilton), i, 78; Thomas, i, 19; ii, 214; William (cl), i, 33; ii, 200; William, ii, 223; iii, 194 (2).
Kaye, Sir John Lister, 5th Bart., i, 206, 207.
Kayley, Thomas (cl), i, 163, 164; ii, 168; iii, 105.
Kegg, William, i, 178.
Keighley, —, ii, 67; Samuel, iv, 93.
Kellingley, Widow, iii, 77.
Kelsall, Mr. John, iv, 110.
Kelsey, Robert, i, 95.
Kemp, Peter, ii, 93; William, i, 167.
Kempley, James, i, 146.
Kendal, George, iii, 154.
Kendall, Dr. G. (R), iv, 194; John, ii, 58; Richard, ii, 95.
Kendrey, Kendrew (Q), ii, 58; iv, 237.
Kenion, John, i, 222.
Kennedy, Prof. W. M. P., Intr., viii.
Kennet, Benjamin (cl), i, 59, 60; iii, 189; Henry (R), iv, 199.
Kent, John, iii, 23.
Kenyon, Adamson (cl), iii, 191; Thomas, i, 168.
Kerr, Joseph (cl), ii, 189.
Kerrich, Samuel, Intr., v.
Kettlewell, John (cl) (1695), i, 35, 95; John, ii, 186.
Key, Robert, iv, 74; William (cl), i, 14; William, iv, 81.
Keys, Thomas, iv, 183.
Keyworth, John, ii, 54; Richard, iv, 94.
Kidd, William (Q), ii, 62; iv, 237.
Kildill, John, iii, 209.
Kildrith, Francis, i, 209.
Kilham, Francis, iv, 57.
Kilks, William (cl), iv, 162.
Killener, Peter, iv, 106.
Kilvington, Charles, ii, 219; George, ii, 158.
King, Henry, i, 88; ii, 113; James, ii, 34, 39; John, ii, 203; iii, 251; Robert, ii, 9; Samuel, iii, 50; Thomas, ii, 4; iii, 147.
Kingston, Duke of, *see Places* (Hull).
Kippax, Robert, iv, 39.
Kirk, Andrew, iv, 45; Christopher, iii, 180; Edward, i, 154; Henry, iv, 182; John, i, 6; iv, 160.
Kirkby, Family of, ii, 99, 100; John (P), i, 61; iv, 225, 227; Mr. John, ii, 100; Mr. Mark (senior), i, 150, 151; Mr. Mark (junior), i, 151; Nicholas, iv, 122; Richard (cl), iv, 10; Robert, ii, 19.
Kirkbyson, George, ii, 122.
Kirke, John, Esqr., iv, 99.
Kitchen, Kitcheon, Philip (cl), ii, 190, 191, 223; Richard, iv, 80.
Kitching, Richard, ii, 51; Thomas, i, 33; iii, 65; William, i, 183.
Kitchingman, Robert, i, 147; Mr. Thomas, i, 89.
Kitson, Roger, i, 89; Samuel, ii, 209; Sir Thomas, iv, 201.
Knaggs, John, i, 185; William, ii, 157.
Knapton, Robert, iii, 109.
Knight, Bulleine (cl), i, 223; ii, 209; Robert (cl), ii, 24; Thomas, iv, 149; Mr. William, iv, 205, 221; Mrs. William, iv, 221.
Knights Hospitallers, iv, 231.
Knowles, George, i, 44; Henry, ii, 113; Joseph, i, 13; Law: iii, 183; Matthew (cl), i, 51; iii, 16.
Knowsley, John (cl), i, 111, 121; ii, 19, 138; iii, 37; Richard, i, 162.

Laborne, William, ii, 205.
Labray, Mr., iv, 176.
Lacey, Thomas, iv, 183.
Lake, Family of, ii, 198; David, iii, 187; Sir Edward, ii, 198.
Lakeing, Jonathan, ii, 158.
Lakeland, Robert (cl), i, 145; ii, 158; iii, 99, 111.
Lamb, John, i, 116.
Lambert, Lord, ii, 4; George, ii, 111; John, ii, 3; Major Gen. John [1683], iv, 227; John and Mrs., iv, 227; Margary, iii, 81; Matthew, ii, 115; Richard, iii, 253; Robert (cl), ii, 76; Robert, ii, 89; Thomas, iii, 24; iv, 28.
Lamplugh, Thomas (cl), i, 43.
Lancaster, John, i, 82; ii, 4.
Lane Fox, Fox; George, Esqr., i, 79; ii, 44.
Langdale, Family of, iv, 207, 213, 214; Lord, ii, 72; iv, 190; Christopher, ii, 121; Jo: iii, 151; Jordan, Esqr., iv, 213, 219; Marmaduke, 4th Baron, iv, 207.
Langley, Joseph, iii, 5; Richard, ii, 115; Mr. [L. Thomas], ii, 19.
Langstaff, John (cl), ii, 191; iii, 207; Thomas (cl), ii, 62, 63.
Lascelles, Francis (cl), ii, 222; iii, 4.
Lascells, Ralph, iii, 92.
Lautene, *see* Hawtene.
Laverack, George, ii, 129; John (cl), iv, 183, 185; John, i, 174; Robert, iii, 200.
Lavrack, Lavarrack, Richard, iii, 73, 81.

Lawne, John, i, 161.
Lawson, Benjamin, iii, 63; Richard, ii, 7; Richard, gent., ii, 190; Thomas (cl), i, 137; iii, 24; Thomas, ii, 157; Thomas, S.J. (R), iv, 210.
Lawton, Edward, yeoman, iii, 78, 80; George [*Collectio*], i, 70, 101, 153, 200, 205; ii, 29, 127, 223; iii, 111, 112; iv, 218, 233; John, yeoman, iii, 78, 80; John, iv, 52.
Lax, Samuel, iii, 188; Thomas (P), i, 112; iv, 225, 226.
Laybourne, Henry (cl), i, 189; ii, 73; Thomas, iii, 126.
Laycock, Mr. Edward, junior, i, 126; James, i, 91.
Layroyd, Leyroyd, Abra: iii, 20.
Layton, William, i, 116.
Lazenby, George, i, 181; John, ii, 56.
Leabarron, William, iii, 92.
Leach, Mr., iv, 229; Thomas (*al.* Leech) (cl), iv, 183, 184.
Leache, Joseph, ii, 178.
Leak, *see* Leake, Thomas.
Leake, Thomas (*al.* Leak) (cl), i, 99, 153, 156; William, i, 183.
Leaper, Robert, ii, 67; William, ii, 93.
Learey, Thomas, iv, 171; William, iv, 116.
Leathley, John, iii, 230.
Leatson, John, i, 115.
Ledger, John, iv, 38; Richard, iv, 38.
Lee, Edward, ii, 161; George, iii, 12; John, ii, 7; iii, 12, 23, 56; Ralph, iv, 26; Thomas, i, 165; Timothy (cl), i, 202; iii, 4.
Leech, John (cl), i, 169; Joseph (cl), ii, 53; Thomas, *see* Leach, Thomas.
Leeds, Duke of, ii, 47, 48, 49; iii, 148, 154; iv, 68.
Leek, Herbert (cl), iv, 33, 34; Mr. William, iv, 112.
Leeke, Samuel (cl), iv, 34, 79, 141, 185.
Lees, Thomas, iv, 75.
Leeson, John, iv, 184.
Leetham, Thomas, iii, 86.
Legg, James, i, 31.
Legget, Daniel, i, 221.
Legh, George, LL.D. (*al.* Leigh) (cl), i, 64, 131; ii, 31, 34, 36, 149; iii, 50, 51; iv, 194, 227; Helen, iv, 213; John, iv, 213.
Leigh, *see* Legh, George.
Leking, Abell, ii, 142.
Leppington, Robert, iii, 118.
Lewis, John (cl) [*Church Catechism Explained*], i, 162; ii, 129; Sir John, ii, 144; Squire, iii, 230; William, ii, 63; iii, 206.
Lexington, Lord, *see* Sutton, Robert.
Leybourne, Talbot (cl), i, 81.
Leyland, John (cl), iv, 96, 106; John, i, 51.
Leyroyd, *see* Layroyd.
Liddell, Thomas (R) (*al.* Liddle), i, 186; iv, 195, 196, 198, 203; William, gent., iv, 195.
Liddle, *see* Liddell.
Lightfoot, John, iii, 79; Richard, ii, 55; Thomas (P), ii, 210; iv, 231; Thomas, i, 27; William, iii, 238.
Liley, William, iii, 184.
Lincolne, Richard, ii, 9.
Lindley, George, i, 202; Henry, iii, 250; Ralph, ii, 112; Richard, i, 180; Samuel, ii, 142.
Lindsey, John (cl), ii, 156; John, ii, 112.
Linley, Thomas, iii, 154.
Linney, William, iv, 104.
Linsley, William, iii, 203.
Linthwaite, Mr. William, iv, 107.
Linton, Matthew, iii, 107; Ursula, iii, 107.
Liptrott, Mr. Richard, iv, 182.
Lister, Anthony (cl), ii, 6; James, i, 12; ii, 152; John, i, 50; Robert, iii, 200; Thomas (cl), i, 221; ii, 94, 95; Thomas, i, 203; ii, 150; William, i, 12.
Little, Henry, iv, 71; Mr. John, ii, 136.
Littlewood, John, i, 136; Joshua, ii, 50; Thomas, i, 169; ii, 222.
Liversedge, Joe, iii, 152; William, ii, 114.
Lloyd, John (cl), iii, 22.
Lock, John, i, 104.
Lockey, Richard, ii, 208.
Locksmith, George, ii, 60.
Lockwood, John, i, 14.
Lodge, John, ii, 30; Otwell, ii, 30.
Lofthouse, Francis, iii, 12; Henry, i, 56; Robert, ii, 56.
Lolley, William, ii, 93.
Lomax, —, iv, 34, 241.
Long, James, iv, 71; Thomas, i, 92.
Longburne, John, i, 188.
Longcaster, John, i, 83.
Longhorne, Longhorn, Robert, yeoman, iii, 78, 80.
Longley, John, ii, 117.
Longmire, George (cl), ii, 220; iii, 175, 176.
Longthorne, Roger, iii, 237.
Lonsdale Peerage, iii, 43.
Lonsdale, Lonsdayle, Lowndsdale, Christopher, iii, 81; John, iii, 72.
Lord, Edward, ii, 148; Henry (B), i, 131; iv, 241.
Lorriman, Edward, ii, 220.
Lounsdale, Robert, i, 196.

Lovell, John, iii, 172.
Lovett, Thomas (cl), iii, 12, 229.
Lowndsdale, *see* Lonsdale, Christopher.
Lowry, Mr. John, ii, 142.
Lowther, John (cl) (V. Eastrington), i, 194; John (cl) (A.C. West Leake), iv, 86; Mrs. [L. 'Mary'], i, 13; Richard (cl), Intr., xiii; iii, 43, 222; Sir Thomas, ii, 191; Sir William, iii, 42, 43.
Lowthorpe, William, iii, 222.
Loxley, John, i, 207; Thomas, i, 180.
Luck, Robert (cl), ii, 73, 74.
Ludlam, John (cl), iv, 74, 102, 182.
Ludlow, Thomas, iv, 113.
Lumley, Benjamin, ii, 222; Lady Elizabeth, iii, 168; Thomas (cl), i, 173; iii, 172; Thomas, iii, 42.
Lund, Henry, i, 57; John, i, 50, 210; ii, 142; Richard, ii, 208; Thomas, ii, 148, 199.
Lunn, Richard, i, 45.
Lupton, Francis, iii, 239; John, i, 51; Robert (cl), ii, 113; William, ii, 140; iii, 235.
Lutheran, iii, 190.
Lutherington, John, i, 172.
Lutwyche, Mr. Thomas, iii, 59, 60, 62.
Lynam, James (cl), iv, 98, 147.
Lysle, John (cl), i, 201.
Lyth, Robert, iii, 8.
Lythe, Michael (cl), iii, 12.

Machin, —, i, 126; Joseph (B), iv, 102, 242; Richard (B), i, 112; iv, 241.
Machon, William, iii, 55.
Mackereth, John (cl), i, 192; ii, 136; iii, 126.
Mackin, Samuel, ii, 115.
Mackley, John, i, 175; Thomas, ii, 74.
Maire, Christopher (R), iv, 195; Henry (*al.* Mayer, Mayor) (R), iii, 229, 234, 236; iv, 195, 198, 210; Peter, S.J. (*al.* Mayer) (R), ii, 199; iv, 195, 198, 210, 221, 222; William (R), iv, 195.
Major, John, i, 218.
Makin, Richard, iii, 86.
Malborn, Thomas (cl), ii, 49, 50.
Mallinder, Mark, iii, 201.
Mallison, James (P), i, 161; iv, 226, 229; Thomas, ii, 51.
Maltby, Hugh, iv, 72.
Malton, Earl of, ii, 47, 186, 188; iii, 86, 193, 194; iv, 189; Lady, ii, 55; William (cl), iv, 33.
Man, *see* Mann, William.
Man [L. Mann], Charles (cl), ii, 59.
Manby, Catherine, iii, 209.
Mander, *see* Maunder.
Manknowles, Mr. Lawrence, ii, 43.
Manley, Robert (cl), iv, 31, 69.
Mann, James, i, 11; Thomas, ii, 149; iii, 55; William (*al.* Man), i, 194 (*see* Man, Charles).
Mannatt, Abram, ii, 51.
Mannock, Sir Francis, iv, 220; Francis (S.J.) (R), iv, 220, 222.
Mansell, Robert (cl), i, 143; ii, 8, 125; William, iii, 96.
Marfitt, James, iii, 169.
Markham, Family of, iv, 211; Catherine, iv, 211; Thomas, Esqr., iv, 211; William, Abp. of York, Intr., vi.
Markland, Matthew (cl), iv, 122.
Marlborough, Duke of, ii, 123.
Maro, P. Vergilius, i, 80.
Marr, Robert, i, 156.
Marriott, Joseph, iv, 9; Randolph (cl), i, 168; T. Esqr., iv, 225; Thomas, iv, 24, 113.
Marsden, John (cl), ii, 179; Joseph, ii, 222; Robert (cl), iv, 119; Samuel (cl), ii, 18, 19, 157; Thomas, ii, 176.
Marsh, George, ii, 49; iv, 184; Josias, i, 171; Robert, iii, 192.
Marshal, Thomas, ii, 184.
Marshall, Benjamin, i, 167; Bryan, ii, 155; Edward (cl), i, 204, 205; ii, 152, 181; Francis, iv, 107; George, ii, 212; Gervas, iv, 185; Henry, ii, 147; Jacob, iv, 31; James, ii, 221; John, ii, 54; iii, 210; Joseph, i, 178 [L. Paul or Ralph], i, 186; Thomas (cl), iv, 115; Thomas, ii, 72.
Marson, John, ii, 160.
Martin, Jervas, iv, 62; Thomas, iv, 3; William (I), ii, 77; iv, 229.
Marum, Stephen, iii, 212.
Mary, the First, H. M. Queen, iv, 178.
Maslen, Matthew (cl), i, 138; iii, 198.
Mason [L. Francis], i, 127; John, i, 83, 86; ii, 60; Thomas (cl), ii, 201; iii, 169; William (cl) (R. Huggate), i, 161; ii, 73; William (cl) (V. Holy Trinity, Hull), Intr., xix; ii, 78; William (poet), ii, 78; William, i, 27; ii, 5.
Massey, Gabriel, iii, 18; John, iii, 65; William, i, 101.
Masterman, Francis, ii, 58; John, ii, 215; iii, 66; Richard, i, 14.
Masters, B.D., Robert (cl), Intr., v.
Mastin, Samuel, iv, 183.
Matchan, Mr. William, ii, 220.

Matchen, Mr. John, ii, 87.
Mather, Mr. Walter, iv, 91.
Matlock, John, iv, 183.
Matson, Francis (cl), i, 216, 217, 218, 219; ii, 90, 91, 196; iii, 135.
Matthew, Tobias, Abp. of York, iii, 73, 74, 75, 76, 80, 81, 82, 83, 84, 85.
Matthewman, John, i, 69.
Matthews, Andrew (cl), iv, 5, 91, 110; Edward (R), i, 221; iv, 197; John, ii, 142; Thomas, i, 221.
Mattison, James, ii, 213.
Maud, William, ii, 142, 209.
Maude, Lady Eveline, iv, 186.
Mauley, Lords de, iv, 202.
Maunder, Henry (cl), i, 143; ii, 8, 125 (*al.* Harry Mander).
Maw, Samuel, iv, 182.
Mawde, John, i, 7, 50.
Mawltby, Hugh, i, 198.
Mawson, John, ii, 108; Matthias, Bp. of Chichester, Intr., xiv; Thomas, i, 223; William, iii, 230.
Maxwell, Lady Winifrede, iv, 204.
Mayer, *see* Maire.
Mayes, Family of, iv, 219.
Mayfield, Edward, iv, 160.
Maynards, John, i, 101.
Mayor, Henry, iii, 58 (*see also* Maire).
Meades, Joseph, iv, 156.
Meadley, Theophilus, iii, 125.
Mease, Thomas (cl) (R. Scorborough), i, 99, 104, 106; iii, 113; Thomas (cl) (junior) (V. Cottingham), i, 156; iii, 116.
Medd, John, i, 92; Robert, ii, 68; Thomas, ii, 58.
Medley, James, ii, 114; John, iv, 25; Stephen, ii, 93.
Meek, Thomas, iii, 111.
Meggit, Robert, iii, 25.
Meller, John, iii, 6.
Mellings, Richard, iv, 39.
Melton, Abram, i, 19; *Lord*, iii, 192.
Mennel, *see* Meynell.
Mense, John (cl), i, 222.
Menthrop, Samuel, ii, 196.
Merchant Taylors Company, i, 122.
Merry England, iv, 189, 215, 218.
Merryett, John (cl), iv, 138.
Messenger, John (S.J.) (R), iv, 200; John, Esqr., iv, 200, 212.
Metcalf, Leonard, gent., iv, 216; Richard (cl), ii, 222 (2); Thomas, iv, 216; William, iv, 216; William (R), iv, 216.
Metcalfe, John (cl), ii, 37 (*al.* Metcalf), iii, 19; John, iii, 251; Robert, iii, 205; Thomas, i, 148; William, iii, 95.
Metham, Mr., iii, 160.
Methley, William, iii, 48.
Methodist Revival, Intr., xi, xxi, xxiii; iv, 224, 234, 235.
Methodists (*see also* Moravians), Intr., x, xi; i, 1, 9*, 10*, 49*, 59, 60 and 61 (12 or 13 M.H.), 129***, 133, 134, 179, 201; ii, 5**, 6, 26*, 27*, 30*, 113, 141, 148*, 178*, 210; iii, 4*, 18*, 21, 89*, 153; iv, 81, 82*, 83, 109*, 181, 191, 197, 230, 234, 235, 236, 242.
Meynell, Family of, ii, 120; iv, 190, 197, 208; George, Esqr., iv, 197; James, S.J. (R) (*al.* Meynhill), i, 127; iv, 195, 212; Roger, Esqr. (*al.* Mennel), iii, 170; iv, 218, 221; Roger, Esqr. (junior), iv, 222.
Meynhill, *see* Meynell.
Meyrick, John (cl), iv, 40, 53, 115, 116, 118.
Miall, J. G., iv, 223, 232.
Michell, Gilbert (cl), iv, 48.
Micklefield, Edward, ii, 171; James, i, 220; Joseph, iii, 138.
Micklethwait, Thomas, ii, 146.
Middlebrough, William, i, 126.
Middleton, Family of, iv, 208; Digby, iv, 211; Francis, 2nd Baron, iv, 103, 155, 167, 211; Henry, 5th Baron, iv, 211; Mrs. Jane [L. Jane Vickers], i, 134; John, i, 81; Thomas, iii, 234; Sir Thomas, 1st Baron, iv, 211; William, ii, 102.
Midgley, Mr., ii, 149; Jonathan, i, 46; Joseph, ii, 40; Joshua, i, 6; Robert (cl), Intr., xix; i, 147; ii, 69; Robert (M.D.), ii, 69; Robert, i, 143; Samuel (cl), ii, 121; iii, 250.
Midleton, Charles, iii, 250; Daniel, i, 165; John, ii, 41; Thomas, iii, 86.
Milbourn, George, iv, 184.
Millar, *see* Milner, John.
Miller, John (cl), ii, 4; John, i, 180, 223.
Mills, Christopher, i, 33; John, i, 33; Mr. Thomas, iv, 107; William (cl), i, 41; iii, 217, 224.
Milman, Catherine, iii, 79.
Milner, John, ii, 139, 187; iii, 154, 155 (*al.* Millar); Jonathan, ii, 191; Joseph (cl), iv, 8; Jos: iii, 149; Thomas, i, 38.
Milnthorpe, Joseph, ii, 198.
Minett, William, iv, 57.
Minskip, William, iii, 199.
Minto, John, ii, 126; William, ii, 11.
Mirfield, Thomas, iii, 152.
Mitchel, Samuel, i, 61; William, i, 61.
Mitchell, Henry, i, 50; John, i, 132; iv, 138; Samuel, i, 41; Timothy,

ii, 114; William, iii, 234; William (B), iv, 241.

Mitchelson, Robert, iii, 127; William, i, 118.

Mitchil, Mitchill, William, yeoman, iii, 78, 80.

Mitton, William, ii, 115.

Moiser, John, i, 86.

Moises, Edward (cl) (senior), Intr., xix; iv, 76, 134, 160, 183; Edward (cl) (junior), iv, 11, 12, 120; Hugh (cl), iv, 12, 160.

Molyneux, Molineux, Sir Charles, iv, 78, 79.

Montgomerie, Esqre., Hugh, ii, 74.

Monthly Review, The, iv, 228.

Monzor, Richard, iii, 55.

Moody, William, iv, 151.

Moor, Francis, i, 199; George, i, 146; James, ii, 15; Ralph, iii, 214; Robert, ii, 89; Mr. Thomas, i, 72; Thomas (senior), ii, 28; Thomas (junior), ii, 28; William [L. Moore], i, 134.

Moore, Jo: iii, 148; William, i, 87 (*see* Moor).

Moorhouse, Edward (cl), iii, 52; John, ii, 5; iii, 151.

Moravians, Intr., x, xi; i, 61; ii, 32, 178; iv, 234, 236, 240.

More, Family of, iv, 195, 198; Mrs., iv, 195, 210, 221; Anne (Mrs. Charles Waterton), iv, 214; Christopher Cresacre, iv, 221; Mrs. Chr. Cres., iv, 221; Thomas, Esqr., iv, 195, 198, 221; Sir Thomas, iv, 198, 214.

Morehouse, H. J., Intr., xiii; ii, 116.

Morfitt, John (cl), ii, 222.

Morland, Richard, i, 209.

Morley, — (B), iv, 181, 242; Martin, i, 194; Richard, ii, 197; Thomas (cl), i, 92; ii, 59; Thomas, ii, 98.

Morrell's *Hist. of Selby*, iv, 215; William (cl), i, 104.

Morris, John, iv, 67; Henry, iv, 68; M.C.F. (cl), ii, 138; William, iii, 52; iv, 183.

Morrit, George, iii, 62; Mrs. Sarah [L. Morritt], i, 138.

Mortimer, John, ii, 31; Marmaduke, i, 82; Michael, i, 129; Thomas, i, 61.

Morton, George, iv, 23; John (P), ii, 20; iii, 143; iv, 229, 232; John, i, 200; Robert, iii, 154; Thomas, iii, 160.

Morvill, Thomas, i, 50.

Moseley, Esqre., Francis, ii, 73.

Mosey, William (cl), ii, 133, 162; iii, 113; William, i, 216.

Mosley, John (cl), iv, 168; Joseph, i, 171; ii, 180; iii, 6; Nicholas (cl), i, 121; ii, 20; [Sir Oswald], iv, 168; Richard (cl), iii, 40, 142, 210, 211; iv, 222; Thomas (cl), ii, 208; iii, 2.

Moss, John, i, 223.

Mote, George, iv, 103; Thomas, ii, 119.

Motherby, Henry, iii, 82, 84; Isabel (*al.* Issabel), iii, 82, 84; William, iii, 82, 84.

Mottershaw, Thomas (cl), iv, 23, 24, 169.

Mottram, Samuel, iv, 184; Thomas, ii, 151.

Mould, Thomas, gen., ii, 132.

Mounshill, Martin (R), *see* Hounshill.

Mount, James (cl), iii, 182, 183.

Mountain, John, iii, 230.

Mower, Edmund (cl), iv, 39, 73.

Moxon, Jacob, i, 202; John, iii, 158 (*see* Hervey, Monox).

Moyser, Esqr., John, i, 42.

Mudd, William, iii, 40.

Mullin, Henry, ii, 49.

Munkman, Thomas, ii, 124.

Murgatroyd, John (cl), ii, 143; iii, 49; Thomas (cl), ii, 156; Thomas, i, 57.

Murray, Alexander, ii, 221; Gideon (cl), ii, 221, 222; James, ii, 221; Patrick, *see* Elibank.

Murton, Robert, i, 22.

Musgrave, Richard (cl), i, 210; ii, 185; iii, 108; Richard, i, 10; iv, 240.

Mussey, John, ii, 190; Robert, ii, 58.

Myers, Mr., i, 40; John, i, 129; Thomas, ii, 119.

Myres, John, i, 83.

Naish, James (cl), iv, 69, 80; Richard (cl), iv, 2, 69.

Naylor, James (Q), iv, 232; John, i, 15, 51, 223; Oliver (cl), ii, 219, 220; Richard, ii, 38; Thomas (cl), i, 101; iii, 189.

Neesome, John, ii, 192.

Nelson, Edward (cl), ii, 130; Jesse, i, 61; John (M), Intr., xi; i, 61, 133; iv, 240; Richard (cl), iii, 202, 203; Robert, ii, 168; William, ii, 65.

Nesfield, John (cl), iii, 26, 162; Samuel, iii, 221; William, ii, 18.

Netleship, George, iv, 73.

Nettleton, Mr. [L. George], i, 205; Robert, i, 16.

Nevell, James, iii, 145.

Nevill, Widow, i, 181.

Neville, *see* Scarisbrick.
Newbold, Mr. George, i, 167.
Newburne, George, ii, 216.
Newby, Francis, iii, 86; Jo: iii, 185.
Newcastle, Duke of, iv, 20, 53.
Newham, W., iv, 3.
Newlove, Christopher, iii, 252; Michael, ii, 134.
Newman, Walter (Q), iv, 121, 238.
Newstead, George, iii, 18; Thomas, i, 210.
Newton, Daniel, iv, 168; Sir Isaac, ii, 147; Jo: iii, 151; John, ii, 63; Jonas, ii, 117; Matthew, ii, 162; Stephen (cl), i, 79, 199; Thomas, ii, 157.
Nichols, Francis, i, 114; Jonathan, i, 124; Nicholas (cl), iii, 9.
Nicholson, Edmund, Esqr., iv, 96, 105; Gervas, iv, 131; Joseph, i, 137; Richard, i, 33; William, ii, 47.
Nightingale, Thomas, i, 29.
Nithsdale, 5th Earl of, *see* Herries.
Nixon, Francis, i, 71.
Noble, Laurence, iii, 180.
Nobles, James, ii, 117; Thomas, i, 19, 20.
Nockalls, *see* Nuckalls.
Nodder, John, gent., i, 180; Thomas, i, 65.
Noel, Esqr., Thomas, iv, 76.
Norcliff, Esqr., Thomas, ii, 139, 162.
Norfolk, Dowager Duchess of, ii, 175; iv, 194, 210; Edward, 9th Duke, i, 44; iv, 188, 190, 198, 215, 219; Thomas, 8th Duke, iv, 210; Christopher, i, 139.
Normanton, Benjamin, i, 131.
Norris, Christopher, iii, 240; Thomas, iii, 95.
Norrish, William, iv, 131.
North, Lord, *see* Guilford; Matthias, iii, 226.
Northin, Joshua, i, 131.
Norwood, John, iii, 212.
Nottingham, Edward, i, 128; Mr. John, i, 36.
Nourse, D.D., Peter (cl), iii, 21.
Nowell, Thomas, i, 132.
Nuckalls, Nockalls, Richard (cl), ii, 87.
Nudding, Michael, ii, 63.
Nuttall, Joshua (cl), i, 123, 124.
Nutter, El. [L. Ellis] (cl), i, 57.
Nutting, Walter, ii, 171.

Oakeley, Richard, iii, 110; William (cl), iii, 110, 111.
Oastler, George, iii, 166; John, iii, 167; William, ii, 172.
Oates, George, iii, 195; James, ii, 111; William, i, 124.
Oats, Martha, iii, 79, 80.
Ockerhausen, Ockerhousen, Occashouss (Mor), i, 49; ii, 178; iv, 240.
Oddie, Richard, iii, 23.
Ogden, Amos, iii, 50; Edward, i, 132; James, ii, 39; Samuel (cl), Intr., xix; i, 131.
Oldfield, Jonathan, ii, 209; William, i, 200; iii, 180.
Oldham, Samuel, iv, 13.
Oldridge, Peter, i, 204.
Oldroyd, Samuel, i, 223.
Oliver, Jo: iii, 185; Joseph, i, 166; Joshua, i, 166.
Olliver, Christopher, iii, 230; John, iv, 69; Stephen, iv, 113; William, i, 221.
Ombler, Peter, iii, 13; Thomas, iii, 174.
Orange, H. R. H. Princess Anne of, Intr., xiii; iii, 43; iv, 2.
Ord, John Walker, iv, 202.
Ordidge, Senior, iv, 147.
Orton, Job (P), iv, 230.
Osbaldeston, Richard, D.D., Dean of York, Intr., xiii, xix; i, 216; ii, 63, 91, 196; William, ii, 90.
Otley, George, ii, 124; Henry, ii, 53; John, iii, 92; Thomas, ii, 204; William, iii, 64.
Ott, John Henry (cl), Intr., xiv, xx; iv, 31, 32, 64.
Outhwait, William, iii, 235.
Outhwaite, Richard, ii, 9.
Overend, George (cl), iii, 106.
Owston, Peter, iii, 122; William, ii, 124.
Owthwaite, John, iii, 42.
Oxford, Countess of, iv, 111.
Oxley, Abraham, ii, 51; George, ii, 50; Matthew, iii, 63.
Oxspring, Joshua, i, 180.
Oxtaby, Stephen, ii, 195.
Oxton, John, iii, 122; Thomas, iii, 132.

Padget, John, ii, 150.
Page, John, i, 203.
Paige, Ralph, iii, 170.
Palliser, Mark, iii, 90.
Pallisser, Walter (cl), iv, 6, 42, 149.
Pallister, George, i, 26; ii, 20; John, ii, 71, 121.
Palmer, Mrs., iv, 95; Raymond (O.P.) (R), iv, 189; Thomas (B), i, 98; ii, 78; iv, 241, 242.
Pape, Thomas, iii, 130, 178.
Papists, *see* Roman Catholics.
Parcival [L. Percival], Mr. Nathanael, i, 138.

Park, William, i, 110; iii, 7.
Parke, Roger, iii, 7.
Parker, Mr. Christopher, iii, 42, 182; George, i, 78; Jeoffrey, ii, 113; John, i, 62; John, Esqr., iii, 182, 251; Mr. John, iv, 124; Colonel John, C.B., F.S.A., Intr., xxiv; iv, 186.
Parkin, Bartholomew, ii, 48; John, i, 22, 186; Mary, iii, 154; William, ii, 127; Mr. William, iii, 58, 59, 61.
Parkinson, John, ii, 5; iii, 7, 183; Robert, ii, 111; Simeon, ii, 5; Stephen, i, 197.
Parkyns, Mrs. Ann, iv, 27; Lady (the late), iv, 11; Sir Thomas, iv, 11; Sir Thomas (the late), iv, 27.
Parne, Thomas (cl), iii, 251.
Parnell, William, ii, 181.
Parr, Benjamin, iv, 92; Mr. Job, iv, 182.
Parsons, John, iv, 169.
Pashley, John, i, 180.
Patrick, Jacob (Q), iii, 238; iv, 238.
Pattison, James (cl), iii, 240; Richard, i, 143; Thomas, iii, 128.
Pawson, Thomas, i, 224.
Payler, Esqr., Nathaniel, iii, 178.
Payley, Robert, ii, 147; William, ii, 7.
Payne, M.A., J. Orlebar, iv, 187, 206, 213, 218.
Peacock, Mr., iv, 229; Benjamin, i, 145; John, ii, 156; Thomas, ii, 156; William, iii, 163.
Peal, *see* Peile.
Pearson, Family of, iv, 238; James (cl), i, 146; ii, 193; James, i, 60; John (cl), i, 118; ii, 137; John, ii, 10; iii, 9; Nathaniel (cl), iii, 55; Peter, i, 121; Richard, i, 130; Thomas, ii, 16; iii, 56, 60, 157; Mr. Thomas, iv, 182 (*see also* Pierson, Robert).
Pease, Jos: ii, 106.
Peat, Thomas, iv, 163.
Peck, William, iv, 173.
Peckett, James, i, 33.
Peel, John, ii, 111.
Peers, William, ii, 221.
Peete, Thomas (cl), iv, 99.
Peile, Peal, Benjamin (P), iii, 249; iv, 229.
Peirson, John, iii, 27; Robert (cl), i, 28.
Pendlebury, William (senior) (P), iv, 230; William (junior) (P), iii, 21; iv, 230.
Penn, Alexander (cl), iv, 53, 116.
Pennington, Richard, iii, 144; William, ii, 102.
Pennock, William, ii, 190.
Penny, —, gent., ii, 99.
[Pennyman], Penyman, Sir James, i, 103.
Penock, John, i, 160.
Peploe, Samuel, Bp. of Chester, Intr., xxiv.
Pepper, Mrs. Jane, iv, 176.
Percival, *see* Parcival.
Perkin, Joseph, i, 20.
Perkins, Henry, gent., iii, 91; Jonathan (cl), i, 171; iii, 6.
Perrott, Andrew (cl), i, 79, 80.
Petch, John, i, 185.
Peter Mary of St. Theresa, *see* Seel.
Peterkin, Robert, ii, 162.
Petra, Cardinal, iv, 188.
Petre, Bishop, iv, 187, 210, 220; Lady, iv, 190, 214; Robert, 7th Baron, iv, 214.
Pettinger, John, iv, 100.
Petty, George, iii, 42; John, i, 123; Richard, i, 124.
Petyt, Mr. [L. Silvester Petyt], iii, 45.
Philips, William, ii, 67.
Phillips, Daniel (M.D.), iii, 61; Philip, i, 95.
Piatt, Pyatt, S.J., John (R), iv, 221, 222.
Pickard, Leonard, ii, 208.
Pickering, Capt., iv, 232; Dennis, iii, 185; James, iii, 56; Joseph, ii, 159; Matthew, i, 29; Richard, ii, 176; iii, 29; Robert, i, 99.
Pickersgill, William, ii, 178; iii, 18.
Pickman, James, i, 201.
Pidding, John (cl), i, 96.
Piercy, James, ii, 16; Michael, iii, 251.
Pierrepont, Pierpoint, Family of, iv, 210; Dame Frances, iv, 8.
Pierse, Mr., ii, 70; John, gen., i, 105.
Pierson, Bradshaw, Esqr., iv, 188, 217; Robert (*al.* Pearson) (Q), iii, 7; iv, 238.
Pigate, John, iii, 198.
Pighells, Pighell, Richard, ii, 107, 108.
Pigot, Hollis (cl), i, 166, 167; ii, 151.
Pilkington, Mr., iv, 167.
Pilley, William, iii, 156.
Pilling, John (*al.* Mr. John), i, 167; Joseph, ii, 35; William, ii, 31.
Pimm, John, iv, 12.
Pindar, John, ii, 124; Joshua (Q), ii, 12; iv, 236; Robert (cl), iv, 102, 149, 151; William, ii, 195.
Pinder, Edward, ii, 93; James, iii, 124; William, i, 186.
Pinkard, John (R), iv, 216, 217.

Pinkney, Christopher (Q), iii, 238; iv, 238.
Pirkin, William, iv, 64.
Place, Christopher (cl), iii, 94; Mr. John, iv, 110.
Plaskett, William (cl), ii, 16; iii, 221.
Plaxton, John (cl), iii, 112, 213.
Pleydell, *see* Downe.
Plompton, Family of, iv, 190, 216; Elizabeth (Mrs. Knight), iv, 221; Robert, Esqr., iv, 216.
Plummer, George, iii, 162.
Plumpton, Edward, iii, 253; Henry (cl), ii, 55; iii, 25, 67, 86.
Plumptre, Mr., iv, 181.
Poad, Richard, iii, 8.
Pogson, John, iv, 63.
Pole, Poole, Family of, iv, 201; James, S.J. (*al.* Pool, *al.* Foxe) (R), iv, 199, 214.
Pollard, Benjamin, iii, 148; Richard (cl), i, 221; Richard, i, 131; Samuel, ii, 42.
Pool, William (cl), ii, 70, 71; iii, 107 (*see also* Pole).
Poole, Edward (cl), iv, 87 (*see also* Pole).
Pooles, John, iii, 194.
Popish Plot, iv, 210.
Popplewell, Joseph, iii, 154; Richard, ii, 35.
Porrit, Peter, iii, 104.
Porritt, Jonathan, i, 62.
Porteous, Andrew (P), i, 29; iv, 225.
Porter, Christopher, ii, 205; Thomas, i, 223.
Portland, Duke of, iv, 184.
Posket, Joe, iii, 144; John, i, 44.
Postgate, Nicholas (R), iv, 188, 204, 222.
Potter, John, Abp. of Canterbury, Intr., v; Robert (cl) (V. Stillingfleet), iii, 91, 92; Robert (cl) (V. Collingham, Yorks.), i, 124; ii, 144; Robert, iii, 179; William (cl), i, 93; ii, 67; William, ii, 124.
Pottinger, William, iv, 64.
Potts, Dom. Bede, O.S.B. (R), i, 189; iv, 204; Luke (R), iv, 203.
Pouls, Thomas, iii, 194.
Powell, Christopher, i, 80.
Poynton, Thomas (cl), iv, 11, 120.
Precious, William, iii, 210.
Presbyterians, Intr., x, xi; i, 4, 5, 10, 13, 25*, 29*, 43-45, 47-49*, 52, 53, 58* (59), 60*** (61), 62*, 63, 73*, 74*, 75, 80, 93, 98*, 101-103*, 112*, 115, 118, 121, 122, 124, 125, 128**, 129*, 130*, 131*, 133, 149, 150*, 161*, 162, 166*-168, 176, 179, 180*, 193, 194, 197, 199, 201, 204*, 210, 212*; ii, 3*, 4*, 8, 20*, 23, 24, 26, 32, (7 M.H.), 35, 39 (4 M.H.), 41, 53, 66, 74, 75, 77, 78*, 79, 88, 92*, 93, 95*, 96*, 106*, 113, 116*, 131, 140**, 148, 149, 167, 169, 170, 178*, 185, 187*, 190, 202, 203, 205, 207, 209*, 215, 220; iii, 3*, 4*, 5*, 14-16, 18, 19, 21*, 30, 39*, 40, 45, 49*, 50*, 54, 57*, 65*, 66, 113, 114, 116, 133*, 136, 140, 141, 143*, 144, 148*, 150, 158, 162, 182, 185*, 187*, 188*, 190, 196, 197, 207* (208), 211, 221, 239*, 244, 246-249**; iv, 2, 3*, 11, 13, 14, 16-18, 23, 49, 61, 63*, 66, 75, 80*, 84, 86, 90, 92, 94, 97, 102, 107, 114, 118, 121, 123, 124*, 133, 142, 143, 146, 152, 153, 155, 156, 163*, 169, 170, 174*, 176*, 178*, 180*, 213, 223-225, 227, 228, 230, 232, 235, 242 (*see also* Independents).
Pressick, George, ii, 157.
Prester, Robert, ii, 28.
Prestley, John, iv, 111.
Preston, John (cl), ii, 131; John, i, 13; ii, 65; Joseph, i, 13, 223; 3rd Viscount (*see* Graham of Esk).
Pretender, The Old, iv, 230.
Priaulx, Peter (cl), iv, 182.
Priest, Elizabeth, iii, 6.
Priestley, Thomas, ii, 148.
Prince, Edward, iii, 196; Thomas, iii, 66; William, iii, 3.
Prior, John (cl), ii, 140.
Procter, Metcalf, Esqr., iii, 18; Ninian, iii, 240.
Proctor, Bradford, iii, 86; John, iii, 86; William, ii, 148.
Prudhom, Prudom, Joseph (cl), i, 114, 218.
Prudom, George, ii, 89.
Prust, Richard, ii, 60.
Pudsey, George (cl), ii, 134.
Pugh, Maurice (cl), iv, 175, 176, 177 (2).
Pullein, Henry, iii, 42; Moses, iii, 244; William, ii, 178.
Pulleine, John, i, 46.
Pullen, Henry, ii, 168; Robert, iii, 23, 153; William (cl), ii, 214.
Purslove, Matthew, iii, 18.
Purston, William, i, 53.
Pyatt, *see* Piatt.
Pybus, John, iii, 209.
Pyle, Mr., Intr., xiv.

Quakers, *see* Friends.
Quick, Canon O. C. (cl), Intr., xxiv.

Radcliffe, John, i, 24.
Radclyffe, John (cl), ii, 35.
Radley, John, i, 28; Joseph, iii, 24.
Ragdale, John (cl), iv, 180.
Ragnall, Jo: ii, 145.
Rainder, Joseph, i, 125.
Raine, Thomas, ii, 139.
Raines, Family of, iv, 216 (*see also* Watson, Joseph (R)).
Rainforth, John, iii, 151.
Rakes, John (cl), iii, 230, 231.
Ramsbottam, Mr. Francis, ii, 96.
Ramsden, James, ii, 95; John, iii, 150; Sir John, i, 16; Mr. Robert, ii, 96.
Ramstar, Richard, i, 21.
Rand, Raines, *see* Watson, James.
Randall, William, iii, 222.
Rands, Richard (cl), i, 200.
Rankey, *see* Rankin.
Rankin, Rankey, Thomas (M), i, 49; iv, 240.
Ransom, Thomas, iii, 31.
Ransome, John, i, 116.
Ranson, George (cl), i, 89; ii, 120.
Raper, Brian, i, 204; Edward, i, 148; iii, 166; John, iii, 163, 165.
Rase, Richard, ii, 187.
Raskill, William, i, 118.
Rastall, W. Dickinson, Intr., vi.
Ratcliffe, John, ii, 150; iii, 20.
Raunes, Jo: ii, 173.
Rawdon, William, i, 47.
Rawling, Richard, i, 183; William, iii, 235.
Rawson [L. Widow], i, 126; Mr. Joseph, iv, 230; Samuel, iv, 184.
Rawstorne, William (cl), i, 65.
Ray, Josiah (cl), ii, 21; iii, 144; Richard, iii, 42.
Rayner, Joseph, iii, 5.
Raynor, Thomas, iv, 92.
Read, Joseph, iv, 63; Richard, ii, 84; William, iii, 217.
Reasby, Reasbye, *see* Reresby.
Redfern, William, i, 20.
Redish, Charles, iv, 185.
Redman, Esqr., Thomas, i, 195.
Reed, Mr. [L. Charles], i, 164; Thomas, iii, 253.
Rees, Delanoy (cl), iv, 184; Oakeley (cl), iv, 178, 179.
Regium Donum, iv, 235.
Reid, Farindon (cl), iv, 96.
Remington, Thomas (cl), i, 176; iii, 213.
Renard, William, i, 52.
Rennison, John, i, 43.
Renolds, John, iv, 20.
[Reresby], Reasby, Reasbye, Esqr., John [later Sir John, Knt.], iii, 68, 69, 70, 71, 72.
Retford, Richard, iii, 148.
Rether, Richard, iii, 126.
Revell, Family of, iv, 199; Anne, iv, 199; Mr. Richard, iv, 199.
Rewell, Henry, i, 72.
Reynard, William, iii, 151.
Reynolds, Robert (cl), i, 122, 162; iii, 141.
Rhoades, Edward, iii, 42.
Rhodes, Abraham, iii, 63; David, ii, 209; Edward, iii, 182; Robert, i, 79, 133; Thomas (cl), i, 63; William, i, 221; ii, 3; iii, 21, 187.
Richard, William, i, 167.
Richards, Edward, iv, 110.
Richardson, Alexander, iv, 164; Charles (cl), i, 107; George, ii, 19; Henry (cl), iii, 146; James, i, 91; Jo: i, 197; John (cl), iv, 111, 147; John (Q), Intr., xxiii; ii, 124, 153; iv, 236, 237, 238; John, ii, 160; iii, 229; Joseph (cl), i, 219, 220; Nicholas, i, 30, 120; Robert, iv, 157; Thomas (cl), iv, 25, 103, 173; Thomas, i, 221; ii, 133; iii, 36; William (cl), iv, 100, 159; William, i, 222; ii, 93; iii, 66; iv, 114, 237, 238.
Richinson, William, iii, 18.
Richmond, Henry, ii, 197.
Rickaby, Cornelius (cl), i, 113, 114, 218; ii, 18.
Rickard, John, iii, 81, 82, 84; William, iii, 73.
Riddel, Family of, iv, 207.
Ridley, William (cl), iii, 184.
Ridsdale, Christopher, i, 208; William, iii, 175.
Rimer, Richard, i, 89.
Ringrose, Matthew, ii, 57; Thomas, i, 38.
Ripley, George, ii, 168; Henry, ii, 98; John, i, 26; iii, 106; Richard, ii, 157.
Riply, John, iii, 230.
Rippon, John, iv, 140.
Rishton, Edward (cl), i, 15, 19; ii, 44.
Rivett, John (*see* Hervey, Monox); Margaret, iv, 196.
Roberts, — (P), i, 166; iv, 226; Elias, i, 69; J. (cl), iii, 192; John, i, 126; Samuel (cl), iv, 27; Thomas, i, 168 (*see also* Busby); William, ii, 113.
Robertshaw, Joseph, ii, 150.
Robertson, Eleazar (cl), i, 35, 95, 174.
Robinson, Anne, iv, 238; Arthur (cl), ii, 195, 196; iii, 130, 225; Christopher (cl), ii, 184; Cuthbert,

gent., iv, 216; Edward (cl), i, 177; ii, 87; Franc: ii, 22; Francis, ii, 198; iii, 130; Henry (cl), i, 190; ii, 133, 161; iii, 136, 223; Henry, i, 9; Humphrey Algood, ii, 172; James, iii, 203; Joe, ii, 21; John (cl), iv, 155; John, i, 211; iii, 156; Jonathan (cl), i, 187; ii, 10, 11; Lawrence, O.S.F. (R), iv, 206; Nicholas (Nicolas) (Q), iii, 29, 110; iv, 237, 238; Richard (cl) [later, Abp. of Armagh, Baron Rokeby], Intr., xix; i, 190; ii, 61; Richard, ii, 127; Robert (cl), i, 212; iii, 12; Robert, i, 211; Samuel, i, 25; Stephen (cl), iii, 147; Thomas, i, 33, 72, 108, 146; William, i, 174; ii, 53.

Robson, John, ii, 74; Ralph (cl), ii, 223; iii, 13, 14, 178, 179; Thomas, iii, 252; William (cl), iii, 10, 126, 127, 173; William, ii, 122.

Rodger, Michael, iii, 44.

Rodgers, Robert, i, 28.

Rodginson, John, ii, 13.

Rodwell, Thomas (cl), ii, 23.

Roebuck, John, iii, 54; William, ii, 47; iii, 6.

Rogers, Dom. Edward Dunstan, O.S.B. (R), iv, 197; Gilbert, iii, 231; Joseph, iii, 24; John, ii, 145; Philip, S.J. (R), iv, 200; Thomas, iii, 8.

Rogerson, Jos: ii, 142.

Rokeby, Baron, *see* Robinson, Richard (cl).

Rolleston, Mr., iv, 167.

Roman Catholics; Papists, Intr., x, xvii, xxiii; i, 4, 6, 9, 25, 28, 31-34, 36, 39, 44*, 47, 49, 54*, 57, 64*, 73, 74*, 75*, 77-80, 82-84, 88, 91, 100, 117, 121-123, 125 (2), 127*, 133, 136, 139*, 140, 142*, 145*, 147, 149, 162-164, 168, 172, 173, 177, 179, 182, 183*, 184, 186*, 189, 193, 195, 198, 199, 202*, 203, 207, 208, 210; ii, 2-5, 8-10, 12, 20, 21, 24, 32*, 47, 51, 53, 55, 57, 58, 60-63, 65, 69, 72, 80, 85, 88, 92-94*, 97, 104, 105, 111, 120*, 121, 124-126, 128, 130, 136, 139, 146, 151, 155*, 157, 166, 167, 169-172, 175*, 177, 180, 184, 191-193, 196, 197, 199*, 203, 207, 208, 211, 213, 215, 217, 218, 220; iii, 3, 10, 11, 13, 16, 21, 28, 39, 41*, 43, 45, 46, 54, 57, 62-65*, 66, 91-95, 99, 101*, 103, 107, 111, 113, 118, 123, 126, 127**, 133, 136, 138-141*, 142-144, 151, 156, 159, 162, 164, 166, 170*, 178, 180, 181, 184, 187, 192, 194, 196, 197, 199, 203, 205, 207, 210, 211, 222, 226, 227*, 229*, 231*, 233*-236*, 237, 239, 241, 244-248*, 249**; iv, 2, 6, 9, 18, 21*, 22, 27-29*, 38, 39, 42, 46, 47, 51, 52, 55, 56, 67, 70, 74, 75, 89, 90, 92, 95, 102, 106, 107*, 109, 111*, 115*, 116, 123 (2), 124, 167, 168, 171*, 172 (2), 180, 224 [*see* Appendix A *passim*].

Romley, William (cl), iii, 200.

Rook, Mark, i, 83; Marsh, ii, 194, 217.

Rooke, Michael, i, 222.

Rooksby, Esqr., Sherner, iii, 222.

Root, Routs, John (P), iii, 39; iv, 229, 233.

Rose, John (cl), iv, 72, 135, 157; Thomas (cl), iv, 28, 30, 36, 37 [38]; William, iv, 117.

Rostern, Mr. Jerome, iii, 157.

Rotheram, D.D. [Caleb] (P), iv, 229, 231.

Rotherford, Joseph, i, 205.

Rothes, John, Earl of, iv, 69.

Rothwell, *see* Wrothwell.

Routledge, Thomas, i, 220.

Routs, *see* Root.

Rowe, Matthew, iii, 66.

Rowland, William, iii, 230.

Rowley, Benjamin, iii, 185; Jo: iii, 148.

Rowntree, Mr. J. S., iv, 235.

Rowth, Sir John, iii, 73.

Rudd, James (cl), ii, 139; iii, 173, 174; John (cl), ii, 84; iii, 31, 32, 122, 123.

Ruley, John, iii, 253.

Rumfitt, Thomas, iii, 230.

Rumons, Robert, iii, 29.

Rushforth, Thomas, i, 50.

Rushworth, James, ii, 41; John, i, 166.

Russel, Radcliffe (cl), i, 183.

Russell, Christopher, ii, 196; Jacob, ii, 97; Stephen, iii, 250; William, ii, 34.

Ruston, Thomas, i, 117.

Rutland, Bridget, Duchess of, iv, 80; John, 3rd Duke, iv, 80, 88.

Ryal, James, iii, 160.

Rycroft, Thomas, ii, 5.

Ryley, Dan., iii, 252; Matt., ii, 3.

Ryther, William, iii, 230.

Sadler, Thomas, iii, 243.

Sagar, Robert (cl), ii, 180.

Sagg, George, iii, 9.

St. Aidan, St. Barnabas, St. Bede, and St. Chad, Intr., vi.

St. Clair, Brigadier, iii, 22.

St. John, ii, 123.

St. Luke, iv, 82.
St. Martin-in-Winter (Martinmas), ii, 84; iii, 70, 75, 79, 83, 85, 213, 219.
St. Michael (Michaelmas), *passim*.
St. Paul, Intr., vi; i, 194; ii, 17.
St. Peter, iv, 92; St. Peter ad Vincula (Lammas), ii, 123, 136; iii, 75, 79, 83, 85.
St. Philip and St. James (May Day), iii, 75, 83, 85.
St. Quentin, Robert, i, 177; Sir William, 4th Bart., ii, 19; iii, 123.
St. Stephen, i, 219.
St. Thomas, i, 12, 100, 186, 199; iii, 12; iv, 13, 74, 169.
Salvin, Family of, iv, 203; Thomas, Esqr., iv, 202, 203, 217; William, Esqr., iv, 203.
Sample, James, ii, 68.
Sampson, Abraham (cl), iv, 158, 182, 185; Alexander, iv, 7; Joshua (cl), iv, 124, 125.
Sanders, John, i, 57; Matthew, iii, 187.
Sanderson, Christopher, i, 215; Henry, ii, 65; James, i, 121; ii, 181; John, ii, 65; iii, 56; Richard, i, 43; William, i, 41.
Sandford, Benjamin (P), iii, 3; iv, 231; Samuel (cl), ii, 114.
Sandy, John, i, 112.
Sandys, Edwin; Abp. of York, Intr., vi.
Sansome, William, iv, 97.
Saundby, Henry, iv, 184.
Saunders, John (cl), iv, 16; Richard, iv, 184; Samuel, iv, 143.
Savage, John (cl), iv, 153; Thomas (*see* Savege).
Savege, Savage, Thomas (cl), iii, 54.
Savile, Family of, i, 167; iv, 211; Mrs., ii, 182, 183; Madam, ii, 177; Sir George, iii, 147.
Sawden, James, iii, 252; Robert, iii, 35; William, iii, 252.
Sawrey, —, gent., ii, 99; John, ii, 211.
Sawyer, Roger, iii, 228; Thomas, iii, 228.
Saxon, Richard, ii, 104.
Saxton, Mr. [L. Henry], iii, 157.
Sayer, William, ii, 219.
Sayle, Mr. Benjamin, i, 165.
Scaife, Thomas, ii, 131.
Scarborough, Scharborough, 2nd Earl of, iv, 62; 3rd Earl, ii, 180.
Scarfe, William, iii, 251.
Scarisbrick (*al.* Neville), S.J., Edward (R), iv, 201.
Scarth, John, iii, 207.
Scatcherd, Samuel, iii, 86.
Scaton, Jervis, iii, 4.
Scatshard, William, i, 14.
Schloss, Sloss, James (I), iv, 116, 230, 231.
Schofield, John, ii, 106; Joseph, iv, 44.
Scholefield, Abraham (cl), i, 224; John, i, 119; William, i, 129.
Scholes, Jonathan, iii, 43.
Scholey, William, i, 140.
Scholfield, Joseph, i, 62.
Scorrah, Matthew, ii, 35.
Scots, The, iv, 225.
Scott, Gilbert, iv, 22; James (cl) (V. Bardsey), i, 46; ii, 146; James (cl) (junior), i, 46; James (P), ii, 3; iv, 225, 227; James, i, 56, 161; John (cl), Intr., xix; ii, 42; iii, 186, 187; John, ii, 119; iii, 179, 183; Richard (cl), ii, 4, 108; Rookby (cl), iii, 92; William, i, 200.
Scowthorn, William, iv, 183.
Screeton, Robert, iv, 161.
Seales, Aaron, iv, 185.
Seaman, John, iii, 31.
Seamer, John, iii, 12.
Searson, John, iv, 133.
Seaton, Jo: iii, 20.
Secker, Thomas; Bp. of Oxford, Intr., v.
Sedgewick, John, iii, 251.
Sedman, John, iii, 133; Richard, i, 211.
Seel, Family of, iv, 194; Peter, O.D.C. (R) (Fr. Peter Mary of St. Theresa), iv, 194, 210.
Selby, Family of, iv, 221; Mrs., iv, 222; Edward Gregory, O.S.B., iii, 248; iv, 209; Francis, iv, 46; John, iv, 62; Thomas William, Esqr., iv, 221.
Sellar, John, iii, 40.
Sellarr (Seller), Thomas, ii, 183; Thomas (junior), ii, 183.
Seller, William (cl), iii, 121, 172; William, ii, 57.
Semley, Henry, ii, 60.
Senior, Elias, ii, 50.
Seton, Christopher-Raleigh (cl), iv, 50.
Sewsby, John, ii, 87.
Shackleton, Jonathan, i, 52; Marmaduke, i, 79; Robert, ii, 108; William, ii, 39, 222.
Shadforth, Francis, i, 211.
Shann, John, iv, 179.
Sharp, Isaac, i, 50; John, Abp. of York (also Sharpe), Intr., vi, xiv; ii, 36, 109; iii, 88, 120, 168, 239; iv, 67 [100], 119, 148, 178, 190, 225; Abp. Sharp's MS., i, 218; iv,

178; John, iv, 60; Joseph, iv, 60; Richard, iii, 217; Stephen, ii, 91; Mr. T., iv, 225; Thomas (cl), Intr., xiv, xix; Thomas, i, 200; William, i, 111.
Sharpe, —, iv, 53 (*see* Sharp).
Shaw, Mr. (P), iv, 178, 230; Abra: ii, 96; Benjamin (P), iii, 5; iv, 231; Ferdinando, iv, 230; Henry, i, 167; iv, 134; Ingram (cl), iii, 188; James, ii, 179; John, ii, 60; iv, 62; John, Esqr., i, 97; Jonathan, iii, 251; Joseph, iii, 195; Mr. Laurence, iii, 46; Thomas, i, 19; iii, 48; William, iv, 130.
Sheard, Benjamin, i, 61.
Sheepshank, Richard, ii, 183.
Sheffield, Sir Edmund, iii, 73, 74, 75, 76; George (cl), i, 39, 160; iii, 132; Ignatius, S.J. (*see* Anderson); Thomas, i, 218; ii, 222.
Shepard, John, i, 72.
Shepherd, Christopher, ii, 174; Joseph (cl), ii, 56, 66, 140; Joseph, ii, 186; Thomas, i, 86.
Shepley, Thomas, i, 142.
Sheppard, James, i, 72; Joshua, iii, 88, 194.
Sherard, Benedict (cl), iv, 88.
Sherbrook, Mr., iv, 3.
Sherburne, Mary Maria Winifred Francisca (*see* Norfolk); Sir Nicholas, ii, 175; iv, 210.
Shercliff, William, iv, 125.
Sherman, John, ii, 152.
Sherwin, Mr., iv, 181; Mrs. Elizabeth, iv, 136.
Sherwing, Anthony, ii, 24.
Sherwood, Robert, ii, 80.
Shileto, Shillito [L. Shillitoe], Mr. Richard, i, 126, 127.
Shillito, Thomas, ii, 106.
Shillitoe, John, iii, 86; Samuel, i, 127.
Shires, Emanuell, iii, 46.
Shirt, John, iii, 201.
Shirtcliffe, Thomas, i, 140.
Sholefield, Mr. (P), iv, 232.
Shores, Robert, iii, 86, 200.
Shott, George, ii, 87; James, ii, 88.
Shutt, William, ii, 125.
Shuttleworth, Family of, iv, 199; George (senior), iv, 199; George (junior) (R), iv, 199; John (R), iv, 199.
Siddal, Sydal, Siddle, Charles (*see* Hopkinson, S.J., Charles).
Siddel, Richard, iii, 156.
Simkin, Thomas, iii, 115.
Simon, Frances, iii, 10; Peter (cl), iii, 252.
Simondson, Leicester (cl), ii, 105; iii, 250.
Simpson, Alex., iii, 253; Bartholomew, ii, 30; John (cl), iv, 23; John, i, 117; ii, 67; iii, 63, 106, 145; iv, 155; Joshua, ii, 148; Matthew, iii, 184; Thomas, ii, 22, 147; iii, 142; William, ii, 103, 203; iii, 221.
Singleton, Thomas, i, 136.
Sison, Philip, iv, 168.
Sissison, Seth (cl), iii, 173, 174.
Sissons, James, i, 161; Thomas, ii, 76; iii, 191; William, iv, 15.
Siver, Michael, ii, 17.
Skelton, James (R), iii, 229; iv, 195, 198; Robert, iii, 98; William, iii, 179; iv, 165.
Skilbeck, John, i, 181.
Skirrow, Holroyd, i, 50.
Slack, Joseph (cl), i, 33.
Slater, Christopher, i, 221; John (Q), i, 125; iv, 236; John, ii, 95; iii, 251; Laurence, i, 5; Mary (Q), i, 125; iv, 236; Philip, iii, 104; Samuel, i, 129; William (Q), i, 125; iv, 236.
Slayter, Joseph, iii, 65.
Sleight, Mr. J. G., iv, 186.
Slinger, Robert, i, 51.
Sloss, *see* Schloss.
Smailes, William, iii, 169.
Smales, Samuel, iii, 36.
Smalpage, Daniel, iii, 187.
Smelt, Luke (cl), ii, 154.
Smiles, Christopher, iii, 169; Robert 'senior,' iii, 169.
Smith, of Egton Bridge, iv, 203; Mr., iv, 203; Mr. (P), iii, 66; iv, 231; Mr. (I), iii, 57; iv, 231; Mr., ii, 59; Mr. Abel, iv, 109, 176; Ambrose, ii, 216; Benjamin (cl), ii, 146, 147; Benjamin, ii, 111; Canon C. J. (cl), Intr., xxiv; Edward (cl), i, 145; Edward, iv, 2, 116; George (cl), ii, 20; iii, 182; George, i, 58; Henry, ii, 173; iii, 166; iv, 58; Hugh, ii, 111; Isaiah, iii, 51; John (P), ii, 32, 96; iv, 225, 226, 228, 229; John, i, 69, 81, 135, 136, 168; ii, 75, 93, 159; iii, 28; iv, 78, 116; John, Esqr., iii, 189; Joseph, i, 76; iv, 66; Joshua (cl), i, 130; ii, 31; Matthew (P), iv, 228; Nathaniel, ii, 219; Richard, ii, 67, 80; Robert, iii, 129, 171; Rowland, ii, 111; Samuel (P), iii, 251; iv, 225; Simon, iii, 240; Thomas (R), i, 142; iv, 196, 202; Thomas (Q), ii, 12; iv, 236; Thomas, i, 23, 158; ii, 207; iii, 102, 107, 252; iv, 14, 169; Timothy, i, 79; William (cl),

iii, 189; William, i, 81; ii, 214.
Smithies, John, i, 39.
Smithson, John, i, 40; iii, 93; Richard, iii, 162; William, i, 46.
Smyth, Mr. John, ii, 198.
Snaith, John (cl), ii, 85, 86; iii, 220; Nicholas, iii, 176.
Snary, Roger, i, 28.
Snell, Anthony, ii, 209; Joshua, ii, 209.
Snowdin, John, iii, 230.
Socinianism, iv, 224.
Sollitt, Isaac (Q), iii, 133; iv, 238; Joshua, gent., iii, 135; Sarah, iv, 238.
Somerset, Duke of, ii, 183; iii, 143.
Somersgill, Anthony, i, 52.
Sommers, Joseph (cl), i, 213, 214; ii, 165, 204, 205; iii, 38.
Sotheran, Sotheron, Mr. William 'the younger,' iii, 78, 79, 80.
Sotthill, Family of, iv, 204.
South, Jonathan, i, 70.
Southby, Elizabeth (Mrs. Willoughby), iv, 211; Thomas, iv, 211.
Southey, Robert (poet), iv, 236.
Sowden, Franc: ii, 106; John, iii, 151.
Sowermire, Christopher, iii, 50.
Sowray, Richard (cl), i, 8, 47, 149.
Spalding, Henry, ii, 94.
Spalton, William, iv, 141.
Spangenberg, August Gottlieb (Mor), ii, 32; iv, 240.
Speck, William, i, 216.
Speight, Benjamin, i, 223.
Spence, Francis, iii, 230; Simeon, i, 149; William, i, 99; iii, 108.
Spencer, John, i, 14; iii, 251; iv, 52; Thomas, iv, 86.
Spenseley, George, ii, 126.
Spenser, John, i, 44; Thomas, ii, 181.
Spink, Edward, i, 9; Jo: iii, 3; John, iii, 139, 209; Thomas, iii, 230.
Spoole, Myles, ii, 24.
Spoone, Richard, iv, 225.
Spooner, John, iii, 58.
Spurr, Mr. William, i, 48.
Squire, Edward, i, 35; iii, 65.
Stable, John (cl), i, 216; iii, 135.
Stables, James, ii, 3, 222.
Stacey, John, iv, 71; Richard, iii, 154; Thomas, iii, 154; William, iii, 154.
Stackhouse, William (cl), iii, 51.
Stainburn, John, iii, 144.
Stainforth, William, iii, 52.
Stainthorpe, George (cl), ii, 65; iii, 28, 206.
Stainton, Henry, iii, 40; Mrs. Jane, i, 4; Thomas, i, 95.
Standfast, M.D., William (cl), Intr., xii; iv, 28, 169.
Standing, Thomas, iii, 251.
Standish, George, iii, 42.
Stanes, Thomas, i, 188.
Stanfield, S.J., Robert (R), iv, 221, 222.
Stanhope, Henry (cl), iv, 10.
Staniland, George (cl), iii, 54, 195.
Stanley, Matth., iii, 6; Robert (cl), iv, 26, 117, 182.
Stansfield, Robert, S.J. (R), iv, 208; Robert, iv, 225.
Stapilton, Esqr., Philip, iii, 178.
Stapleton, Nicholas, Esqr., i, 139, 140; iv, 201.
Stather, William, i, 119.
Stavelow, Robert, i, 46.
Stavert, F.S.A., Canon W. J. (cl), i, 51.
Stead, John, ii, 95; Joshua, ii, 115; William, iii, 18.
Steadman, William, iv, 24.
Steel, George, iii, 159; Thomas, ii, 178.
Steer, Charles (cl), ii, 54; William (cl) (senior), i, 180; William (cl) (junior), iii, 88.
Steers, Edward, i, 165.
Stephenson, Christopher (cl), ii, 55; iii, 23; Henry (cl) (*see* Stevenson), John, gen., i, 164; Jonathan (cl), iii, 153; Thomas, ii, 93; William (cl), iii, 21; William, ii, 12, 54.
Sterne, Stern, Jaques (cl), Intr., xx; i, 36; ii, 89, 90; iii, 36; iv, 209, 219, 220; Lawrence (cl), Intr., xvi, xix, xxii; iii, 36, 93; Richard, Abp. of York, i, 103.
Stevenson [Stephenson], Henry (cl), iv, 54, 124; Thomas, iv, 8.
Stilborn, Thomas 'the elder,' i, 120.
Stillington, Esqr., Jos: iii, 91.
Stock, Evan (P), i, 61, 129, 'Stott'; iv, 225, 226, 229; William, ii, 205.
Stockdale, Mr. William, ii, 147.
Stockhill, Robert, ii, 189.
Stockton, William, ii, 124.
Stoker, John, ii, 119.
Stokes, John (cl), iv, 9.
Stokoe, Alexander (cl), iii, 247 (2), 248.
Stone, Dr. Darwell (cl), Intr., xxiv; John, ii, 112; Thomas, iv, 120, 121.
Stonehouse, Christopher, iii, 252; George, i, 143; Thomas, iii, 206.
Stoneley, Martin, ii, 93.
Stonor, Family of, iv, 192; Dr. John Talbot, Bp. of Thespiae (R), iv, 192.
Store, William (cl) (C. Aughton), i, 36, 157, 191; William (cl) (A.C. Catton), i, 149; William, iii, 169.
Storer, Richard, iii, 21.

Stores, Cordal, iv, 147.
Storey, William, i, 31; iv, 182.
Stork, Robert, i, 104.
Storr, Joseph (cl), i, 186.
Storrey, William, ii, 15.
Story, Jo: ii, 140; John, ii, 190; iii, 209.
Stott, *see* Stock.
Stourton, Family of, iv, 197; Charles, 14th Baron, iv, 214.
Stowes, George, i, 180.
Strafford, Lord, iv, 29, 201.
Strangwayes, Christopher, ii, 131.
Strelley, Mr. Philip, iv, 108; William, iv, 37.
Stringer, John, iii, 196; Thomas, i, 81.
Strode [L. William] (cl), ii, 183.
Strother, Thomas (cl), i, 11.
Stubbs, Katherine, iii, 203.
Study, Thomas, i, 142.
Sturdle, Richard, i, 86.
Sturdy, Christopher, i, 209; John (cl), i, 165, 166; John, ii, 9.
Sugar, William, i, 58.
Sugden, John, ii, 39; iii, 150; Joseph, i, 19; Thomas, ii, 209; William, ii, 108.
Suger, Mr., i, 208.
Suggit, Richard, iii, 92.
Summerton, William, iii, 106.
Sumner, Thomas, iv, 48.
Sunderland, Peter, Esqr., i, 59; Thomas, ii, 38; iii, 20; William (cl), ii, 37; iii, 20.
Surr, John, ii, 215.
Sutcliffe, James, ii, 39; Jobe, ii, 150; John, i, 132; iii, 51; John (senior and junior), ii, 39; Thomas, ii, 39; Tobit (cl), i, 132; ii, 37; William, iii, 20.
Suter, Thomas, iv, 85.
Sutton, Charles, iv, 36; John (cl), iii, 168; John, iii, 25; Richard (cl), Intr., xiii; iv, 2; Robert, Lord Lexington, iv, 80; Sir Robert, iv, 63; Lord Robert, iv, 80; Stephen (cl), ii, 102.
Swailes, John, i, 164.
Swallow, Mr. [L. Richard], i, 205.
Swann, George, iii, 161.
Sweetaple, William (cl), iv, 57.
Swift, James, i, 169; Timothy, iii, 64; William, ii, 119.
Swindell, James, iii, 250.
Swire, Thomas, i, 57.
Sykes, Henry, iii, 86; John, ii, 115; Joseph, i, 19, 20; Sir Mark (cl), Intr., xx; iii, 34; Sir Mark Masterman, iii, 34; Samuel, ii, 44; Sir Tatton, iii, 34; William, iii, 48.
Symondson, Mr. Anthony, ii, 112; Thomas, ii, 121.

Tailbey, John, iv, 115.
Tallboyes, John, i, 105.
Tanfield, Robert, i, 7.
Tasker, Lancelot, iii, 213; Robert, iii, 146; William, iii, 146.
Tate, Jo: ii, 119; Richard, ii, 2; Thomas, i, 44; William, i, 164.
Tatham, Mr. John, ii, 7.
Tattersall, William, ii, 5.
Tayler, Esqr., Richard, iii, 239.
Taylor, Anby, i, 164; Daniel, i, 64; David (M), i, 201; iii, 89; iv, 240; Francis, iii, 156; Henry, iv, 138; James, i, 23; Jeffry, i, 90; Jeremiah, iii, 204; John, D.D. (P), iv, 230; John, i, 223; ii, 162, 171; Joseph, i, 43; ii, 211; iii, 93; Joshua, i, 24; ii, 108; Margaret, ii, 17; Mathew, i, 183; Richard, ii, 164; Robert, ii, 24; iii, 205; Mr. Robert, ii, 16; Thomas, i, 45, 47, 106, 157; ii, 166; William, ii, 205.
Tayloure, Mr., iii, 241.
Teal, Richard, iii, 90.
Teasdale, John (cl), i, 165 (*see* Teesdale).
Tebb, William, ii, 209.
Tebott, Christopher, iv, 3.
Teesdale, Teasdale, O.P., John Vincent (R), iv, 207.
Tempest, Family of, iv, 190, 200, 219; Mrs., of Tong, iv, 186; Arthur, (cl), Intr., xx; i, 54, 77; Sir George, iv, 219; Sir Henry, iv, 219; Nicholas, iv, 219; Robert (cl), i, 25; Robert, ii, 175; Stephen, Esqr., i, 55, 56, 57; iv, 191, 200; William (R), i, 139; iv, 196 [*al.* Thomas], 201.
Temple, William, i, 186.
Tengate, Joseph (cl), i, 116.
Tennant, Calvert (cl), Intr., xix; i, 127; Henry (cl), i, 126; James, ii, 30; Thomas (cl), iii, 158, 185; Thomas, i, 60.
Territt, William (cl), Intr., xviii; i, 98.
Terry, George, iii, 230; Thomas, iii, 253; William, iii, 230.
Tetlow, James, i, 223; Mark, ii, 34.
Thackaray, Peter, ii, 103; William, i, 80.
Thackera [L. Thackerah], i, 126.
Thackray, Franc: ii, 105; Joseph, ii, 22.
Thaddeus, O.F.M., Fr. (R), iv, 187, 212, 216, 217.
Thanet, Earl of, iii, 45; late Earl, iii, 45.

Theaker, Thomas, iv, 42.
Thespiae, Bp. of, *see* Stonor.
Thew, Francis, iii, 225.
Thirkold, Mr. William, iii, 187.
Thistle, Thomas, i, 187.
Thomas, Jacob (cl), i, 129; Joseph (cl) ['John'], i, 48; Richard (B), ii, 35; William, ii, 202.
Thomason, James, i, 222.
Thomlinson, Christopher, i, 126; John, iii, 175.
Thompson, Edm., iii, 18; Edward, iv, 54; Mr. Edward, i, 151; Mr. George, ii, 79; Isaac (cl), ii, 79; John, i, 72; ii, 3; iii, 2, 16, 86, 156; iv, 102; Jonathan, iii, 149, 150; Leonard (cl), i, 82, 83, 85; iii, 161; Matthew, i, 196; Peter Antoninus, O.P. (R), iv, 206; Richard, ii, 148; Mr. [L. Richard], i, 83; Robert, i, 81; ii, 215; iii, 203; Samuel, iii, 193; Thomas, i, 61, 111; William (cl) (A.C. Burnsall), i, 51; William (cl) (R. Escrick), i, 183; William (cl) (C. Holmfirth), ii, 222; William, iii, 86, 105.
Thomson, Henry (cl), i, 143; ii, 67, 68; Jo., iii, 2.
Thorbarn, Thomas [Robert Thorburne] (P), ii, 106; iv, 229.
Thorburgh, Thornburgh, Jane, iii, 73; Robert, iii, 81.
Thornhill, Jos: iv, 237.
Thorns, Joseph (cl), iii, 49.
Thornton, John, i, 60, 129, 130; ii, 179; iv, 135; Richard, ii, 28; Robert, i, 60; iii, 231; William, ii, 95; Sir William, ii, 103.
Thorp, Henry, ii, 173; Joseph, ii, 189; Thomas, iii, 96 (*see also* Thorpe).
Thorpe, Mrs., iv, 213; Robert (*al.* Thorp), ii, 93.
Thowlis,' *see* Fowlis.'
Thelkeld, John (cl), ii, 93.
Thurlby, Clifford (cl), iii, 156.
Thwait, John, ii, 117.
Thwaites, James, iii, 63; Thomas (cl), iii, 102.
Thwing, Thomas, iv, 188, 222.
Tiberiopolis, Bp. of, *see* Williams, Dr. Thomas, O.P.
Tickell [John], iv, 242.
Tilburn, Richard, ii, 213.
Tilford, Jo: ii, 169.
Tillotson, John, Abp. of Canterbury, iv, 229; John, iii, 20.
Tim, John, ii, 52.
Timm, George, iv, 125.
Tindall, Richard, iii, 93.
Tinegate, Henry, i, 214.
Tinker, Richard, iii, 21.
Tipson, Richard, iii, 213.
Tireman, Henry, ii, 172.
Tod, William, i, 83.
Todd, Abraham (cl), iii, 205; John, iii, 66, 96; Robert, iii, 251; Thomas, i, 204; ii, 89; William, gent., ii, 45.
Tomes, John, i, 35.
Tomlin, Heneage (cl), i, 37; ii, 90; Thomas, iii, 237; William (cl), ii, 14, 223; iii, 36, 129, 130, 178, 226.
Tomlinson, Matthew (cl), iv, 5, 22, 74, 147; William (cl) (R. Sigglesthorne), iii, 125; iv, 90; William (cl) (R. Skelton, Bulmer), iii, 109.
Tompkin, Thomas, iv, 159.
Tomson, William, ii, 113.
Tongue, Richard, iv, 141.
Topham, Godfrey, ii, 5; Mr. [John] (cl), i, 218; Lupton, ii, 111; Matthew (cl), Intr., xix; i, 178.
Toppin, John (cl), iii, 246.
Torre, Torr, Esqr., Nicholas, ii, 198.
Tower, Henry, ii, 7.
Towneley, Townley, Mr. Charles, ii, 32; iv, 194, 205.
Townend, Jeremiah, iii, 48; John, iii, 18; Richard, ii, 55; iii, 194.
Townrow, Henry, i, 137.
Townsend, John (cl), iv, 112; Meredith (I), iv, 229.
Townshend, *Colonel*, ii, 123; *Lord*, iv, 214.
Towse, John, i, 107.
Trainholm, William, i, 174.
Trance, Thomas, i, 135.
Trant, Thomas (cl), i, 73; ii, 46.
Trappes, Margaret [Mr. Trappe], i, 205.
Trapps, Esqr., Francis, iv, 212.
Travers, Henry (cl), Intr., xx; ii, 138, 207.
Travis, John, ii, 212; William, iii, 48.
Trench [Richard Chenevix], Abp. of Dublin, Intr., xix.
Trevet, John (R), iv, 209.
Trippet, Joseph, iii, 156.
Trout, Mr. (P), i, 167; iv, 226; George, iii, 194.
Trowell, Thomas (cl), iv, 17.
Trowsdale, Jonathan, iii, 99.
Tundale, William, iii, 229.
Tunin, Matthew, i, 181.
Tunsdill, John, ii, 7.
Tunstall, Tunstal, Mrs. (Q), ii, 29; iv, 236, 237; Cuthbert (*see* Constable, Cuthbert); John (Q), i, 12; ii, 236, 237; Mr. Marmaduke, iv, 189, 192; P.B. (R), iv, 210.
Turie [Robert] (cl), iii, 201.

Turnell, John, iv, 165.
Turner, Mr., ii, 129; Cholmley, Esqr., i, 29; Francis, ii, 183; George, iii, 204; Hammond (cl), iii, 154, 155; iv, 69; James (cl), i, 174; iii, 27; James, i, 100; Jo: i, 62; John (cl), i, 72; John, i, 87; iii, 195, 253; iv, 185; Jonathan (cl), i, 170; Matthew, ii, 168; Nicholas, iii, 126; Richard, ii, 24; William, iii, 145.
Turnis, Robert, iii, 239; Thomas (cl), iii, 239.
Turton, John, ii, 182.
Twibel, Joseph, iii, 61; Sarah, iii, 61; Sarah (=Sarah Wright), iii, 61.
Twibell, James, i, 28.
Twigg, Joshua, i, 25.
Twistleton, John, Esqr., i, 164; William (cl), i, 223.
Twittey, William (cl), i, 24; iii, 193.
Tyas, Mary, ii, 180; Robert, ii, 180; Thomas, ii, 61.
Tyerman, L., iv, 236.
Tyers, William, i, 73.
Tymperon, Mr. William, ii, 88.
Tyrwitt's *Eccles. Law*, Intr., xxi.
Tyson, Leonard (cl), ii, 82; William, ii, 102.

Uliatt, Henry, iv, 81.
Uppleby, George, ii, 66.
Usher, Ellis, iii, 38.
Usherwood, Francis, iii, 97.
Ustler, James, ii, 27.
Uthersill, William, iii, 99.

Vaine, William, iii, 101.
Vanne, Robert, ii, 136.
Varley, John (Q), i, 131; iv, 236; Richard, i, 45.
Varwell, Robert, iii, 118.
Vassey, Jervas, iv, 12.
Vassin, Richard, iv, 90.
Vaux, *Alderman* [L. John], ii, 56; John, iii, 2.
Vavasour, Family of, iv, 200, 218; Sir Walter, iv, 190.
Vawkes, William, i, 138.
Venn, J. and J. A., Intr., xxiv; i, 30; ii, 87, 147, 191; iii, 31, 46, 54, 148, 192, 199; iv, 98, 107, 116, 129, 144.
Vevers, William (cl), i, 133; William, gent., i, 44.
Vicars, John, i, 69.
Vickerman, John, iii, 135; Peter, iii, 128; Robert, iii, 174.
Vickers, Mrs. (*see* Middleton, Mrs. Jane); Thomas, iii, 54; William, ii, 182.
Victoria, H.M. Queen, iv, 235.
Vincent, Esqr., Thomas, iii, 68, 69, 70, 71, 72.
Virgil, *see* Maro.

Waddington, Elkanah, ii, 96; Joshua (cl), iv, 66, 170; Ralph, iii, 83; Robert, ii, 24; Samuel, ii, 26; Thomas, i, 53.
Wade, Bartholomew, iv, 174; Thomas, iii, 199.
Wadsworth, Field Sylvester (P), iv, 224; Mr. Henry, ii, 96; John (P), i, 25; iii, 57 ('Wordsworth'); iv, 224, 227, 232; Jonas Bancroft, ii, 39.
Wager, John, iii, 213.
Wagstaff, Robert, ii, 222.
Wailes, Thomas, ii, 58.
Wailsby, William, ii, 206.
Waines, gent., William, i, 102.
Wainesforth, Mr., ii, 208.
Wainewright, Humfrey, iv, 12.
Wainman, Benjamin (cl), ii, 111; iv, 225, 231; John (P), i, 128; ii, 109; iii, 4; iv, 225, 226, 231; Thomas (P), i, 49; ii, 109, 110; iv, 225, 231.
Waite, Hugh, ii, 105.
Waits, Christopher, iii, 230.
Wake, William, Bp. of Lincoln, and Abp. of Canterbury, Intr., vi, viii, xiv; iv, 64.
Wakefeild, John (cl), iii, 90.
Wakefield, George (cl), Intr., xx; iv, 107; John, ii, 94; Thomas (cl) (V. Orston), iv, 113; Thomas (cl) (R. Rowley), iii, 31; Thomas, ii, 173.
Waldby, Thomas, iii, 114.
Wales, H. R. H. the Prince of, ii, 3.
Walker, Anthony, iii, 140; Charles, iii, 86; Francis, i, 120; iii, 211; George (cl), iii, 65; Henry, iv, 118; J. W., O.B.E., F.S.A., Intr., xxiv; ii, 116; John (cl), i, 188; iii, 7, 8, 211; John, i, 150; ii, 81; iv, 62; Matthew, ii, 171; Richard, i, 53, 61, 95, 114; ii, 35; iv, 12; Robert (cl), ii, 102; Roger, ii, 125; Samuel, iii, 90; Silvester, iii, 203; Thomas, iii, 109; iv, 74; William, i, 120; ii, 191.
Wall, Mr. Abraham, ii, 36.
Wallace, Richard, ii, 220.
Waller, Bryan, ii, 6; James, iv, 39; Nicholas, Esqr., 'the elder,' iii, 68, 69, 71, 73-76; Nicholas, Esqr., 'the younger,' iii, 68, 69, 71, 73-76, 80-85; Nicholas, gent., iii, 74, 80-85; Thomas, i, 107; iii, 101.
Wallew, John, iv, 110.
Wallis, Edward, iii, 253; James, iv,

153; Tedwall, iii, 194; Mr. [L. Towers], i, 190.
Walls, John, iii, 10.
Walmesley, Family of, iv, 214, 215; Bartholomew, iv, 214; Catherine, iv, 214; Francis, iv, 214; Mrs. Juliana, iv, 214.
Walmsley, Peter (cl), ii, 186, 187, 188, 189.
Walsh, John, ii, 175.
Walsham, Joseph, i, 178.
Walter, John, iv, 103.
Walters, W., iv, 4.
Waltham, Christopher, ii, 206.
Walton, James, iii, 6; Martin, i, 58.
Wand, Edward, i, 165; Thomas, iii, 252.
Wande, William, ii, 167.
Wanley, Francis (cl), ii, 222; iii, 165, 166.
Ward, Dr., iii, 96; Jeremy, i, 65; John, i, 138, 221; Mathew, iii, 81; Peter, ii, 106; Samuel, ii, 152; Thomas, i, 95; iii, 243; William (cl), i, 160; iii, 133, 169, 228; William, iv, 141.
Warde, John (cl), iv, 67; Richard, i, 220.
Wardell, James, i, 177; Mr. John, senior and junior, i, 151, 152; Thomas, ii, 89.
Wardrobe, Thomas (P), iii, 249.
Wardrope, Thomas, i, 135.
Ware, Mr., iii, 110.
Wareing, John, iii, 196.
Warham, Richard, iii, 23.
Warmworth, George, i, 127.
Warneford, Richard (cl), ii, 138, 172.
Warrell, John (cl), iv, 89.
Warren, Mr., iv, 167; Mr. J. C., iv, 223, 240.
Warrender, Sir George, Bart., i, 22; Hugh (cl), i, 22.
Warriner, Richard, iv, 61.
Warrington, Samuel, i, 222.
Warton, Mr. Charles, i, 102, 103; Sir Michael, i, 103, 104; Robert (cl), ii, 127; iii, 100, 101.
Warwick, John, iv, 3; Thomas (cl), i, 32.
Waterhouse, Edmund, i, 101; James, i, 129; Mr. Nathaniel, i, 132; ii, 37, 148, 149; iii, 50; Thomas, i, 194.
Waterton, Family of, ii, 177; iii, 46; iv, 190, 214; Charles, Esqr., iv, 214; Thomas, iii, 55.
Waterworth, John, ii, 176; iii, 105.
Watkin, John, i, 194; William, iii, 102.
Watkinson, Dr. [L. Henry], iii, 11.
Watson, Mrs. Ann, iii, 13, 130; George, i, 45, 174; ii, 223; iii, 77; Henry, iii, 46; Hugh, ii, 111; James (R) (*al.* Rand or Raines, Richard), iv, 216; John (cl), iii, 232 (2), 233, 234, 240; John, i, 87; ii, 59, 183; iii, 201, 222; Peter (R) (*al.* Adams), iv, 211; Peter, iii, 89; Robert, ii, 187; iii, 27; Sampson, iii, 163; Samuel, iii, 158; Thomas, ii, 208; iii, 109; Mr. Timothy, ii, 142; William, iii, 44, 176.
Watt, James (cl), iii, 69, 71; Mary, iii, 69, 71.
Waugh, Richard, iii, 18.
Wayne, Gabriel (cl), iv, 121, 136; George, i, 221.
Wayte, George (cl), iv, 93, 123, 182; Henry (cl), iv, 161, 163.
Weatherhead, Anthony (cl), iii, 185; Christopher, iii, 143; John (*al.* Wetherhead) (cl), i, 53; Thomas, i, 51.
Weatherill, Michael, iii, 102.
Webster, Bernard, i, 93; George, ii, 213; John, ii, 97, 156; iv, 65; Ralph, ii, 200; Robert, iii, 124; Wriggan (cl), iv, 11, 67.
Weddell, Esqr., Charles, iii, 182.
Weighill, John, ii, 219.
Weightman, John, iv, 5; Thomas, iv, 168.
Welack, William, ii, 5.
Weld, Family of, iv, 210; Cardinal, iv, 210.
Welesby, Matthew, iii, 173.
Wellburn, William, i, 218.
Wells, gent., John, iv, 19.
Welsh, John (cl), iv, 182, 183; Thomas, iv, 78.
Wenman, Richard (cl), iv, 133.
Wentworth, Mrs. Elizabeth, ii, 43; Sir Thomas, 1st Earl of Strafford, iii, 73, 80-85; Sir Thomas, 3rd Earl, ii, 47; iii, 86, 87; Thomas, Esqr., iii, 74.
Wesley, Westley, Westly, Mr. Charles (M), Intr., xi; i, 61; ii, 211; iv, 240; Mr. John (M), Intr., xi; i, 61, 133; iv, 60, 225, 240; *Journals*; iv, 234, 236, 240; *Life*; iv, 236, 240.
West, Aholiah, iii, 61; Francis, i, 222; John, iv, 6; Thomas, i, 117.
Westaby, William, i, 40.
Westbrooke (*al.* Darell), O.S.B., Dom. William Maurus (R), iv, 205, 218.
Westby, Esqr., George, i, 152.
Westeneys, Benjamin, iii, 154;

Edmond (*al.* Edmond Wastneys), iii, 154, 155; Edward, iii, 154; Joseph, iii, 154.
Westerman, William, iii, 4.
Westland, William, ii, 9.
Westley, Westly, *see* Wesley.
Westwood, Robert, i, 7.
Wetherell, Jas., iii, 145; Robert, iv, 51.
Wetherhead, Thomas, ii, 28 (*see* Weatherhead).
Wetwang, Robert, ii, 76.
Whalley, John, ii, 111.
Whalmsley, Thomas, ii, 176.
Wharham, John, ii, 183; Mr. John, iii, 88.
Wharram, John, ii, 135; Thomas, iii, 252.
Wharrey, Robert, iii, 66.
Wharton, Edward, ii, 171; John, ii, 152; Robert, i, 26; Thomas, ii, 208.
Wheatcroft, John, iii, 192.
Wheatley, Jonathan, iii, 230; William, iv, 162.
Wheeler, Robert, iv, 175.
Wheelhouse, John, ii, 208.
Wheelwright, Mr. [L. Francis], ii, 59.
Wheler, Granville (cl), Intr., xix; iv, 86, 87.
Whinnerall, John (cl), ii, 119.
Whitaker, Christopher, i, 197; Jas., i, 204; Joseph, iii, 152; Matthew (cl), i, 119; Thomas (P), iv, 228; [Thomas], iv, 236; Timothy, i, 60; William (P), iv, 231.
White, George, iv, 149; Luke, iv, 117; Robert, ii, 69; Sampson, iii, 40; Thomas, iii, 24, 215; iv, 169; Thomas, Esqr., iii, 239; William, iv, 41, 103.
Whitefield, Mr. George (M), Intr., xxiii; iv, 240.
Whitehead, Beaumont (cl), i, 70; ii, 45; George, iii, 154; Jas., gent., iii, 140; John, junior, iii, 192; Jonathan, ii, 41; Robert (cl) (*see* Wrightson); Robert, iv, 27; Thomas, ii, 217; William, i, 10, 14; iii, 154.
Whiteheads, Gervase, iii, 154.
Whiteley, Edward, i, 167.
Whitfield, George, ii, 89.
Whiting, Richard, i, 108.
Whitley, Elkanah (Q), iii, 19; iv, 238; Mr. W. T., iv, 236, 241, 242.
Whitlock, John (P), iv, 224; Nathaniel (P), iv, 3, 224.
Whitmore, Esqr., William, i, 97.
Whittaker, William (P), iii, 133.
Whittell, Richard, ii, 67.
Whitter, Witter, John (P), ii, 78; iv, 229, 233.
Whitwell, James, iii, 119; Valentine, i, 90.
Whitwham, John, iii, 63.
Whitworth, John, iv, 173.
Wickham, Wickam, Henry (cl), ii, 3, 144.
Wickins, John (cl), ii, 184; iii, 144.
Widdrington, William, 4th Lord, ii, 200.
Wiggins, John (cl), i, 128.
Wighton, Gilbert (cl), i, 14; ii, 2.
Wilberfoss, Robert [L. Thomas], iii, 111.
Wilbey, Joseph, ii, 211.
Wilcock, Edward, iii, 6.
Wild, Christopher, iv, 175.
Wildboar, Wildbore, Timothy (I), ii, 77; Tobias (I), iv, 229.
Wilde, Mr. Leonard, iv, 232.
Wildon, Thomas, ii, 57.
Wildrington, Esqr., Peregrine, iv, 210.
Wiley, Richard, i, 4.
Wilkes, George (cl), i, 22.
Wilkinson, Mr. Caleb, iii, 46; David, ii, 111; Francis, i, 56; Henry, iii, 23; iv, 180; James, i, 96; Jo: iii, 189; Jonathan, ii, 175; Joseph, iii, 206; Leod., iii, 166; Matthew (cl), iii, 46; Richard (cl), ii, 121, 122; Richard, iii, 4, 199; Mr. Richard, ii, 96; Robert, iv, 3; Thomas, iii, 86; William, i, 57; ii, 3, 191; iv, 94.
Wilks, Fran: i, 79; John, i, 137.
Willan, John (cl), i, 87; iii, 164; Thomas (cl), iii, 222.
Willats, Charles (cl), iv, 116.
William III, H.M. King, i, 22; ii, 21; iv, 171, 235.
William, John, iii, 146; Richard, ii, 5.
William and Mary, iv, 223.
Williams, Dr. [Daniel] (I), iv, 223; Dr. Thomas, O.P., Bp. of Tiberiopolis (R), iv, 188, 189, 213, 215, 218, 219.
Williamson, Christopher, iii, 233; James (cl), iii, 167; James, iii, 238; John, i, 191; Michael, i, 86, 90; Samuel, i, 184; Thomas, i, 56, 58, 120; William, i, 56.
Willis, Mathew, iii, 56.
Willoughby, Family of, iv, 211; Cassandra, iv, 211; Mrs. Elizabeth, iv, 107, 211; [Mrs. Emma], iv, 103; Francis, Esqr., iv, 211; James (cl), iv, 211; Thomas, iv, 211.
Wills, William, iv, 88.

Willson, John, ii, 2.
Wilmott, Thomas, iv, 27, 106.
Wilson, Mr., ii, 144; Benjamin (cl), ii, 198; iii, 187; Bernard (cl), Intr., xix; iv, 107, 165; Christopher, iii, 143; Edmund, ii, 7; Edward (cl), i, 128; iv, 156; Edward, ii, 89; Mr. Edward, ii, 166; Henry, iii, 200; Isaac (cl), i, 87; James, ii, 67, 96, 111; John (cl) (A.C. Lockington), ii, 160; John (cl) (C. Winksley), iii, 244; John (B), iii, 16; iv, 241, 242; John, i, 10, 52; ii, 8, 47, 96, 102; iii, 169; Michael, i, 81, 163; Miles (cl), ii, 29, 30; Robert, i, 79; Roger, i, 28; Samuel (P), iv, 144, 232; Samuel, i, 200; Thomas, i, 183; Walter (*MS.*), iv, 223, 227-232; William, i, 190; ii, 26; iii, 56, 99; iv, 25.
Wilton, Henry, iii, 230; Canon (Richard), ii, 159; R. C. Esq., Intr., xxiii; ii, 159; iv, 186, 205; Robert, iii, 130.
Winch, Edward, iv, 20.
Winch, John (cl) (late R. Thirkleby), i, 89; John (cl) (R. Kirkby Knowle), i, 89; ii, 120; iii, 166; John, ii, 127.
Windle, Christopher, i, 129.
Windsor; Robert, ii, 176.
Winfield, John, i, 180; iv, 160.
Winn, John, ii, 65; Sir Rowland, Bart., ii, 117; William, i, 164.
Winter, Thomas, ii, 106.
Winteringham, Edward, ii, 137.
Wise, John (cl), i, 43; Robert, ii, 115.
Wiseman, Henry, iv, 45; John, i, 183; iv, 113.
Witelay, George, iii, 240.
Withers, Edmund (cl), ii, 212; William (cl), iii, 152.
Withrow, Mr. W. H., iv, 236.
Witter, *see* Whitter.
Witton, William, iii, 251.
Wolfe, General, iv, 228.
Wollans, Francis, i, 213.
Wolley, Edward (cl), iii, 53, 54.
Wolsey, Cardinal, Intr., vi.
Womersley, Joseph, ii, 114.
Wood, Anthony, iii, 239; Christopher, ii, 69; David, iii, 253; George (cl), Intr., xx; iii, 24; George, i, 78; Sir George, iii, 24; Henry, ii, 82; Isaac, ii, 142; Jo: iii, 149; John, ii, 103, 114, 115; iii, 86; iv, 54, 99; Jonas, iii, 50; Noah, i, 201; iii, 89; Ralph, i, 187; Richard, i, 143; iii, 49, 156; Robert, ii, 8; Stephen, ii, 142; Thomas, i, 150, 210; iii, 112, 213, 'I. Wood'; William (cl), ii, 106; iii, 250; William, i, 133; iii, 239; iv, 20.
Woodall, William, iii, 56, 138.
Woodburn, William, ii, 102.
Woodhead, John, ii, 179; Joseph, ii, 44; Sarah, ii, 49.
Woods, Henry (cl), iv, 90, 131, 132; John (cl), iv, 27, 164.
Woodward, Thomas, i, 33.
Woodyear, Mr., ii, 208.
Woolby, Mr. Simon, iv, 124.
Woolfe, Nicholas (cl), i, 39, 111, 112, 113, 159, 217.
Woollin, John (cl), i, 178.
Wordsworth, Canon Chr., Intr., xxiv; George, i, 203; Mr. [L. Josias], iii, 5; (*see also* Wadsworth).
Worrell, Anthony, i, 75.
Worsley, John, iv, 35.
Worthington, O.P., Dr. Thomas (R), ii, 94; iv, 206, 213, 219.
Wortley, John, ii, 117; Robinson, i, 122.
Wragg, John, i, 22.
Wraith, John, ii, 179.
Wrangham, Francis (cl), ii, 124; Robert, ii, 189.
Wray, Augustine, ii, 148; Robert, iii, 230; Thomas (cl), i, 134.
Wreakes, George, ii, 148.
Wright, Barnard, i, 202; Griffin, ii, 143; John (cl), iv, 179; John, i, 181; ii, 71, 209; iii, 61, 180, 183, 194, 199, 235; iv, 25, 86, 97; Joseph, S.J. (R), ii, 120; iv, 208; Marmaduke, ii, 193; Peter, i, 41; Richard, iv, 88; Robert (cl), iv, 65; Robert, iii, 4, 144; Sarah, iii, 61; Thomas (cl) (R. Birkin), i, 44; Thomas (cl) (A.C. Halifax), ii, 34; Thomas, i, 47; William, i, 14; iii, 48; iv, 8.
Wrightson, of Cusworth Park, ii, 45; May, ii, 45; Robert (cl) (*al.* Whitehead), ii, 45.
Wriglesworth, Ralph, i, 192; ii, 88.
Wrothwell, Rothwell, S.J., John (R), iv, 208.
Wykes, Isaac (cl), i, 144, 189; ii, 125, 153, 154, 189.
Wyley, Peter, ii, 154.
Wynn, Apralum, ii, 34; Francis, i, 204.
Wyrell, John, i, 199.
Wyrill, John, i, 47.

Yarburgh, Edmund, gent., iii, 83, 84, 85; George, iii, 73; Henry, Esqr., ii, 139; Nicholas, Esqre., iii, 68-73; Sarah (Saray), iii, 83, 84, 85, 68, 69, 71, 72, 73; Thomas, gent., iii, 68-72.
Yarr, Richard, i, 202.

Yates, Bernard, O.S.F. (R) (*al.* Yeates; Yate), iv, 203, 206, 217; Francis (cl), ii, 5; iii, 250; Thomas, iii, 242.
Yelland, Gervas, iv, 130.
Yeoman, John, i, 189.
York, John, iii, 95; Stephen, ii, 157.
Young, Anthony (cl), ii, 22; iii, 251; James (cl), i, 158, 224; ii, 86; Matthew, i, 58; iii, 46; Peter, iii, 238; Samuel, iii, 194.
Youngson, Thomas, i, 37.
Yoward, Mr. Ra., iv, 99.

Zimmerman, Dr. B. (R), iv, 187, 194, 210.
Zouch, Charles (cl), Intr., xx; iii, 46, 48; iv, 214; Henry (cl), iii, 48; Thomas, D.D. (cl), ii, 124; iii, 48; iv, 129 ('Charles').

MISCELLANEA.

Act of General Free Pardon (Grace), ii, 189 (*passim*).
Alehouses, i, 35, 154; ii, 100, 174.
Assembly of Divines, iv, 58.
Baron of the Exchequer, iii, 24.
Black servant, i, 105.
Blasphemy, i, 17.
Blue Coat Boys, iii, 134.
Broad Seal, i, 171; iv, 54.
Canons, 6, 20, 21, iv, 127; 13, 14, 15, ii, 211; 35, ii, 109; 39, ii, 110; 41, ii, 111; 48, iii, 8, 211; 59, ii, 164; 62, ii, 114; iv, 127; 70, i, 156; 79, ii, 40, 210; 102, i, 156; 103, i, 18.
Chaplains: Royal, i, 168; ii, 3; iii, 21, 42, 43, 251; iv, 2; Naval, ii, 115; iii, 173; Military, ii, 123; iii, 22; Domestic, i, 21, 96, 140, 223; ii, 104, 183, 219, 220; iii, 31, 102, 120, 148; iv, 20, 55, 62, 64, 69, 119, 134, 157, 171.
Church: Bell, i, 206; Bell-ropes, iv, 170; 'Body and Isles,' i, 63; Book of Homilies, iii, 15; Bread and Wine, iii, 145; Chest, iv, 28; Clock, i, 12; ii, 198; Communion Cup, iv, 77; Communion Money, ii, 155; iv, 129; Confirmation Press, iv, 137; Consecration Deed, ii, 142; Easter Book, ii, 76, 78; iii, 128;Fees,i,156; Fence, iv,50; Frame, Pannel, Table, ii, 172; iii, 17, 18, 137; iv, 18, 86, 97; Galleries, i, 101; ii, 189; iii, 252; Minister's Gown, ii, 50; Pews, i, 55, 207; Poor John's Money, i, 132; Porch, i, 42; iii, 71; Rates, ii, 142; iii, 169; iv, 7; Register Book (*passim*); Silver salvers, iv, 169; Steeple, iii, 125; iv, 19, 145; steps, iii, 208; Vestry Meeting, iv, 57; Wakes, iv, 72; White Sheet, ii, 114; Wall of Churchyard, i, 119; Wine, i, 206; Wine-Penny, ii, 135.
Churchwardens: Dissenters, iv, 22, 142, 145; their 'Forebearance,' i, 108, 154; Oath, iii, 33.
Civil Wars, i, 103; ii, 39; iv, 231.
Clandestine Marriages, i, 156.
Clergy with two Christian Names, ii, 13, 195; iii, 7; iv, 32, 50, 55, 156.
Clerical Decency, ii, 83; iv, 70.
Clerical Difficulties, 'accidental distress,' iii, 91; age, iii, 29; bad cold, i, 85; broken leg, i, 68; craziness, i, 218; debt, i, 145; derangement, iv, 10; daughter disordered, iii, 194; dullness of hearing, ii, 52; fatigue in preaching, iv, 142; fever, iv, 49; gout, ii, 211; mountains, moors and snowdrifts, ii, 30; iii, 27; 'ill-set' for a text, iii, 88; ill-housed (*see* Parsonages); interruption and abuse, ii, 51; lameness, iii, 105; lunatic brother, iv, 136; lunatic wife, ii, 162; melancholic patron, ii, 136; melancholic wife, iv, 126; negligent parishioners, iv, 14; overwork, i, 18; palsy, iv, 28; phrenzy, iv, 9; prop'd by physick, iv, 15, 17; salary withheld, iii, 237; 'sinking' inconveniences (i.e., dilapidations), i, 66; Valetudinarian, iv, 16.
Clerical Types, acquiescent, ii, 94; cautious, i, 169; complacent, ii, 15; devout, iii, 96; disciplinarian, iv, 20; economiser, ii, 144; 'eruditus,' ii, 147; evasive, Intr., xii; xv; iii, 105; iv, 114, 148; even-tempered, ii, 141; famed for Piety, i, 67; generous, i, 84; genial, iii, 190; 'grand voice and manner,' ii, 138, 172; grateful, iv, 133; humble, iv, 160; humorist, ii, 138; ignorant, ii, 102; ingenuous, ii, 221; laconic (shortest Return, 46 words), iii, 111; militant, iv, 123; negligent, i, 224; ii, 75; iv, 140, 142; pathetic, iv, 135; persistent, iv, 4; poetical, iii, 190; iv, 83; prolix (fullest Return, 9,919 words), iii, 67; sedulous, iv, 112; studious, iv, 128.
Compendious Schoolmaster, The, ii, 69.
Door to Door, ii, 16, 168, 172.
'Eldest Brother,' ii, 197.
Embezzling, i, 135.
Excise office, i, 194.
French Refugee, ii, 124.
Gentlemen's Society, iv, 107.
Gleaning, iii, 164.

Grand Donation (1660), i, 22.
'Heathen Temples,' iv, 64.
Highest endowments; Church, i, 104; Pious Uses, iii, 142; Education, iii, 45.
'Hurry of seed time,' iv, 70.
Indentures (extracts), iii, 68, 73, 80.
'Iniquity of Mankind,' iv, 8, 58, 59.
Justice Book, ii, 162.
King's Business, iii, 42.
Knitting, i, 113; ii, 144; iii, 213.
Largest—Man in Yorkshire, iv, 241; Parish, ii, 23; Parsonage, iv, 59; Population, ii, 140.
Lay Baptism, ii, 25.
Layes (Poor Rates), i, 169; iv, 36, 59.
Lecture Day (Presb.), ii, 210.
Lecturers, i, 59, 60, 99, 101, 102, 104, 113, 153, 156, 191; ii, 33, 34, 41, 78, 142, 143; iii, 66, 134, 186, 187, 193, 249; iv, 14, 15, 104, 105 (*see* Addenda), 179; 'Concionator,' 180.
Living held for a Minor, iv, 62.
Marriage Licences and Fees, , 18; iii, 240; iv, 127; Certificate, iii, 201.
Merchant Taylors Co., i, 122.
'*Merry England*,' iv, 189, 215, 218.
Mongrells, iv, 16.
Mortmain Act, i, 153; iii, 12.
Non-juror, i, 35.
Norrisian Professor, ii, 142.
Occupations; alum workers, ii, 156; apothecary, iii, 187; barrister, i, 22; carpenter, ii, 161; clothier, iii, 51; constable, i, 100; iii, 112, 113; iv, 170; Flaxdresser, iv, 34; Forgemen, iii, 20; Husbandman (*passim*); Keeper, ii, 59; Lead miner, iii, 245; midwife, iii, 209; iv, 161; Physician, iii, 135; Praeceptor, ii, 19; sail-maker, iv, 232; sailors, iv, 102, 150; ship's carpenters, iv, 102, 150; Soldiers, i, 224; ii, 97, 111, 123; iii, 20, 22, 58; iv, 78; surgeon, ii, 108; tailor, iv, 53; traveller, i, 187; weaver, ii, 11; iii, 34; iv, 53.
Oldest Clergymen (in Cleveland), i, 145; (in these Returns), i, 54.
Parental Pride, iii, 114.
Parsonages uninhabitable, &c.; cottage low-thatched (mud, mean, poor), ii, 136; iii, 154, 177; iv, 12, 45; conveyed away, iii, 239; crowded out by Curate, iv, 131; damp, ii, 129; iv, 15; demolished, ii, 6; frequent floods, iii, 110; ruinous, ii, 134; iv, 124; swallowed up by Humber, iii, 10; small, iv, 101; uninhabitable, ii, 146, 211 (*passim*); walls studded with clay, iv, 53.
Perambulation Day, iii, 137.
Pew Rents, i, 130, 207.
Physique Garden, ii, 125.
'Plow Day,' ii, 208.
Popish Books, iii, 245; Catechism, iv, 172.
Rack tenants, i, 141.
Rape Seed, ii, 181.
Refusal of Holy Communion; i, 61, 63, 154, 158, 199; ii, 55, 68, 87, 139, 162, 177; iii, 9, 66, 135, 152, 168, 182, 216; iv, 4, 18.
Restoration, The, iv, 58.
Roguery, iv, 174.
Roman Catholic Living, i, 64.
Ruinous Bridges, i, 16.
Rustat Scholar, i, 73; ii, 61, 163; iv, 33, 51.
School Payments, i, 37, 66, 68, 131; iv, 80.
Sequestrators, i, 112; ii, 133; iii, 17, 106, 224; iv, 27, 113, 115, 124, 155, 162.
Sermon, 5/-; iv, 107, 151, 165; 40/-, i, 132; Lecture, 5/-, i, 113.
Sinecure, ii, 127.
Smallest Parishes, i, 157, 193.
Song School, iv, 106.
Spinning, i, 101, 113; ii, 144.
Stormy Easter Day (Apr. 3rd, 1743), i, 74, 213; ii, 131, 132, 134, 154; iii, 128, 200, 217.
'Tale of a Tub'; Intr., xi; iii, 153.
Terriers (extracts), i, 54, 56; iii, 72.
Test Act, iv, 223.
Thebaean Legion, ii, 124.
Toleration Act, iv, 50, 223.
Town Feast, iv, 84.
Town Stock, ii, 73; iii, 197.
Union, Act of (1707), iv, 223.
Unitarianism, iv, 224, 229, 235.
Usurpation, The, ii, 223.
Waistcoats for Widows, i, 12.
Wears and Water Brinks, ii, 43.
Westmoreland Scholar, i, 209.
Whinns and Furrs, iii, 177.
White Mule, iv, 10.
White Penny Loaves, Bread, &c., i, 113, 138, 160, 171; ii, 59, 75, 105, 123, 197; iii, 25, 40, 77, 93, 110, 132, 166, 215, 242; iv, 19, 21, 86, 92, 102, 118, 129, 136, 168.
Wills (extracts), i, 151; iii, 12, 59, 60, 76; iv, 150.
Woodward Professor, i, 131.

ADDENDA AND CORRIGENDA.

VOLUME 1.

Page xiii, line 7, for Friezland read Frizeland.
Page xiii, line 9, for 'on the King's business' read 'upon King's business.'
Page xx, line 2, for Jacques read Jaques.
Page 8, line 21, for *Bilbrough* read *Bilborough, Yorks.* (also on page 149).
Page 12, line 6, for *Bolton Chapel* read *Bolton Chapel, Craven* (also on page 53).
Page 19, line 41, for *Marsden Chapel* read *Flockton Chapel.*
Page 26, after John Coates, add Master of Gr. School, Skipton (par. Overton).
Page 27, line 18, for 'acted also as A.C. Hooke Chapel,' read see *Hook Chapel*; for *Thropham* read *Thorpe St. John.*
Page 38, 5 lines from bottom, after *Barmston*, add 'and *Harpham.*'
Page 39, line 12, for *Fraisthorp* read *Fraisthorpe*, also on pages 111, 112, 159.
Page 40, line 8, delete (Harthill).
Page 49, line 17, for *Weston* read *Weston near Otley.*
Page 51, add after William Carr: 'see *Holbeck Chapel.*'
Page 58, line 30, for *Bolton* read *Bolton by Bolland.*
Page 60, line 14, for Kennett read Kennet, and add 'see *Wibsey Chapel.*'
Page 61, add after Gr. Sch. Master: Usher, William Brooke, above; Petty Master, John Belcher (see *Wibsey Chapel*).
Page 64, 7 lines from bottom, for *Skelbrook* and *Ealand*, read *Skelbrooke* and *Elland.*
Page 74, line 21, for *Middop* read *Midhope.*
Page 88, 9 lines from bottom, for *Felliskirk* read *Felixkirk.*
Page 89, after R. John Wind add 'and *Thirkleby.*'
Page 92, line 12, after *Helmsley* add 'and *Kirkdale.*'
Page 93, line 6, for *Skelton* read *Skelton-in-Cleveland.*
Page 95, 12 lines from bottom, for *Deighton* read *Deighton* (*Cleveland*); for Eleazer read Eleazar, and add (see *Allerton* and *Deighton* (*Cleveland*).
Page 97, 2 lines from bottom, read *Grimston* for *Grimeston.*
Page 102, after V. Samuel Johnston add (see *Beverley St. Nicholas*).
Page 104, line 41, read Thomas Mease (senior) (also on page 106); last line but one, for Clark read Clarke, and for sizer, sizar.
Page 107, line 7, for *Norton* read *Norton-juxta-Malton.*
Page 108, after R. Samuel Dennis, add (see *Lissett Chapel*).
Page 110, line 8, for *Agnes Burton* read *Burton Agnes* (also on page 193), and add 'and *Harpham.*'
Page 111, 7 lines from bottom, for *Ruston* read *Rustone*; for *Millington* read *Givendale*; for *and* read and.
Page 117, 13 lines from bottom, after *Hedon* add *Preston-in-Holderness.*
Page 118, line 24 and last line, for *Kayingham* read *Keyingham.*
Page 121, line 7, delete *Millington.*
Page 133, after line 27, add V. Charles Zouch (see *Sandal Magna*).
Page 138, line 5, for *Peniston* read *Penistone.*
Page 143, for *Gillamore* read *Gillamoor.*
Page 144, after *Kirkby Grindalythe* add, 'and *Newton Chapel, Ryedale.*'
Page 146, 8 lines from bottom, for in, read it.
Page 150, line 28, after *North Newbald* add, 'and *Sancton.*'
Page 156, after V. Thomas Mease read (Junior).
Page 157, 8 lines from bottom, delete *Eskdale* (also on page 89), for *Fylingdale* read *Fylingdales.*
Page 163, line 22, after *Naburn* add 'and *Stockton-on-the-Forest*' (also on page 164, line 15).
Page 167, after A.C. John Holme, add (see *Loversall*), and Gr. Sch. Master, Edmund Withers (see *Owston*).

Page 171, lines 22 and 23, for Peniston read Penistone.
Page 172, line 20, after *Rufforth* add 'and *Murton Chapel.*'
Page 173, line 7, for *Thorp* read *Thorpe.*
Page 178, line 6, delete [Woolin].
Page 180, after V. William Steer read (Senior).
Page 183, last line but one, for Dons read Dom, for Hardisty read Hardesty.
Page 188, line 12, after *Pickering* add 'and *Newton Chapel, Ryedale.*' Line 13, after *Wilton Chapel* and *Newton Chapel* add *Ryedale.*
Page 190, line 29, for 11th Febr., 1742 read 4th May, 1738; last line, delete 'see *Weighton.*'
Page 192, line 25, after Elstronwick Chapel add [Elsternwick]; 2 lines from bottom, for *Aldborough* read *Aldborough, Holderness,* and add *Humbleton.*
Page 193, line 18, after *Barmston* add 'and *Harpham.*'
Page 198, line 17, after *Leeds* add *Parish Church.*
Page 203, line 28, for *Hutton Pannel* read *Hooton Pagnell.*
Page 204, line 11, for *Sherburne* read *Sherburn.*
Page 208, last line, for Whitestoncliffe read Whitestone Cliff.
Page 211, 3 lines from bottom, for *Carleton* read *Carlton.*
Page 214, 11 lines from bottom, for *Ruston* read *Ruston Parva.*
Page 216, line 24, after A.C. John Stable add (see *Speeton*).
Page 218, line 6, after *Hunmanby* add *Fordon Chapel.*
Page 221, line 10, read V. John Browne; for *Elstronwick* read *Elsternwick*; 3 lines from bottom, for Carthagena read Cartagena.
Page 222, line 19, after William Bowman add (see *Alborough, Boroughbridge* and *Dewsbury*).
Page 223, line 4, delete *Farnley Chapel*; 12 lines from bottom, for *Burgwallis* read Burghwallis; line 15, after *Walton* add 'and *Whiston.*'
Page 224, line 10, after *Otley* add 'and *Pool Chapel.*'

VOLUME II.

Page 9, 9 lines from bottom, for *Wilton* read *Wilton-in-Cleveland.*
Page 13, line 23, for *Elstronwick* read *Elsternwick* (also page 88).
Page 19, line 6, for *Rudston* read *Rudstone.*
Page 45, line 27, for Cusworth read Cusworth Park; after line 32, add, for Abp. Holgate's Sch., see below.
Page 49, end of Harthill, add Gr. Sch. Master: Bartholomew Parkin.
Page 51, line 25, for *Little Sandal* read *Kirk Sandal.*
Page 55, line 5 after *Snaith* add 'and *Rawcliffe*'; line 6 for *Armin* read *Airmyn*; line 37 add (see *Rotherham*).
Page 56, line 23, for *Lawrence* read *Laurence.*
Page 60, line 2, after *Kirkdale* add 'and *Bilsdale.*'
Page 67, line 6, add (see *Barlby*).
Page 72, line 26, delete *Notts.*
Page 81, 12 lines from bottom, for *Sowerby, Pontefract* read *Sowerby-juxta-Halifax.*
Page 82, 4 lines from bottom, for *Aslaby Chapel* read *Wintringham.*
Page 87, line 4, for *Dripool* read *Drypool.*
Page 88, for *Aldborough* read Aldborough, Holderness.
Page 89, for *Linton* read *Linton-in-Craven* (also on page 90); after Hornsey cum Riston add [Riston].
Page 90, line 27, delete *Riston.*
Page 92, for *Agnes Burton* read *Burton Agnes,* and add '*Ergham* and *Barmston.*'
Page 105, line 10, for *Kirkby with Broughton* read *Kirkby-in-Cleveland*; line 12, for *Pannall* read *Pannal.*
Page 106, line 29, add (see *Ryther*).
Page 108, line 14, for *Gisburne* read *Gisburn.*
Page 111, line 13, delete (see *Silsden Chapel, Bingley* and *Pudsey*).
Page 119, line 22, for *Stainburne* read *Stainburn.*

Page 120, line 23, for Ransom, read Ranson.
Page 124, after line 14, add, Sch. Master: Mr. Henry Allerston.
Page 125, lines 8 and 11, for *Gillamore* read *Gillamoor.*
Page 126, line 27, after *Helmsley* read 'and *Bilsdale.*'
Page 133, 8 lines from bottom, add *Shipton, Harthill.*
Page 134, after *Bugthorp* add *Preston-in-Holderness.*
Page 135, line 24, after *Levisham* add *Middleton, Ryedale, Cropton, Lockton,* and *Newton Chapel, Ryedale.*
Page 142, line 13, for *Farnley Chapel* read *Farnley-juxta-Leeds.*
Page 147, line 3, for *Hornsea with Riston* read *Hornsea* and *Riston*; one line from bottom, read *Skipton-in-Craven.*
Pages 153, 155, 190, for *Grindalyth* read *Grindalythe,* and add 'and *Newton Chapel, Ryedale.*'
Page 159, line 25, for Kirk-Heaton read Kirkheaton.
Page 161, line 7, add *Shipton, Harthill.*
Page 165, for Joseph Somers read Joseph Sommers; for *Ruston* read *Ruston Parva* (also page 205).
Page 166, line 10, for *Cottam* read *Cottam, Yorks.*
Page 168, 10 lines from bottom, for *S. Dennis in Walmgate* read *York, St. Denys* (also Vol. 3, page 105) and add *Stockton-on-the-Forest.*
Page 172, 8 lines from bottom, for *Kildwick* read *Kilnwick* (also on page 207).
Page 179, after Q. XI. (No. 164) add V. Edward Rishton, V. of Almondbury.
Page 184, line 16, for Wickens read Wickins.
Page 186, line 13, for *Useburn* read *Ouseburn.*
Page 193, line 21, for *Craythorne* read *Crathorne.*
Page 194, line 15 after *Osbaldwick* add *Dunnington* and *Rufforth.*
Page 200, 1 line from bottom, for Graham, of Esk read Graham of Esk.
Page 202, 5 lines from bottom, for *Gisbrough* read *Guisbrough.*
Page 204, line 22, add *Skirlaugh.*
Page 205, for *Lowthorp* read *Lowthorpe.*
Page 206, after *North Cave,* add 'and *Sancton.*'
Page 209, line 29, read *Farnley-juxta-Otley* and *Pool Chapel*; line 31, delete '*Farnley Chapel* (*Otley*).'
Page 213, after the A.C., add, Gr. Sch. Master: John Coates (see *Acomb*).
Page 216, line 20, add (see *Eston,* below).
Page 219, line 17, for *Carleton* read *Carlton.*
Page 222, line 9, after Gideon Murray, add (see *Hackness*).
Page 223, for Midhop, read Midhope; line 14, for *Bolsterston* read *Bolsterstone*; 5 lines from bottom, for *Preston* read *Preston-in-Holderness.*

VOLUME III.

Page 7, 10 lines from bottom, for *Ellerburn* read *Ellerburne,* and add 'and *Newton,* Ryedale'; 7 lines from bottom, for Ellerburn read Ellerburne, and add Ryedale, after *Newton* and *Wilton* Chapels.
Page 8, line 34, after *Pickering* add 'and *Ellerburne*'; line 35, after *Wilton Chapel* read Ryedale; and for *Ellerburn* read *Ellerburne*; line 36, after *Middleton, Ryedale* add, '*Cropton, Lockton, Levisham* and *Kirkby Grindalythe.*'
Page 10, 5 lines from bottom, after *Skeckling with Burstwick* add 'and *Thorngumbald.*'
Page 12, after V. Thomas Lovett, add (see *Yapham-with-Meltonby*); add, Usher: Richard Donn (see *Seaton Ross*).
Page 14, lines 34 and 37, for *Preston* read *Preston-in-Holderness* (also on page 179).
Page 16, after C. Matthew Knowles, add (see *Burnsall*).
Page 23, line 5, for *Hoyland Chapel* read *Hoyland-juxta-Wath.*
Page 25, 11 lines from bottom, for *Hooke* read *Hook* (also on page 86, line 3).
Page 37, line 16 for *Bielby* read *Beilby.*

Page 42, line 10, add (see *Tunstall*).
Page 54, line 1, for Woolley read Wolley.
Page 58, top, add 'A.C. William Humpton (see *Eccleshall*).
Page 65, line 21, for D. and Ch. of York, read D. and C.
Page 67, last line but one, for Dowrne read Downe.
Page 87, last line, for Hutton read Hooton.
Page 99, line 20, for *Brompton* read *Brompton-with-Snainton*.
Page 101, line 1, for *Kirkby cum Broughton* read *Kirkby-in-Cleveland*.
Page 106, line 15, for Comm. read Commissary.
Page 108, line 7, for *Marton in Bulmer* read *Marton-on-the-Forest*.
Page 109, line 6, after *Normanby* read *Yorks*.
Page 111, 3 lines from bottom, for Nether read Over.
Page 113, line 32, for *Kildwick near Watton* read *Kilnwick-on-the-Wolds*.
Page 114, 13 lines from bottom, read (see *North Newbald* and *North Cave*) instead of present bracket.
Page 120, after R. Heneage Dering, add (see *Ripon*).
Page 120, line 21, for *Thorp* read *Thorpe*.
Page 127, line 1, for *Thorgumbald* read *Thorngumbald*; add School Master: Richard Rether; Parish Clerk: same Richard Rether.
Page 135, line 12, for *Stainton* read *Stainton-in-Cleveland*; line 17, read Buckrose after *Sherburn*; 3 lines from bottom; for *Marton* read *Muston*, and add *Fordon*.
Page 136, 8 lines from bottom, for *Leckonfield* read *Leconfield* (and elsewhere).
Page 148, line 34, for Nether Stillington read Nether Shitlington.
Page 156, line 24, for Prestwick read Prestwich.
Page 161, line 8, for *Bransby* read *Brandsby*.
Page 162, line 8, for *Raskelf* read *Raskelfe*.
Page 165, after 140, Thirtleby add [Thirkleby]
Page 166, line 5, after *Kirkby Knowle* add 'and *Bagby Chapel*.'
Page 169, line 30, after *Normanby* read Yorks. (also on page 187).
Page 170, line 19, for *Stainton* read *Stainton-in-Cleveland*.
Page 171, line 12, for *North Otteringham* read *North Otterington*.
Page 177, line 22, delete *Eskdale Chapel*.
Page 179, line 27, for *Nun Monckton* read *Nun Monkton*.
Page 180, 7 lines from bottom, after *Dewsbury* add 'and *Whiston*.'
Page 189, after A.C. Thomas Naylor, add (see *Beverley, St. Mary's*, Text).
Page 191, line 39, for D'Oyley read D'Oyly.
Page 197, after C. Joseph Hall, add (see *Tankersley*, Text).
Page 198, bottom, add Parish Clerk: same Thomas Crowther.
Page 201, 7 lines from bottom, for *Thorp* read *Thorpe*.
Page 204, 10 lines from bottom, after *Brompton with Snainton* add 'and *Snainton Chapel*.'
Page 213, line 15, for I. Wood read T. Wood.
Page 227, last line, for Hodgkinson read Hopkinson.
Page 230, line 29, for *Skelton* read *Skelton, Ripon*.
Page 232, line 17, for *Bishop Monckton* read *Bishop Monkton* (also on pages 233 and 234).
Page 249, after C. William Graham, add (see *Hexhamshire*).
Page 250, line 6, for Pannall read Pannal; for Poole read Pool; line 26, for Feliskirk read Felixkirk; line 38, add (see *Kilvington South*).
Page 251, line 1, after Easington read (Craven); line 33, after C. Anthony Young, add (see *Hampsthwaite*).
Page 252, line 28, for Winteringham read Wintringham.

VOLUME IV.

Page ix, for Barmby-in-the-Willows (Barnby) read, Barnby-in-the-Willows (Barmby); for Bothamsall 22 read Bothamsall 20; add Bramcote 18; for Carlton Chapel (*s.v.* Norwell) read, Carlton-on-Trent; for Colston Basset, read Colston Bassett; for Edwinstow read Edwinstowe.

Page x, for Holme Pierpoint read Holme Pierrepont; for Kirkton read Kirton; for Kneesal read Kneesall (also on page xi); for Lindby read Lynby; for Ragnell read Ragnall.
Page 2, line 34, for Boothby Grasse, read Boothby Graffoe.
Page 4, after V. Joseph Chadwick, add School Master: John Warwick.
Page 5, line 13, for *Lindby* read *Lynby*; 6 lines from bottom, delete *Bawtry* (also on pages 22 and 147).
Page 6, for Walter Palliser, read Walter Pallisser.
Page 11, after A.C. Wriggan Webster, add (see *Hickling*); after V. Thomas Poynton add (see *Ratcliffe-on-Soar*).
Page 12, after A.C. Edward Broughton, add (see *Newark*).
Page 15, after A.C. Thomas Clarke, add School Master: Thomas Smith.
Page 20, 3 lines from bottom, for *Kirkton* read *Kirton*.
Page 23, after R. Thomas Heald, add (see *Ordsall*).
Page 25, line 7, after *Kneeton* add 'and *Southwell.*'
Page 28, after R. William Standfast, add (see *North Wheatley*).
Page 34, for Samuel Leake, read Samuel Leeke.
Page 36, line 32, for *Sierston* read *Syerston*.
Page 37, line 28, for Colston-Basset read Colston-Bassett; after Claworth add [Clayworth].
Page 41, line 22, after *S. Mary's, Nottingham* add 'and *Sneinton*' (also on page 68).
Page 42, 9 lines from bottom, after *Askham* read *Notts*.
Page 46, line 11, after *Stanton on the Wolds* add 'and *Nottingham, St. Mary's*'; 7 lines from bottom, for *Barmby* read *Barnby*.
Page 48, 3 lines from bottom, after *Syerston* add 'and *Coddington.*'
Page 52, line 9, for *Missen* read *Misson* (also on page 100).
Page 64, 8 lines from bottom, for Berkswych read Berkswich.
Page 67, after A.C. Wriggan Webster, add (see *Broughton Sulney*).
Page 74, 7 lines from bottom, after *Blythe*, add *Austerfield* and *Sutton-on-Lound*; after *Scrooby* add 'and *Austerfield*'; add, Master of the Hospital: John Ludlam (see *Bawtry* and *Mattersey*).
Page 76, line 8, delete the first (Senior) from text.
Page 77, after V. Richard Hardy add (see *Owthorpe*, below).
Page 78, after C. Richard Hardy add (see *Kinalton*).
Page 84, after Kirkton add [Kirton].
Page 90, line 6, delete *Yorks.* after Sigglesthorne; after Lindby add [Lynby].
Page 98, after A.C., add Parish Clerk: William Sansome.
Page 102, last line, for Pinder read Pindar.
Page 104, line 12, after *Weston* read '*Notts.*'
Page 105, C. Thomas Fellows, add 'Vic. Chor. & Lecturer, Southwell.'
Page 107, after V. Bernard Wilson, add (see *Winthorpe*); for *Barnby* read *Barnby-in-the-Willows*.
Page 110, after R. John Abson add (see *Rolleston*); 7 lines from bottom, for *Lindley* read *Lynby*.
Page 116, line 3, delete whole line; after Plumptree add [Plumtree].
Page 125, after R. Thomas Gylby, add (see *East Retford, East Markham,* and *West Drayton*).
Page 129, for Dr. Charles Zouch, read Dr. Thomas Zouch.
Page 130, after V. Nicholas Howlet, add (see *South Leverton*); after Ragnell add [Ragnall].
Page 136, line 11, for *Ratcliffe* read *Radcliffe*.
Page 141, for A.C. Robert Gunthorpe read Robert Gunthorp.
Page 151, after C. Robert Pindar, add (see *Misterton*).
Page 153, for C. Thomas Heblethwaite read Thomas Hebblethwaite.
Page 154, line 33, for *Barmby* (*Notts.*), read *Barnby-in-the-Willows*.
Page 156, line 1, read George Stanton (Staunton) Brough; after line 6, add A.C. (1st Med.) The same Henry Franceys.
Page 158, line 25, for *Tythby* read *Tithby* (also on page 162).
Page 160, V. Chappell Fowler, add 'Vic. Chor. Southwell.'
Page 163, after A.C. Henry Wayte, add (see *Willoughby*).

Page 166, 6 and 7 lines from bottom, for Mapplebeck read Maplebeck.
Page 170, 7 lines from bottom, for *Greenley-on-the-Hill* read *Gringley-on-the-Hill*.
Page 171, line 33, for *Headon* read *Headon-with-Upton* (also on page 73).
Page 174, after R. Paul Jenkinson, add 'A.C. Henry Clarke' (see *South Muskham*).
Page 177, line 2, after *Eastwood* add 'and *Woodborough*.'
Page 182, line 5, after *Cropwell Bishop* add 'and *Sneinton*'; line 33, after *Mattersey* add 'and *Harworth*'.
Page 183, Hallam, West, add 'R. William Clarke' (see *Mansfield Woodhouse* and *Skegby*); under Kingston upon Soar, delete '*Kingston-upon-Soar*.'
Page 184, 10 lines from bottom, delete (see *Ossington*); 5 lines from bottom, for *Pierpoint* read *Pierrepont*.
Page 188, line 36, for Blackburne read Blackburn (also on last line, page 213); line 39 for Brussells read Brussels.
Page 192, line 9, for Tunstal read Tunstall; 7 lines from bottom, for Harvey read Hervey.
Page 194, line 3, for 32 read 31; 7 lines from bottom, for Glos., read Worcestershire.
Page 195, line 23, for Cliff read Cliffe (also on page 13).
Page 197, 8 lines from bottom, for 222 read 221.
Page 198, line 4, for No. 5 read No. 6.
Page 205, line 14, for 196 read 202.
Page 207, 5 lines from bottom, for at read and.
Page 208, 3 lines from bottom, for Charleton read Charlton.
Page 210, line 1, for Middlestown read Middlesmoor; line 10, for Shereburne read Sherburne; line 17, for chaplan read chaplain.
Page 211, 12 lines from bottom, for 52 read 53.
Page 215, 12 lines from bottom, for 54 read 59.
Page 217, line 12, for 52 read 53.
Page 225, line 23, for *Gisburne* read *Gisburn*.
Page 226, line 1, for Crostone read Cross Stone (also line 32; and on pages 232 and 236); line 11, for *Warley* read *Halifax, Warley*.
Page 227, line 1, for Eccleshall read Ecclesall; 13 lines from bottom, delete (see *Birstall*).
Page 229, 3 lines from bottom, for Thorbarre read Thorbarne.
Page 230, line 4, for Aker's read Akers; line 5, for Kneesal read Kneesall.
Page 231, line 8, for Peniston read Penistone; line 10, for Plumptree read Plumtree; line 22, delete 'and Silsden Chapel.'
Page 232, line 15, after Hulme read 'text, Mr. Hullam.'
Page 236, 7 lines from bottom, for Pinder read Pindar.
Page 238, line 17, for Pearson read Pierson.
Page 239, for Skipton read Skipton-in-Craven.
Page 241, line 10, for Collingham, read Collingham, North; line 14, for Jeffreys read Jefferys.

www.ingramcontent.com/pod-product-compliance
Ingram Content Group UK Ltd.
Pitfield, Milton Keynes, MK11 3LW, UK
UKHW042209080726
473066UK00007B/330

* 9 7 8 1 1 0 8 0 5 8 7 7 3 *